CRIME IN AMERICA

A Reference Handbook

CRIME IN AMERICA

A Reference Handbook

Jennifer L. Durham

**CONTEMPORARY
WORLD ISSUES**

ABC-CLIO

Santa Barbara, California
Denver, Colorado
Oxford, England

Library of Congress Cataloging-in-Publication Data

Durham, Jennifer L.
    Crime in America : a reference handbook / Jennifer L. Durham.
        p.   cm.—(Contemporary world issues)
    Includes bibliographical references and index.
    1. Crime—United States—Handbooks, manuals, etc. 2. Criminology—Handbooks, manuals, etc. I. Title. II. Series.
    HV6787.D87   1996   364.973—dc20   96-9077

ISBN 0-87436-841-3

01 00 99 98 97 96 95   10 9 8 7 6 5 4 3 2 1

ABC-CLIO, Inc.
130 Cremona Drive, P.O. Box 1911
Santa Barbara, California 93116-1911

This book is printed on acid-free paper ∞ .

Manufactured in the United States of America

For Mom and Dad

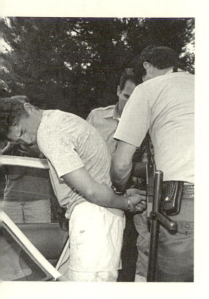

Contents

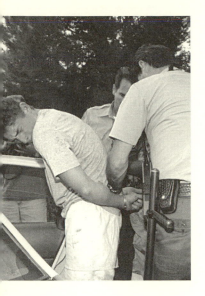

Preface

Crime is a broad and general subject that encompasses many smaller topics; therefore, this book is not intended as an exhaustive reference. Instead, it should serve as an introduction to crime problems in the twentieth-century United States and assist in a basic understanding of how the criminal justice system works. The book provides historical information on landmark Supreme Court decisions, important congressional legislation, and key figures who have tried to study or battle crime in some way. This background, along with the numerous resources at the end of the book, should serve as a springboard for further inquiry into the many aspects of crime in the United States.

I would like to thank the following people for their assistance and support: Sharon Van Meter for her help with Department of Justice materials; the staff of the Walter R. Davis Library at the University of North Carolina, Chapel Hill; the staff of the Cameron Village Library in Raleigh, North Carolina; my editor, Todd Hallman; Deborah Lynes and Darice Whetstone of D&D Editorial Services; Cheryl Carnahan, copyeditor; Mom, Dad, and Michael; and most of all, Mark Moore.

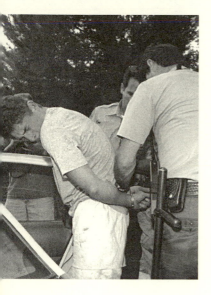

Surveying America's Crime Problem

1

In 1928, Herbert Hoover declared in his inaugural address, "The most malign of all . . . dangers today is disregard and disobedience of law. Crime is increasing. Confidence in rigid and speedy justice is decreasing."[1] More than 65 years later, crime ranks as one of the most talked about and hotly debated national issues in the United States.

On September 13, 1994, President Bill Clinton signed the Violent Crime Control and Law Enforcement Act of 1994, the largest piece of federal legislation targeted at crime ever passed in U.S. history. Yet despite all the anticrime bills, increased funding of law enforcement, Supreme Court decisions, and agencies created at all levels of government to combat the troubles, crime rates continue to rise. The number of crimes committed rises naturally with increases in population, but overall crime *rates* remain well above the level in the 1960s, when crime became a prominent national issue.

Crimes of a heinous nature dominate the local and national evening news around the country. In 1994, a South Carolina woman intentionally rolled her car into a lake, drowning her two young sons buckled inside. A gun-wielding man opened fire on a New York subway in 1993, killing six people

1

and injuring others. Criminals come in all stripes, from white-collar criminals like savings and loan executive Charles Keating, who was convicted of securities fraud, to would-be assassins like John Hinckley Jr., who shot President Ronald Reagan in 1981.

Adding to age-old forms of crime are new technology-related crimes. With the increasing sophistication of computers and large companies that organize information on computer networks, the opportunity for data theft and embezzlement is greater today than it was in the past.

In 1992, people reported 14.4 million offenses to law enforcement agencies around the country, meaning more than 5 percent of Americans were victimized by crimes.[2] Statistics also suggest that law enforcement agencies cannot keep up with the tide of crime. In 1992, only 21 percent of the offenses reported were cleared by arrest.[3] According to the Federal Bureau of Investigation's (FBI) *Uniform Crime Reports*, during that year someone was murdered every 22 minutes, robbed every 47 seconds, and raped every 5 minutes.[4]

What is being done to combat crime? There are thousands of law enforcement agencies nationwide. National and state governments pass anticrime legislation regularly. In 1993–1994, Congress passed more than 75 criminal statutes, as well as the largest piece of federal legislation in U.S. history, the Violent Crime Control and Law Enforcement Act of 1994, mentioned previously.[5] Washington, D.C., has more police per inhabitant than any other U.S. city, yet it consistently maintains one of the highest crime rates in the country.[6] Legislation and stepped-up police presence are not solving the problem.

A wide variety of private organizations dedicated to fighting crime—from inner-city citizen patrol groups like the Guardian Angels to criminal justice research organizations and neighborhood watch programs—have also failed to curb the tide of U.S. crime.

The remainder of this chapter describes in general terms trends in crime, various forms of crime, different approaches to crime control, the criminal justice system, and victims.

How Serious Is the Crime Problem?

If we look at FBI statistics since the 1960s, the crime problem—especially violent crime—has increased greatly. Some optimistic commentators have pointed to slight drops in crime rates in recent years as evidence that the crime situation is improving, but compared to the levels of thirty years ago, the rate of offenses remains high. In 1993, 440.1 aggravated assaults occurred per 100,000 U.S. inhabitants—up from 298.5 per 100,000 in 1980 and 80.4 per 100,000 residents in 1963.[7]

Violent criminal activity is increasing at an alarming rate among juvenile males. According to one writer, "Young criminals have traditionally been less violent, specializing in crimes against property, but the current trend is toward younger violent felons."[8] Nearly 14 percent of all suspects arrested for murder in 1990 were under age 18, compared to about 8 percent in 1963.[9]

Other serious problems law enforcement officials face involve the rise of new kinds of crimes. Investigators are unfamiliar with the cultures of immigrant ethnic groups that are forming criminal organizations in large cities and with the methods of sophisticated new computer criminals. Gun-wielding felons have many more weapon choices than they used to have. New crimes, weapons, and modes of operation force investigators to develop new techniques to combat them, a process that can be both costly and difficult.

Legislation

Prior to the 1960s, state and local governments assumed most of the responsibility for crime control. Federal crime laws like the Dyer Act of 1919, which outlawed the transport, receipt, or concealment of stolen vehicles across state lines, established new offenses but were not intended to significantly reform the justice system.[10]

The twentieth century's first major attempt at reforming the criminal justice system at the federal level came in the late 1920s under the administration of Herbert Hoover. In 1929, the president appointed the National Commission of Law Observance and Enforcement, subsequently nicknamed the "Wickersham Commission" after Attorney General George Wickersham, who chaired the group.

The group's initial purpose was to study law enforcement problems related to the Eighteenth Amendment—already more than a decade old—which outlawed the manufacture, sale, and transport of alcohol.[11] The commission, however, ended up investigating the entire criminal justice system. At the end of its two-year investigation, it produced a detailed report that delineated weaknesses in the criminal justice system and proposed reforms. One problem noted especially involved rampant complaints about police mistreating suspects.

Many of the problems the commission identified still exist today—courts overloaded with cases, inadequate punishment of criminals, and overcrowded prisons. The commission recommended several specific reforms, including increasing funding for law enforcement agencies and expanding federal prisons, but the government took little action on the proposals.

World War II followed the Great Depression, and legislators focused on more pressing economic and wartime issues. During the 1950s, a legislative reform project initially begun in the 1920s was rejuvenated. The American Law Institute, an organization of attorneys, judges, and other legal experts, began the undertaking. By 1931, the organization had drafted a Model Penal Code, but the project essentially vanished during the Depression and the war. In 1950, it was resurrected by its original leader, Herbert Weschler. The model ultimately influenced many states to revise their criminal codes, but it had little effect on national legislation.[12]

In the early 1960s, FBI statistics showed a sharp increase in crime. According to *Uniform Crime Reports,* the rate of violent crime rose by 12 percent between 1958 and 1963, and the overall crime rate jumped by 30 percent during that period.[13] Concern about organized crime and urbanization also contributed to the emergence of crime on the national agenda. Beginning with the administration of Lyndon Johnson, the quantity of federal anticrime legislation exploded.

Crime became a focal point in the 1964 presidential election. Conservative candidate Barry Goldwater accused the Johnson administration of being soft on crime. Goldwater called for law and order and criticized Johnson's socioeconomic approach to fighting crime. In September 1965, Johnson signed the first crime bill passed during his administration. The Law Enforcement Assistance Act created the Office of Law Enforcement Assistance, designed to aid law enforcement officials across the country.

Also in 1965, Johnson appointed the Commission on Law Enforcement and Administration of Justice, chaired by Attorney General Nicholas Katzenbach. The commission spent two years studying the U.S. crime problem and completed reports that consisted of a series of seemingly disconnected recommendations aimed at the police, courts, prisons, narcotics, juvenile delinquency, and other areas.[14] Critics alleged that the reports did more to guard civil rights than to fight crime.

The commission's reports led to the passage of the Omnibus Crime Control and Safe Streets Act of 1968. The final bill bore little resemblance to the proposals Johnson had originally introduced to Congress, but he had little choice but to sign the bill he had initiated. Conservatives criticized the act's antipoverty approach to crime and called for policies designed to punish criminals. Governors across the United States were concerned about the loss of state authority over law enforcement that would result from the bill.

The bill's provisions created block grants to states for law enforcement, authorized wiretapping in some local investigations, and loosened gun licensing restrictions. The bill also created the Law Enforcement Assistance Administration (LEAA), which was designed to aid state and local law enforcement agencies. Congress ended the agency's funding in 1982.

In 1968, Johnson formed the National Commission on Reform of Criminal Laws. The commission submitted a report to Richard Nixon, who was president when it finished its work. The report included stringent anticrime proposals such as mandatory sentences and the abolition of the insanity defense.[15] During the 1968 presidential campaign, Nixon had repeatedly criticized the Johnson administration's approach to crime control. He argued that Johnson's "war on poverty" had not only failed to curb crime but had actually contributed to an increase in the crime rate. Nixon called for policies that punished offenders.

Also at issue during this period were connections between civil rights and antiwar movements and crime. American blacks staged sit-ins and peaceful demonstrations that some felt contributed to a breakdown in the public order. Students opposed to the war in Vietnam held demonstrations on college campuses across the country. Incidences of violence, such as the riots following Martin Luther King Jr.'s assassination, also contributed to perceptions of declining public order.

Nixon's approach to crime control contrasted sharply with that of Johnson. Nixon called for a law-and-order approach that emphasized deterrence and strict punishment. He rejected Johnson's idea of improving economic circumstances in an attempt to reduce crime. Under Nixon's administration, Congress passed several major pieces of anticrime legislation. In July 1970, Congress passed the District of Columbia Crime Control bill; three months later, the Organized Crime Control bill was passed.

Both bills allowed investigators more leeway in gathering evidence by expanding wiretapping and electronic surveillance powers. In 1970, just two years after the passage of Johnson's omnibus crime bill, Congress began hearings on amending the legislation. Nixon signed a final bill in January 1971. Its major stipulations included increased funding for correctional facilities and the revision of block grant rules.

In spite of legislative efforts to curb crime, statistics continued to show rises in illegal activity. Each subsequent administration has continued to push for congressional anticrime legislation. In 1974, President Gerald Ford signed a bill that united federal juvenile justice programs under the Law Enforcement Assistance Administration. Two years later, he signed the Crime Control Act of 1976, which reauthorized the LEAA for another three years.

Initially, anticrime legislation was not a primary focus of President Jimmy Carter's administration. Within a few months, however, the LEAA once again came under discussion. Following lengthy arguments in Congress, the Justice System Improvement Act (Public Law 96-157), passed in 1979, greatly diminished the authority of the LEAA. The act created the Bureau of Justice Statistics, the National Institute of Justice, and the Office of Justice, Assistance, Research, and Statistics. The last of these agencies was designed to coordinate the activities of the others. In 1980, Congress granted the LEAA just enough money to keep it afloat, but the agency was phased out in 1982.

Some critics of crime legislation have complained about the disorganized nature of existing criminal statutes. Once enacted, federal laws become part of the United States Code. Congress passed a number of crime bills in the 1980s, including the Comprehensive Crime Control Act of 1984 and the Crime Control Act of 1990. National criminal laws, one critic has argued, form a "fairly random collection of criminal statutes passed at different times for different purposes, all criminalizing what Congress at that given moment believed should be punished."[16] He further observed that 80 to 90 percent of proposed code compresses or rewrites existing law.[17]

President Bill Clinton, following lengthy debate in Congress, signed the Violent Crime Control and Law Enforcement Act of 1994—the most comprehensive bill in history—which he pushed heavily. The bill expanded the death penalty, imposed bans on many models of firearms and placed new restrictions on gun dealers, imposed mandatory life sentences without parole for federal offenders convicted of three serious felonies, allocated more than a billion dollars for border control, and established several grant programs designed to aid victims and promote crime prevention. (See Chapter 4 for an abridged version of the 1994 bill.)

The vast pool of legislation passed by Congress since crime became a prominent national issue in the 1960s has not stemmed the tide of offenses. On the contrary, crime continues to increase in the United States. Some critics continue to demand additional legislation to combat the problem. Others seek different approaches to fighting crime, including education that emphasizes morals, prevention through alleviating racism and poor economic circumstances, and strengthening families.

Organized Crime

Some states require participation of only two individuals in certain illegal activities to define those activities as "organized crime," which ranks among the most difficult types of crime to curb for several reasons. First, offenses are rarely reported to the police. Criminal organizations abide by unwritten codes that forbid any participants to reveal information to authorities. Those who do so face retaliation and possibly death. People involved in organized crime are not generally disposed to report offenses to the police because they are willing participants. For example, in their own minds both the buyer and the seller of illegal drugs benefit from a transaction between the two. Nobody has been victimized by the sale.

Typical organized criminal activity in the United States includes gambling, loan sharking, bootlegging, money laundering, extortion, racketeering, and other illegal activities. *Loan sharks* lend money to people at very high interest rates, and they expect to be repaid in a short period of time. Much loan shark money is lent to people who lose money in illegal business deals. A hypothetical scenario illustrates the way loan sharks work: Joe is a compulsive gambler and finds himself with a $5,000 debt to a bookie. The bookie has demanded that Joe pay up immediately and tells him he will send someone to collect at three o'clock the next day. Joe knows he had better have the money if he wants to escape physical harm. He contacts a loan shark, who lends him the money to pay the bookie. The loan shark demands to have the money returned in one week with 30 percent interest. The following week Joe does not have the money to pay him back, so the loan shark demands to become part-owner of Joe's restaurant.

Illegal gambling has long been one of the largest moneymaking activities of organized crime in the United States. Profit estimates vary widely among law enforcement agencies, but the annual figures are always in the billions of dollars. One popular form of illegal gambling is the *numbers game.* At the bottom of the numbers betting hierarchy are people who collect bets from individuals. On the next level, people collect the bets and take them to a central location, called a bank, where all the bets are processed.

A *bookie* keeps track of bets in a second form of illegal gambling called *bookmaking,* a system by which people place bets on events such as dog or horse races. Although legal ways to bet at the track exist in some states and legal methods of betting off the track are found in two or three states, illegal bookmaking still flourishes. Its black-market nature enables a winner to hide his or her profits from the Internal Revenue Service (IRS) and to bet on many more sporting events than legal systems allow. Bookies also extend credit to customers.

Organized crime syndicates are responsible for many bootlegging operations in the areas of drugs, counterfeit money, stolen cars, and numerous other commodities. A successful syndicate often has many players. Stolen car rackets, for example, involve people in a number of positions—thieves who steal the cars, their bosses, and "fences" who buy the cars whole or in parts and resell them. Most often, the cars are dismantled and the parts sold individually, although stolen cars are sometimes given new looks, complete with new serial numbers and license plates to obscure their origins.

When illegal enterprises become sufficiently lucrative, the profiteers are likely to launder their money. *Money laundering* involves redirecting large profits from illegal business into legal businesses so the profits appear to be legitimate. Launderers have thus hidden suspiciously high profits from banks and the Internal Revenue Service.

In 1967, President Johnson's Task Force on Organized Crime said, "[Organized crime] involves thousands of criminals, working within structures as complex as those of any large corporation, subject to laws more rigidly enforced than those of legitimate governments."[18]

Since before Johnson's time, numerous pieces of federal leg-islation have been signed into law to combat organized crime. The Racketeer Influenced Corrupt Organizations Act (RICO), passed in 1961, outlawed racketeering in interstate commerce. RICO was amended in 1970 and was used in the 1980s to pros-ecute several organized crime bosses. Congress passed the Money Laundering Control Act of 1986 in an attempt to make it more difficult to hide profits from illegal ventures.

The Mafia

When people speak of organized crime, the *Mafia* almost always comes to mind, and Mafia organizations have indeed played a prominent role in organized criminal activity. The term *Mafia* originated as a name for members of a political resistance move-ment opposed to foreign domination in Italy. Today, the word is used to describe a number of criminal organizations.

The first Italian Mafia members who caused trouble in the United States were recognized by authorities in New Orleans in the late 1800s. Around the turn of the twentieth century, large numbers of immigrants from Eastern Europe and other places began to arrive in the United States, and every group seemed to have its own criminal organizations. Groups of Irish, Jewish, and Italian gangsters sprang up in cities like Chicago and New York, where immigrants were concentrated in ethnic neighborhoods.

Italian organized crime structures differ from others in one important aspect: they are organized around the family. Loyalty and confidentiality reside with relatives, and the bonds are much stronger than those in other ethnic groups, which form criminal structures around friendships and gang membership. Each family has a head boss, known as a don.

In the early 1900s, members of virtually every immigrant group ran organized illegal activities, from bootlegging to gam-bling and prostitution. Irish gangs controlled gambling syndi-cates and political machines; Jewish gangs also controlled some gambling syndicates and prostitution rings.[19]

Italian families did not rise to prominence until the Prohibi-tion period of the 1920s. Perhaps the most famous figure from this era is Al "Scarface" Capone, who dominated the Chicago liquor bootlegging underworld. Capone grew up in an Italian neighborhood in New York, where he originally became involved in mob activities. His career began early—he was a member of a youth gang at age 11. He later moved to Chicago and became a billionaire as a result of bootlegging during Prohibition.

During the period between 1920 and 1933, contraband liquor was usually either brewed in illegal distilleries or brought in from Canada or Mexico. Competition among rival organizations led to hundreds of deaths during these years. After the Eighteenth Amendment was repealed in 1933, crime syndicates continued gambling enterprises, loan sharking, and other illegal activities. Bootlegging did not entirely disappear either, because black-market alcoholic beverages were cheaper than legally produced liquor.

Organized crime rings are shrouded in secrecy and are often difficult for police to crack. If, despite the odds, authorities are able to gather enough evidence to bring a case against a crime boss to court, the organization will use all of its influence to ensure a favorable verdict. The syndicate will threaten or bribe jury members, witnesses, and court officials.

In 1992, the FBI successfully prosecuted Gambino family boss John Gotti on 13 charges of murder, tax fraud, gambling, and racketeering. He bore the nickname "Teflon Don" because the government had difficulty making charges stick to him. Gotti had been acquitted of three previous indictments beginning in 1986. The FBI finally succeeded in prosecuting him, largely because of testimony from Gotti's right-hand man, Salvatore "Sammy Bull" Gravano. Officials also bugged an apartment in which Gotti discussed his criminal activities. Jury members were sequestered and were guarded by U.S. marshals.[20]

White-Collar Crime

White-collar crime is the crime of "respectable people," people who would never think of physically harming someone or who have respectable and often high-paying jobs. Although white-collar crime is often connected to organized crime, individuals are certainly capable of committing offenses such as fraud and embezzlement on their own.

The main arenas for white-collar criminals are not inner-city streets or shopping malls but are instead the corporate world, government offices, communications networks, and mailboxes. These criminals' weapons are not guns but are computers, telephones, and cash. White-collar crime is different from other crimes in that it does not involve physically harming someone and more often victimizes a company or an organization than any particular person.

Banks are easy targets for white-collar criminal activity because money is their business. Numerous bank tellers have been implicated in embezzlement cases for stealing a portion of the cash they handle every day. Some bank presidents and other high-ranking executives have embezzled large sums of money. Employees of credit card companies face similar temptations. They handle payments and credit card numbers for thousands of customers, and a crooked employee can manage to steal either of these.

White-collar criminals do not always work for large corporations. Cashiers embezzle money from cash registers. Passing bad checks is a common offense that does not require access to large banks or corporate accounts, although computer verification systems and an increasing preference for other forms of payment are making it more difficult for criminals to write bad checks. Increasingly, stolen credit cards present a real danger, but companies are also taking steps to combat that problem. Photos appear on some users' cards, and many stores keep computerized records of signatures when a customer signs a receipt.

Other common white-collar crimes are faked deaths to allow one to collect life insurance money and faked accidents or fires intentionally set to allow the collection of insurance money. Counterfeiters manufacture fake currency and forge copies of virtually any document. These schemers may branch out and form entire organizations. For example, if a person stages an accident, a doctor might diagnose severe injuries when there are none, and a corrupt lawyer may serve as the "victim's" attorney. Insurance agents can also participate in the scheme by awarding large sums of money to the supposed victim.

One recent common scheme goes something like this. A crooked entrepreneur seeking to scam people out of money hires a few people to make telephone calls for him or her. The telephone operators are instructed to call people (usually housewives or elderly people) and inform them that they have won a prize if they will just send in a small amount of money. If the organization even bothers to send a prize to its victims after they send the money, it is usually a piece of junk. The spread of such scams led to the passage of the Senior Citizens Against Marketing Scams Act of 1994.[21]

Another scheme involves a salesperson who, for example, goes door to door demonstrating a miraculous new product that

will lift the worst stains imaginable from carpets and uphol-
stery. People are so impressed that they prepay for a bottle or
two of the miracle stain remover, and the salesperson promises
to return with their orders. The salesperson might not come
back at all, or he or she might deliver bottles of an entirely different substance that is much cheaper—in every sense of the
word—than the product that was demonstrated.

Violating environmental laws and regulations is sometimes
considered to constitute white-collar crime. Corporations have
been charged with illegally dumping toxic chemicals into rivers
and lakes, for example.

Because health is so important to people, the health and
medical professions attract many crooked entrepreneurs. These
people offer miracle cures for every conceivable human ailment,
from baldness to cancer, and it is often difficult to differentiate
between effective treatments and fraudulent schemes.

A description of the large number and variety of fraudulent
schemes would occupy a book in itself, and those discussed
here represent only a tiny fraction of the total. But such schemes
can usually be determined by a general rule: if it sounds too
good to be true, it probably is.

One problem with white-collar crime is that it is often difficult to detect until significant damage has been done. For example, if someone diverts a few cents here and there to another account, it is some time before such small thefts accumulate to a
noticeable sum. In another example, by the time supposed prize
winners figure out that they have been scammed, the crooked
entrepreneur will have probably moved elsewhere.

Drugs and Crime

Illegal drugs figure prominently in criminal activity for a number of reasons. Possession, use, sale, and distribution of illegal
drugs all violate the law. Drugs are also often a factor when
other crimes are committed. The Bureau of Justice Statistics
(BJS) defines drug-related crimes as "offenses in which a drug's
pharmacologic effects contribute; offenses motivated by the
user's need for money to support continued use; and offenses
connected with drug distribution itself."[22]

Most violent crime associated with drugs occurs in the
chaotic and ugly world of trafficking. Criminal organizations
orchestrate large-scale drug trafficking rings, and they use

violence to intimidate and defend themselves against law enforcement agents, cheats, and rivals. Violence is also used to expand territory, retaliate against informers, and punish distributors for selling drugs of an inferior quality. The BJS found that

- Drug users are more likely to have criminal records than nonusers.
- Those with criminal records are more likely to use drugs than those who have no criminal record.
- The numbers of crimes rise as drug use increases.[23]

Drugs and alcohol augment violent tendencies in some people. Between 25 and 35 percent of all state prison inmates from 1974 to 1989 committed their offenses under the influence of drugs.[24] Seventy-five percent of inmates surveyed by BJS reported having used drugs during their lifetimes—40 percent within the month prior to their offense. Twenty-seven percent said they committed their crimes while under the influence of drugs.[25]

Heroin and cocaine rank among the most expensive drug habits, and crimes committed to support these habits often involve large sums of money.[26] One writer has estimated that two of every three looters during the 1992 Los Angeles riots were drug or alcohol abusers.[27]

Drug Use Forecasting tests, which test for ten drugs, found that of arrestees tested, more than half of persons arrested in most cities had used drugs recently. Additionally, cocaine was found more frequently than any other drug.[28]

Since by definition inmates are prone to crime to begin with, prisons are often breeding grounds for drugs, which can be smuggled in by visitors and new inmates. In 1996, federal prosecutors targeted an inmate named Larry Hoover, who they alleged controls a 50,000-member cultish drug gang known as the "Gangster Disciples" from his prison cell in Dixon, Illinois. Prosecutors say the gang has members in 35 states, approximately 5,000 of which are in prison.[29] It should be noted, however, that drug use and serious crime are not always connected. Drug users may not be prone to violence and might get high to forget problems or to have fun in social situations. On the flip side, not all criminals use drugs.

Law enforcement officials combat drug crimes in a number of ways. Community policing is gaining popularity; this allows police to interact with the community on a regular basis rather than only showing up to arrest offenders. A citizen tip often alerts police to drug users, dealers, and houses, and law enforcement officials actively encourage residents to report suspected violations. Local agencies target high-crime areas in their districts and are often equipped with special drug units.

At the higher levels of trafficking, bank officials sometimes alert police to large deposits that may point to illegal drug activity. Banks are required to file a Currency Transaction Report on all transactions of $10,000 or more, which allows officials to monitor suspicious activity.

Approaches to Crime Control

With criminologists, politicians, sociologists, psychologists, writers, and others all interested in crime, it is inevitable that widely divergent viewpoints exist on how to control this perpetual problem. Some believe problems originate within the individual, whether for biological, psychological, or moral reasons. Others feel poor social and economic circumstances are responsible for crime. These beliefs, in turn, shape people's views on how to control miscreants.

In the high-profile world of politics, where legislation is written and anticrime policy for the nation is determined, two general philosophies dominate. Large pieces of legislation might have a "conservative" or a "liberal" bent, but they usually require bipartisan support and therefore must make concessions to both viewpoints.

Many conservatives view criminal activity as an issue of individual responsibility and accountability. Their anticrime proposals tend to promote harsh sentences aimed at both punishment and deterrence. A conservative commentator has written, "The conservative solution to crime—putting violent offenders in prison for longer periods of time—works."[30] This view stems from understanding people as individuals fully capable of making choices, who should bear the full consequences of their actions. For some conservatives, stiff sentences are simply practical; for example, they believe the possibility of a lengthy jail term discourages people from committing crimes.

Other conservatives believe crime is a result of declining moral character. Crime, they argue, will not decrease until individuals regain moral character, despite the policies government officials implement. Conservative Christian writer Charles Colson holds this view: "This is the hidden root of violent crime in

America: Our culture has bred a generation without conscience."[31] Conservatives usually support the death penalty for convicted murderers and strict sentences for other crimes. Many criticize efforts to rehabilitate criminals, arguing that rehabilitation cannot replace punishment and often does not work.

Liberals approach the crime problem from a different direction. Many liberals believe poor economic circumstances lead to crime, and they formulate anticrime policies aimed at improving those circumstances. President Lyndon Johnson centered many of his proposals around such thinking and introduced legislation aimed at reducing poverty and providing sufficient education.

When a criminal has committed an offense, liberals tend to favor lighter punishment combined with rehabilitation efforts. They believe drug and alcohol rehabilitation, psychological counseling, education, and job training can help to reform convicted criminals and prepare them to rejoin society. Lamenting the passage of Washington state's Initiative 593, which imposes mandatory life sentences for those convicted of three "most serious" crimes, one liberal writer complained, "The last remnants of rehabilitation as a goal of incarceration have been eliminated."[32]

Another centerpiece of liberal policy has been an emphasis on defendants' rights. During the 1960s, the Warren Court ruled on a number of court cases aimed at ensuring defendants' rights in the justice system, including the famous *Miranda v. Arizona* in 1966, which established a four-part requirement for the admissibility of confessions in court. Arrestees are now read their "Miranda rights."

Computers, Technology, and Crime

In the middle of the night on February 15, 1995, FBI agents in Raleigh, North Carolina, knocked on the door of outlaw computer hacker Kevin Mitnick. Mitnick had evaded them previously, moving from spot to spot across the United States and living under aliases. In addition to having committed many other computer offenses, Mitnick had broken into the computer systems of many communications companies, stolen software, cracked security codes, and obtained more than 20,000 credit card numbers.[33] He is part of a new generation of computer criminals whose crimes grow more complex as technology advances.

Computer crime is among the most difficult crimes to crack. "Hackers," as the offenders are known, can hide behind electronic aliases and reroute signals through a maze of computers net-worked around the world, making their activity very difficult to trace. Police are rarely equipped with the technical knowledge required to begin to trace these hackers and must often call in outside expertise.

Mitnick had been convicted previously on computer of-fenses and eventually returned to hacking. The FBI had almost caught him more than once—in a Kinko's parking lot in Cali-fornia and at his apartment in Seattle—but he escaped both times. He made a mistake that would prove to be his undoing on Christmas Day, 1994, when he broke into the computer of California security expert Tsutomu Shimomura. Shimomura and others were able to track Mitnick to an apartment complex in Raleigh, where FBI agents arrested him.[34]

How do hackers gain the information required to conduct their activities? Sometimes they simply experiment with secu-rity codes until one finally works. They search dumpsters and trash bins outside of companies for discarded computer manu-als or disks and paper that might contain security codes and in-formation on the operating systems. Sometimes an employee can read over the shoulder of another worker who has a higher access level to the company's computer system than he or she does.[35] Mitnick was known to have posed as a technician on the telephone in attempts to gain secret information.[36]

Working inside companies, people can use computers in any number of illegal ways: diverting money to other accounts or locations for personal use, stealing software or privileged in-formation, manipulating data, falsifying records or account statements, intercepting communication, or destroying data.[37] One method, known as the "salami" technique, involves cutting off a small amount of money from each of many computer ac-counts and rerouting the funds into a personal account.[38] The offender may divert only a few cents from each account, which can add up if numerous accounts are involved.

There are various types of computer criminals. Some simply enjoy breaking into protected areas and altering a little data here and there. The more brazen hackers might alter or destroy large amounts of data. Someone may hold a grudge against a particular company or person and may break into their com-puters for revenge. Still others seek to steal information, such as credit card numbers or marketing plans, and sell it.

Technology has also given rise to other high-tech crimes. In 1992, a number of women who had visited a Virginia infertility specialist began to notice that their children resembled the doctor. It was eventually revealed that the doctor had fathered at least 15 children, even though he had advertised a complex and discreet sperm-screening process.[39] In that same year, a drug trafficking ring using Kennedy International Airport in New York City stole expensive airplane guidance systems for the planes they used for smuggling.[40]

Crime Prevention

Legislators and police officers are not the only people who engage in the battle against crime. As with public agencies, private anticrime organizations and programs are abundant. It is little exaggeration to say that for almost every aspect of crime, an organization or group exists that aims to correct it. (See Chapter 5 for further descriptions of these groups' activities.)

Individuals can do many things to lessen the chance someone will harm them or steal their property. Some safety tips follow.

Personal Property

There are several steps you can take to help police identify stolen personal belongings if they are recovered.

- Mark all large valuables with your name and driver's license number. Some good candidates for marking are computers, stereos, television sets, VCRs, video cameras, and other electronic equipment. If the item cannot be engraved, use invisible ink.
- Make a list of valuables, with detailed descriptions. Any special markings, serial numbers, or engraved identification should be written down, because all of this information can help police to identify recovered stolen goods more easily. Photographs of the items are good additions to the list.

Home

There are no foolproof methods of protecting yourself from becoming a crime victim at home. You can make it difficult, however, for a potential intruder to gain access to the premises. You can also make your home appear to be a poor candidate for break-ins and thus reduce your risk of harm.

- Rule number one: keep doors and windows locked. Make sure your lock is a good, secure lock that burglars will have a hard time opening. The screws that hold the lock in place should be long enough so they do not come loose under pressure.
- Strong doors at all entrances, particularly those that are the most obscured, are very helpful. Avoid hollow, wooden doors. It is a good idea to install quality peep-holes in doors.
- Make sure all entrances to your home are well lit.
- Secure all windows and sliding glass doors with quality locks. Additional mechanisms for securing sliding glass doors include a bar in the track and devices that prevent a would-be intruder from lifting the door out of its track. Similar devices can be used on windows that slide side-ways.
- Do not leave spare house keys hidden near the house. If you have to leave them outside, do not pick an obvious spot such as under a rock, under a brick, beneath the doormat, or on top of a ledge. Experienced criminals know where to look for keys.
- If you are going to be out of town, have a neighbor pick up your newspaper and mail. Accumulated mail and newspapers signal potential burglars that you might be gone. Ask your neighbor to put a load of his or her trash in one of your cans.
- It is also a good idea before you go out of town to set timers to cause your lights to go on and off, which gives the appearance that someone is home. If possible, set dif-ferent lights to come on at different times each day.
- Keep tall ladders inside or well hidden. Intruders can use them to reach a top-floor window.
- It is especially important to keep the garage securely locked. It is a hiding place that is often filled with tools that can be used to break into your house. Also be wary of electric garage doors. Some thieves walk around neighborhoods with garage door openers and see which garages their buttons will open.

- A large, loyal dog with a loud bark constitutes good protection.
- If a stranger comes to your door and needs to use the telephone, offer to make the call while he or she waits outside.
- Ask for identification when someone claiming to be a service person, police officer, or something similar knocks on your door. Tell the person you will have to verify his or her ID before you let him or her in.
- If you come home and think somebody who is not supposed to be there might be inside, call the police from a neighbor's house or other nearby telephone.
- If a burglar enters your home while you are there, remain silent. Call the police as soon as you can. If you encounter the burglar, do not provoke him or her unless you are in a good position to take the burglar prisoner. If he or she flees upon seeing you, write down as many details as you can about the person's appearance and car.

Neighborhood Watch Programs

Most police departments have crime prevention sections, and they usually make officers available to talk to groups interested in starting a community watch program.

- Neighbors should take steps, such as those described earlier, to mark and secure their property.
- They can agree to watch for suspicious activity in the area and report it to the rest of the neighborhood.

Children

It is necessary to talk to children to protect them from crime. The steps listed here can help to reduce their risk of being victimized and can help authorities to investigate crimes against them if anything does happen.

- Always make sure young children are supervised.
- Teach your children not to talk to strangers.
- Make sure your children know your name and their full names, as well as their address and telephone number.

Any such information can help police locate parents if children become lost.

- Make sure schools and day care centers know who is authorized to pick your children up.
- Do not allow children to answer the door at home by themselves.
- Watch for sudden changes in your child's personality. Marked changes in behavior can indicate that a child is being abused or can signal that a child has begun to use drugs.
- Hire babysitters you know and trust.
- Have children fingerprinted and take videos or photos to give to police if anything happens to them.

Bus, Car, and Transportation Safety

Trouble can arise without warning when you are in your car or on a bus. You can help guard against those who would harm you or steal your property in these situations.

- Do not arrive at bus stops long before the bus is scheduled to come, especially if you are alone. It is better to ride with a friend.
- When you use public transportation, sit near the driver if possible. If not, sit near a large number of people.
- Always keep your car locked, regardless of whether you are in it. Always keep windows rolled up.
- City dwellers often buy inflatable dummies to allow them fraudulent use of high-occupancy vehicle lanes in which traffic moves more quickly, but it is a good idea to have one beside you to make it appear as though you are not driving alone.
- If someone approaches your car, honk your horn several times and drive away as soon as you can.
- If someone starts to follow you, honk your horn sporadically and keep driving. If you can, drive to a police or fire station. If this is not possible, drive to a well-lit place like a gas station. Never drive home—this will let whoever is following you know where you live.
- Park in areas that are well lit and as close as possible to the door you plan to enter.

- Have your keys in hand before you head to your car. Check to make sure nobody is in the car before unlocking the door.
- Do not stop to help someone who appears to have car trouble. Drive on, and call the police as soon as you can.
- If you have car trouble, stay in your car if possible. Keep an envelope in your car that contains quarters and has the names and telephone numbers of friends written on the outside. If a stranger walks up to your car and asks to help, slip the envelope through a cracked window and ask him or her to call the numbers on the outside.
- Do not give rides to hitchhikers.
- Do not leave valuables in plain sight. It is best to put them in the trunk.

Fraudulent Schemes

These tips can help you to avoid becoming a victim of fraud.

- Do not, for any reason, give money to someone under suspicious circumstances.
- The elderly are frequent targets of fraudulent money-making schemes, and they should be especially wary when someone calls with an offer that sounds too good to be true.
- If someone calls to let you know you have won something, be very careful. If you do not remember entering an official contest, you have probably won either a piece of junk or nothing at all. If there is a catch, such as a requirement to buy something before you get your prize, hang up the telephone.
- Do not give your credit card number out over the telephone unless absolutely necessary.
- Do not carry large amounts of cash.
- If possible, have your paycheck deposited directly into your bank account. Otherwise, it may be lost or stolen from your car or mailbox or may be lost at the post office.
- Call the police if you feel a scam artist has tried to take advantage of you so they can alert others.
- If you are in doubt about any business practice, call the local Better Business Bureau. You can register a complaint,

and they can tell you if others have complained about the same practice.

- Before purchasing a miracle cure that promises to heal an ailment, do some research on the product. Some herbal products, for example, have been used successfully for centuries, and others have appeared on the market only recently. Be alert for new and untested cures that may be useless or even harmful.

Personal Safety

Observing the following tips can sometimes keep you from injury if someone tries to harm you.

- Morning is the safest time to walk; nighttime is the most dangerous. It is always preferable to walk with one or more friends. When walking at night, choose a busy, well-lit street and walk close to the road. Do not walk near buildings where people can hide.
- A woman wearing high heels should kick them off if someone starts to follow her—if possible, toward her pursuer.
- If you receive an obscene telephone call, hang up.
- In many states, it is now legal to carry a concealed weapon, provided you are licensed and trained to do so. If you choose to carry a gun, make sure you know how to use it properly. Similarly, if you carry mace or hot-pepper spray, be sure you know how to handle it. An attacker can seize weapons and use them on you.
- Punches and blows delivered to an attacker's spine can kill or paralyze him or her.
- Beepers and whistles can alert people nearby that someone is trying to attack you. If you do not have such a device, scream as loud as you can to draw attention to the scene. When an attacker perceives that a lot of people might see him, he or she is more likely to flee.
- If someone starts following you, get to a populated area as soon as you can.
- Do not carry your keys in your purse. If someone steals it, your house key and car key will be available along with your address and telephone number.
- If possible, carry money in a secure, hidden pocket.

- Carry purses close to your body. Large purses that hang freely make easy targets.
- If someone tries to steal your purse, try to get a good description of the thief. Call attention to the thief by blowing a whistle or screaming so other people will see him or her. If you resist someone who is much stronger than you or who might have a weapon, you may be hurt.
- Above all, use good judgment when you choose to fight an attacker. Is the attacker stronger than you? Does he or she have a weapon that might be used if you resist? Do not challenge someone who is likely to hurt you unless you think your life depends on it.

Abuses of Power

When an onlooker captured on videotape the end of a beating incident involving the Los Angeles police and intoxicated motorist Rodney King in 1991, complaints about police brutality and other abuses rang from civil rights groups, the media, and others. Police began chasing King, who had consumed several beers with a high alcohol content. King stepped on the accelerator, and a high-speed chase ensued that involved several cars and a police helicopter. When he finally stopped, King taunted officers and resisted arrest. Two Taser darts were used, but King remained defiant, and police began beating him.

It was this last segment of the episode that an onlooker immortalized with his video camera. Clips of Los Angeles Police Department (LAPD) officers beating King played on the evening news around the country for days. State charges were eventually brought against the arresting officers. A Los Angeles jury acquitted them, sparking a deadly riot in the city.[41] After the acquittal, federal civil rights charges were brought against the officers, and a jury awarded King more than $3.8 million.[42]

The King case sparked criticism largely from the left, but another case of alleged abuse of power enraged the political right. Attorney General Janet Reno was widely criticized by conservatives for authorizing a raid on a religious compound in Waco, Texas, in 1993 that led to the deaths of 17 children, more than 60 other cult members, and 4 ATF agents. The ill-fated decision sparked a congressional investigation into the incident.

During a weeks-long standoff, federal agents repeatedly asked Branch Davidian leader David Koresh, who was accused of stockpiling weapons inside the compound and of abusing children, to surrender peacefully. He refused, and agents from the Bureau of Alcohol, Tobacco, and Firearms moved in with tear gas and tanks. Minutes later, the compound burst into flames, and many cult members inside lost their lives. Federal agents claimed cult members had started the fire, and surviving cult members claimed the invading tanks had set off the flames.[43]

Police corruption in our nation is as old as U.S. history itself. Without public officials who looked the other way as a result of threats or bribes, the lucrative bootlegging underworld would not have prospered during the Prohibition era. Confiscated goods such as drugs can be sold for a great deal of money and represent easy temptations for crooked police officers.

Wrongful convictions may not appear to result from power abuse, but the innocent victims often feel that is the case. In 1938, a court wrongfully convicted a man named Bertram Campbell for forgery. Campbell served more than three years in prison before he was paroled. After his release, he read about a man arrested for forgery whose style seemed similar to that of the crime for which he had been convicted. He was later pardoned and awarded $115,000 in damages, but he died less than three months after receiving the award.[44]

Forced confessions were widespread in the early twentieth century. With techniques they called "the third degree," police officers extracted confessions from suspects using different forms of torture. Some common methods were pouring water into a suspect's nostrils and delivering blows to the head at regular intervals.[45]

On June 13, 1966, the United States Supreme Court handed down a landmark decision in the *Miranda v. Arizona* case. Miranda had appealed a conviction on the grounds that police had failed to tell him about his Fifth Amendment right against self-incrimination, and he won. The *Miranda* decision defined four standards for usable confessions: a suspect must be advised that (1) he or she has the right to remain silent; (2) if he or she says anything, it can and will be used against him or her; (3) he or she has the right to have an attorney in the room during any questioning; and (4) if he or she cannot afford a private attorney, the court will appoint one.

Corruption in the criminal justice system is not limited to law enforcement agencies. Judges and jury members can accept bribes or succumb to other pressure, such as threats from Mafia organizations, to fix the outcome of a case. Opportunity exists for misbehavior at all levels.

Offenses

When someone breaks the law, this offense is classified into different categories. A *felony* involves a serious offense such as murder, rape, or robbery; punishment is usually either death or imprisonment. States define *felony* differently. A felony in California is "a crime which is punishable by death or by imprisonment in the state prison." In North Carolina, a felony is defined as "a crime which was a felony at common law; is or may be punishable by death; is or may be punishable by imprisonment in the state's prison; [and] is or is denominated as a felony by statute." Some states do not specify what constitutes a felony.[46]

Less serious offenses are called *misdemeanors*—these include traffic offenses, petty theft, and simple assaults, for example. Misdemeanors are often punished by any combination of probation, fines, community service, and short jail terms.

Within these broad classifications are more specific definitions of crimes that, once again, vary from state to state. In general, homicide, the taking of another's life, is the most serious offense, and depending on the circumstances in which it happened, it can be classified a number of ways. If somebody intentionally kills another, he or she has committed *first-degree murder. Second-degree murder* occurs, for example, if a burglar kills someone he or she did not intend to encounter during the theft. Killings in self-defense are called *justifiable homicides* and are committed by police in the line of duty or by people defending themselves from attack.

The circumstances surrounding manslaughter are often violent quarrels between people who know each other. If a man beats his wife to death in a fit of rage, he has committed *voluntary manslaughter. Involuntary manslaughter* results from negligence such as reckless driving.

A *rapist* forces sexual intercourse on someone who does not consent. In the majority of cases, men rape women. A person commits *statutory rape* if he or she has sexual intercourse with a child who is younger than the age of consent, which differs from state to state but is usually somewhere between ages 12 and 16. Assault and battery often go together. *Assault* is the threat of violence, and *battery* is the actual action. If someone threatens another with a punch, that person has committed assault; if he or she punches another person, he or she is guilty of battery. In *simple assaults,* no weapon is brandished, and the victim is not seriously injured.

Thefts are usually divided into the categories of robbery, larceny, and burglary. Violence or threat of violence is used in *robberies. Larceny* means to steal someone else's property or possessions. Depending on the value of the stolen goods, larcenies can be considered felonies or misdemeanors. For someone to commit *burglary,* he or she must enter private premises—a home or business—to steal.

When a building is intentionally or maliciously burned down, an *arson* has occurred. People commit arson for varied reasons: for revenge, to collect insurance money, or for sport. Females are arrested for *prostitution,* or selling sex, more often than males. Organized prostitution rings are run by pimps or madames. (See the Glossary and other sections of this chapter for descriptions of common offenses in white-collar, organized, and juvenile crime.)

The Criminal Justice System

Law Enforcement Agencies

Law enforcement agencies form the first level in the criminal justice system. When a crime is reported, officials from the appropriate law enforcement agency begin investigating the offense. If a suspect violates federal drug trafficking laws, the Drug Enforcement Administration may take over the case. Local police handle most offenses, however. The thousands of law enforcement agencies in the United States vary in size, purpose, and jurisdiction. The vast majority are local.

Many federal law enforcement agencies are part of the Department of Justice, and a number are under the Department of the Treasury. Major federal law enforcement agencies include the FBI, the United States Marshals Service, the Drug Enforcement Administration (DEA), and the Bureau of Alcohol, Tobacco, and Firearms (ATF). Here is a list of federal law enforcement agencies under their parent agencies.

Department of Justice
Federal Bureau of Investigation (FBI)
Drug Enforcement Administration (DEA)

Immigration and Naturalization Service (INS)
United States Marshals Service

Department of the Treasury
Bureau of Alcohol, Tobacco, and Firearms (ATF)
United States Secret Service
Internal Revenue Service
United States Customs Service

United States Postal Service
Postal Inspection Service

Department of Transportation
United States Coast Guard

For a more complete description of the functions and duties of these agencies, see Chapter 5.

Two or more agencies will sometimes work together on a case. For example, the 1993 Branch Davidian siege in Waco, Texas, involved both the ATF and the FBI.

J. Edgar Hoover, who served as director of the FBI from 1924 to 1972, is largely responsible for the expansion of federal investigation powers. Hoover transformed the poorly organized Bureau of Investigation into the efficiently run FBI. He created a national fingerprint file, a forensics laboratory, a training academy, and a ballistics division. Prior to his tenure, bureau agents had not been allowed to carry guns.

State law enforcement agencies have the power to enforce laws only within the boundaries of their states; other states fall out of their jurisdiction. Every state except Hawaii has its own police force. The power and duties of these agencies vary widely from state to state; some state police primarily patrol the highways, whereas others have much greater authority. State agencies also train and assist local departments.

Local law enforcement agencies play the most important role in fighting crime in the United States. Federal agencies rarely become involved in an investigation unless a suspect has violated federal law or committed crimes in more than one state. Disputes between local departments and federal agencies can surface when the latter decide to participate in or take over a case. Gang and Mafia activity are two good examples of types of cases that invite joint investigations. Local police are familiar with the key players, and federal agencies bring in sophisticated investigation techniques.

City and county police enforce the law only within their jurisdictions. For city police, that jurisdiction is usually the city itself; county police cover cities that do not have their own departments, as well as areas outside city limits. Larger law enforcement agencies may have special teams to handle situations such as hostage takings, bomb threats, narcotics, juvenile crime, and searches.

As discussed earlier, a new approach to law enforcement is gaining popularity around the United States. Community policing puts officers on the streets of the neighborhoods they have been assigned to patrol and is popular especially in inner-city neighborhoods. Police walk the streets and get to know the local residents rather than coming to make arrests only when they are called to the scene of a crime.

The large number of disconnected agencies in the United States invites disputes over jurisdiction and sometimes impedes effective investigation. On the other hand, the absence of a single and unified national police force guards against serious abuses of power.

Investigation, Forensics, and Handling Evidence

Handling evidence is very tricky. Before it can be presented in court, it must be collected and analyzed—a sometimes lengthy process that involves several players. A record is kept of each person who handles evidence. Immediately following a crime, nobody is allowed near the scene until investigators finish collecting evidence. After a photographer has taken pictures of the undisturbed scene, the investigators dust surfaces for fingerprints, collect hair and clothing fibers, and look for any other clues that might lead them to a suspect. When the evidence has been gathered, it is taken to a crime laboratory for analysis. These laboratories use sophisticated equipment to determine what kind of gun fired a bullet, classify the type of blood found at the scene of the crime, identify chemicals and drugs, match hair and fiber samples, and provide many other details.

In court, the proper or improper handling of evidence can seriously influence the outcome of a case. Defense attorneys frequently try to discredit the prosecution's evidence by alleging mishandling, corruption, or inconclusiveness. At the nationally televised murder trial of former football star O. J. Simpson in 1995, defense attorneys launched an assault on the credibility of blood deoxyribonucleic acid (DNA) evidence linking Simpson to the murders of his ex-wife and her friend.

Some controversial methods exist for obtaining evidence, such as the use of lie detector tests, that courts have ruled inadmissible. Investigators may use the tests to lead them to suspects, but they must find other evidence to link those suspects to their alleged crimes. Hypnotizing victims, witnesses, and—less frequently—suspects is another method that yields questionable results.

At the beginning of the twentieth century, the United States did not have a single crime laboratory. Now there are hundreds, with increasingly sophisticated methods of analyzing evidence. New technology has given rise to previously unheard-of crime-solving tools. Investigators can detect fingerprints with a laser, which has the added benefit of finding some fingerprints dusting cannot. Another popular new method of analysis involves DNA identification from blood samples, a practice encouraged by the Violent Crime Control and Law Enforcement Act of 1994, which provides federal grants to help states establish or improve DNA identification programs in forensics laboratories.[47]

A computer system at the Indianapolis Police Department archives lab reports, crime-scene photographs, fingerprints, witness statements, 911 calls, and other information relating to ongoing investigations.[48] In times past, officers might have had to contact the crime lab and look through fingerprint and photograph files to obtain necessary information. Digital cameras put fingerprints on computers, allowing them to be more closely examined and widely distributed among investigators.[49]

In the mid-1980s, law enforcement agencies began wide use of Automated Fingerprint Identification Systems, which can examine 1,200 fingerprints per second and print out possible matches.[50] Agencies are looking into similar possibilities for identifying gun markings on bullets.[51]

Courts

A court settles arguments between parties after a complaint has been formally filed. In *criminal courts,* the parties to the dispute are the government (at whatever level) and a defendant who is accused of breaking at least one law. Two private parties take their dispute to *civil courts.* Civil cases are often heard in the same courts as less serious criminal trials.

Sometimes a case can involve both civil and criminal law. When victims of crime feel the criminal justice system has failed them in some way, they can file suit in civil court. For example, when a Los Angeles jury acquitted O. J. Simpson of two murders, the families of the victims brought a wrongful death suit against him in civil court.

A *judge* presides over trials and appeals. He or she is responsible for keeping order, making sure attorneys follow the rules, and ruling on evidence that will be allowed into the courtroom. Judges also sentence people juries convict and instruct juries on the laws that apply to the case at hand. Each party in a dispute is represented by an attorney who is familiar with the laws of the state. Attorneys argue cases for the plaintiffs and defendants and provide them with legal advice. The district attorney is the plaintiff in criminal trials and represents "the people" of the city, county, or state that is bringing the charges.

Some defendants choose to act as their own attorneys. In a recent example, Colin Ferguson, who opened fire on a crowded subway car in New York City, chose to represent himself in court. Most legal experts do not recommend that defendants act as their own attorneys, because they are unlikely to be familiar with the intricacies of the laws they are accused of violating. In both civil and criminal trial courts, a 12-member jury hears a case. In criminal trials, the jury determines if the defendant is guilty or innocent of the charges brought against him or her. If the members return a guilty verdict, a judge may sentence the new convict, usually at a sentencing hearing. In civil cases, a jury sides with either the plaintiff or the defendant and awards damages accordingly.

State courts are hierarchical systems and are organized differently from state to state. In general, a system of lower courts is in place to hear local and state cases. A *magistrate* issues search and arrest warrants, sets bail, appoints an attorney for defendants when they cannot afford their own, and conducts preliminary hearings. *Small claims courts, traffic courts,* and other courts hear cases involving lesser offenses, whereas *municipal courts, county courts,* and *superior courts* hear more serious cases. Civil suits and minor criminal misdemeanor cases are often relegated to the lowest level of trial courts, whereas superior courts hear felony cases. A state is typically divided into superior court districts, with at least one judge presiding in each. Superior courts also hear appeals from minor courts.

Above these courts are *appellate courts,* which represent the first step in appealing the decision of a lower court. No trials or juries are found in appellate courts. Instead, a panel of judges reviews the decision of the lower court and makes a ruling. The judges make sure that certain or all aspects of the case—the arrest, questioning of the suspect, jury selection, evidence admitted into the courtroom—were handled according to the law. Some states do not have intermediate appellate courts, so appeals must go to the *state supreme court,* the highest court in the state. In states that have appellate courts, the state supreme court can sometimes refuse to hear an appeal.

Federal courts hear cases that involve (1) parties from different states, (2) the United States as a party, (3) constitutional law, (4) violations of federal law, and (5) appeals from lower courts. *District courts* are trial courts; more than 90 are found in the United States and its territories. A state convict may take his or her case to federal courts after exhausting the state appeals process.

Above these courts are twelve *courts of appeals,* one in each district. The cases that reach these courts are generally heard by three circuit judges, although an important case might be heard en banc by all twelve judges. Nine justices serve on the *United States Supreme Court,* the highest court in the nation. Very few cases reach the Supreme Court, and it can hear only a small fraction of those that do. Its decisions are final. Other federal courts such as the *Court of Claims,* the *United States Customs Court,* and the *Court of Customs and Patent Appeals* have jurisdiction over specific cases.

Prisons, Jails, and Corrections

Several different institutions hold criminals. If someone is convicted of a serious crime such as murder, robbery, arson, or rape, he or she will likely be sentenced to spend time in *prison.* Prisons house convicted criminals in cells, and they have different characteristics according to the various types of criminals.

If a prison is not exclusively for men or women, the two sexes are kept in different sections. Violent criminals and those likely to attempt to escape are sent to maximum security prisons. Nonviolent offenders, such as white-collar criminals, are sent to minimum security prisons. Armed guards watch the prisoners both inside and outside, and the institution is surrounded by barbed wire and other security equipment.

The Bureau of Prisons operates federal prisons, where persons convicted of violating federal laws and those who have committed crimes in more than one state are incarcerated. Common federal offenses include breaking immigration laws, tax evasion, and drug trafficking offenses. The most violent felons are usually found in state prisons.

Governments used to have prisoners perform highway construction and other arduous tasks, but that practice has faded as a result of court rulings on its constitutionality and complaints that unpaid labor takes jobs away from free citizens. Modern prisons commonly have a chaplain, religious services, and opportunities for education and vocational training.

Jails hold offenders who are waiting for trial in custody. They are run by local cities and counties rather than the state. Some jails are connected to police headquarters. Separate areas are designated for women and juveniles. People who have been sentenced to a short term of incarceration, usually less than a year, are also kept in jails. Juveniles serve their sentences in *reformatories* or *juvenile detention centers,* which are structured differently from adult prisons. Reform and education are emphasized more heavily in the punishment of young offenders.

Not all convicts are required to serve time. First-time offenders who have not committed serious crimes might be sentenced to *probation,* or supervised release. During his or her specified period of probation, the offender is required to report to a probation officer at certain intervals. The probation sentence might have additional conditions, such as staying away from criminal friends, finding steady work, or submitting to periodic drug tests.

The probation sentence is given inappropriately at times to ease prison overcrowding, which has become a serious problem in the United States. Overcrowding contributes to violence and rioting among a prison population already prone to such activities.

Parole, or early release, is granted by a parole board to prisoners who behave well and who are no longer deemed a threat to society. Some sentences, usually for murder, forbid parole. Parolees are required to report to a parole officer, and their early release can carry extra conditions.

Arrests, Convictions, and Sentencing

To further understand how the players in the criminal justice system work together, let us trace a fictional 26-year-old man named Ned through a murder case. After receiving an anonymous report of a dead body next to a dumpster behind a local grocery store, police arrive at the scene. After a brief look at the evidence, they determine that the murder occurred at this spot. They secure the scene and bring in a criminalistics team to gather evidence, which is taken to a forensics laboratory for analysis.

The police spend the next two days questioning relatives of the victim and combing the neighborhood for potential witnesses. The information they gather and lab results from the forensics specialists lead them to suspect a former friend of the victim—Ned. After obtaining a warrant for his arrest from the magistrate, they approach Ned, read him his rights, and drive him to the police station. They obtain a search warrant for his apartment, where they hope to find additional evidence linked to the murder.

At the police station, an officer "books" him, or enters a charge in the book. Ned is charged with first-degree murder and is taken to jail. When he arrives, he is ordered to empty his pockets, and the contents are held for safekeeping. At this point, he might be allowed to call friends, relatives, or a lawyer, although an officer might call for him. He is then fingerprinted, and his picture (known as a mug shot) is taken. Ned will soon face arraignment—that is, he will be brought into court and officially charged. A magistrate decides whether a grand jury should consider the case or whether the charges should be dismissed. Between 14 and 23 citizens sit on a grand jury, and a specified number—frequently 12—have to agree to bring an indictment.[52]

The grand jury can either dismiss Ned's murder charge or indict him. In Ned's case, the evidence is too strong to dismiss, so the jury unanimously indicts him on one count of first-degree murder. Ned will then be required to enter a plea, and a judge will set bail.

Bail is a set amount of money a defendant pays for his or her freedom until a trial. Its specific purpose is to make sure a defendant appears in court on his or her appointed day, and it is refunded when the defendant does so. A judge denies Ned bail because of the seriousness of his crime and orders him to be held in jail until his trial. If he had committed a misdemeanor rather than a murder, he might have faced very low bail or none at all.

He pleads "not guilty by reason of temporary insanity" on the advice of his lawyer, who thinks Ned's stormy family history can be used to influence the jury in his favor. Strong evidence links Ned to the murder of his former friend who, police discovered, had cheated him out of more than $6,000.

A psychiatrist who examined Ned determined that he could have been, but was not necessarily, insane at the time he murdered his former friend. The psychiatrist will serve as an expert witness, even though her diagnosis was inconclusive.

The insanity defense is defined differently from state to state. In essence, the argument holds that the defendant did not know what he or she was doing at the time he or she committed the crime. Insanity can be temporary, can stem from psychological and emotional problems, or may result from a disease such as multiple personalities.

The district attorney who prosecutes the case will sometimes offer a plea bargain, allowing the defendant to plead guilty in exchange for reduced charges, a lighter sentence, or both. The district attorney thus avoids a lengthy trial and all of the work associated with prosecuting; the prisoner receives lighter punishment than might have been the case if a jury had convicted him or her. Plea bargaining lightens the caseload of an already overburdened court system, but many oppose reducing the sentences of criminals. District attorneys sometimes refuse to offer a plea bargain.

Although Ned committed his crime in a state that has the death penalty, prosecutors decide not to pursue the death sentence because of his family history, his youth, and the fact that this is his first offense. A trial date is set, and lawyers on both sides begin preparing for their time in court. Since Ned faces state charges, he will be tried in a state court.

Ned's lawyer tries to bar some of the prosecution's evidence from the courtroom on legal technicalities but has little success. During the trial, he tries to evoke sympathy among the jurors by strongly emphasizing Ned's abusive upbringing.

The trial lasts for nine days, and after six hours of deliberation, the jury convicts Ned on the charge of first-degree murder. A judge sentences him for a minimum of 35 years to a maximum of life in prison. Will Ned ever see the outside world again? That depends. He is unlikely to receive a pardon from the governor, because there is little doubt that he is guilty. Depending on his behavior in prison, he might be granted parole after 35 years.

Murder is the most serious crime tried in state courts, and if Ned had committed a lesser felony or a misdemeanor, his treatment throughout the system would have been very different. He would likely have been allowed bail before the trial. If convicted, he would have faced less prison time and possibly been sentenced to probation.

Juvenile Delinquency and Justice

The overall juvenile delinquency rate was about the same in 1993 as it was in 1963 (around 17 percent of all arrestees were juveniles), but there is evidence that crimes committed by minors are becoming more serious. In 1993, 17.1 percent of all arrestees were juveniles under age 18. Also in that year, 16.2 percent of those arrested for murder and 16.3 percent of those arrested for forcible rape were under 18. In 1963 those numbers were 7.8 percent for murder and 17.5 percent for forcible rape—this represents a sharp increase in murder and a slight decrease in forcible rape. Statistics also suggest that very young children are committing more crimes. In 1993, more than 35,000 children under age 10 were arrested. "Under 10" offenses were not even listed in the 1963 *Uniform Crime Reports*.[53]

In many states, juveniles are defined as children under age 18, although in some states the age is 16. Some offenses, such as underage drinking or driving, can only be committed by juveniles. But many of their crimes are equally illegal for adults. As is the case with adult crime, juvenile offenses occur most often in urban areas, and they are frequently associated with gang membership.

The juvenile justice system is less tightly organized than the adult criminal justice system. A minor who commits an offense is taken to the police station. Sometimes the offender is given a warning, and police note the offense on the offender's record. He or she is subsequently released to parents' custody. If the crime is serious enough or is not the person's first offense, the police will refer the case to a juvenile court.

Juvenile courts do not have juries. Instead, a judge listens to both sides of a case and sentences the youth. Juveniles, like adults, have the right to know the charges against them, the right to an attorney, the right against self-incrimination, the right to be heard, the right to cross-examine witnesses, and the right to appeal. They do not have the right to a jury trial.[54] Juvenile courts face the same problems that plague the rest of the criminal justice system. Many are overburdened as a result of the number of cases, and young offenders often receive impersonal treatment.

When a judge finds a juvenile guilty, he or she may sentence the youth to probation, place the offender under the care of a public or private agency, or order the offender to spend time in a reformatory. Because of juveniles' youth, juvenile justice places more emphasis on reform than does adult corrections. Juveniles typically receive much shorter sentences than adults and are required to continue with schoolwork and undergo psychological counseling while detained.

In 1978, the killing of a seminary student by a 13-year-old boy in New York sparked criticism of the juvenile justice system. By law, the boy could only be tried in family court, and he received an 18-month renewable sentence—the maximum. The case led to the passage of a state law that allows juveniles to be tried as adults and to similar laws in other states.[55]

Criminals and Their Victims

In one sense, there is no typical criminal. Different circumstances provide different opportunities for different crimes. A potential criminal who is raised in poverty and in a broken home is likely to commit offenses such as robbery and other violent crimes. A bank executive who shows a penchant for crime is more prone to commit embezzlement and other forms of white-collar crime. Statistics show, however, that most criminals—and most victims—are minorities, males, and young people.[56]

Criminal activity may also take on certain characteristics with levels of intelligence. Many repeat and violent offenders have low IQs,[57] but some experts predict that the increasing sophistication of technology will give rise to a new breed of intelligent criminals.[58]

Victims of violent crime frequently know their attackers. In 1992, 47 percent of murder victims knew the person who took their life.[59] Similarly, women are often acquainted with the men who rape them.

The link between poor social and economic conditions and violent crime is indisputable, but the reasons for this correlation are hotly debated among sociologists and politicians. Some say poor conditions encourage broken homes, violence, and unemployment; others believe all of these problems originate with moral decay. Psychological factors also contribute to crimes. Many arsonists are pyromaniacs and compulsively burn down buildings for sport. Some rapists and other abusers develop sexual obsessions. Emotionally unstable people may be more prone to violence than those who are stable emotionally.

Some researchers have asserted that biological factors contribute to crime, but the results of their studies are highly controversial and largely unproven. Italian psychologist Cesare Lombroso and, later, U.S. anthropologist E. A. Hooton tried to identify genetic traits common to criminals. Lombroso identified features such as long lower jaws and flattened noses that he believed appeared disproportionately in criminals.[60] Some modern researchers have looked for genes that make a person prone to violence. Genetic mapping has been used to identify common defective genes in people with diseases; scientists have also used the technique to try to identify common genetic traits in criminals—a practice many fear will lead to attempts to manipulate human genetic material in future generations.[61]

Most crime occurs in cities, where large numbers of people live crowded together. Cities such as Washington, D.C., New York, and New Orleans have reputations for having consistently high crime rates. Metropolitan areas are breeding grounds for all types of crime. Within cities, most violent crime takes place in downtown areas known as inner cities, where large numbers of low-income people live close together in run-down housing complexes. Drugs, murders, robberies, and gang activity grip these neighborhoods.

Lower- and middle-income neighborhoods are perfect targets for the numbers racket and other illegal gambling, because they contain many people who will take risks to earn extra money. Too often, though, they only enslave themselves further to bookies or loan sharks. Upper-class criminals also live in cities. Many downtown areas are home to large headquarters of banks and corporations that offer a multitude of temptations to those inclined to embezzle money.

Politicians have begun to pay more lip service to crime victims. In a 1993 proclamation that established National Crime Victims' Rights Week, President Bill Clinton boasted, "Much has been accomplished during the past two decades to institutionalize victims' rights in this country. Bills of rights have been enacted at the federal level and by 49 state governments to codify certain essential protections for victims. All 50 States now have crime victim compensation programs."[62]

Gangs

Crime-ridden inner cities have been marked in recent years by an increasing number of youth gangs. A gang is usually made up of males of the same ethnic group, and it engages in criminal activity that is often violent. A typical gang might have 30 members, go by a name such as "the Panthers," and have panther symbols on the members' jackets. Perhaps the most famous gangs in the United States are the "Bloods" and the "Crips" in Los Angeles.

Many gangs are composed of recent immigrants to the United States, and different cities have problems with different ethnic gangs. Los Angeles has many Mexican, or Chicano, gangs, whereas New York has problems with Haitian, Puerto Rican, and Jamaican gangs.[63] Los Angeles County claims the highest number of gangs in the United States—more than a thousand gangs and 136,000 gang members.[64]

Some gangs are organized around a specific illegal venture such as drug dealing, and these groups tend to be tightly organized. Others are structured more loosely and do not specialize in any particular type of criminal activity.[65] In any case, gang loyalty is of utmost importance. When a member of the gang is hurt or killed, the other members plot revenge. If the police catch a gang member because of illegal activity, he will not give away information on member-friends who were also involved.

Once a young boy joins a gang, it is difficult for him to quit. If he leaves the group, fellow members become suspicious, and he becomes a target. The group may put him through an exit ritual, such as having him walk through two lines of gang members who beat him as he walks by.[66]

Some gangs are controlled from the top down by a powerful leader, who is often an older, respected boy in the neighborhood. Others have a few different leaders, each of whom specializes in a certain activity and who takes charge when the rest of the gang engages in that activity.[67] For example, one leader might acquire a reputation for stealing automobiles, so whenever gang members decide to steal a car, he takes charge. Members are often ranked by age. The youngest are called "juniors," "pee-wees," or another name that indicates the inferior status conveyed by their age.[68]

Although gangs vary from place to place in size and structure, some common problems are associated with them. Gang fighting, or fighting between gang members, frequently results in murder and other violence. Such confrontations can occur on a small scale between two members of rival gangs or on a much larger scale involving many members from each gang. A large percentage of juvenile homicides is associated with gang violence.

Gang fighting erupts when two rival groups want control over the same undertaking or territory, when a member of one gang ventures into the territory of another gang, or when revenge is sought for the death of a fellow member. The drive-by shooting is the preferred method for murdering rival gang members. Unfortunately, innocent bystanders who are caught in the crossfire lose their lives too. Rapes, violent assaults, stabbings, robberies, and muggings are just a few of the other crimes frequently associated with gang activity.

Specific gangs control territories within a community. Gangs might divide a neighborhood into regions or may simply claim control of a gymnasium, school, or other building. They may organize initiation rituals potential members must undergo to join the group. The rituals often involve committing crimes.

Very few exclusively female gangs exist, but young girls might be members of gangs or might assist the boys in their criminal activities. For example, girls may keep guns for the boys. The female gangs that do exist are sometimes associated with a particular male gang.[69] Although they might have similar structures, their activities are less violent.

"Good guy" gangs such as the Guardian Angels in New York have formed in some cities to patrol crime-ridden areas and stop crime when they see it happening. Although some people have objected to these organizations as unauthorized law enforcement agencies, law-abiding residents of high-crime areas are usually happy to have them.

The federal government—the DEA, the FBI, or the ATF, for example—sometimes aids local law enforcement agencies in battling serious gang problems. These organizations provide wiretaps and other assistance to local agencies that are familiar with the area's gangs.[70]

Gun Control Laws

Handguns are by far the murder weapon of choice in the 1990s,[71] and many legislative attempts have been made to keep them out of the hands of violent criminals. One of the most hotly debated issues in crime today involves the effectiveness and constitutionality of gun control laws.

Until 1993, the Gun Control Act of 1968 contained the main federal gun regulations, which included attempts to prohibit convicted criminals and other risky groups from buying guns, to curb gun traffic between states, and to ban the import of guns used for purposes other than hunting and sport.[72] In 1993, Congress passed the Brady Handgun Violence Prevention Act, better known as the Brady Bill, which established a national instant criminal background check system and a five-day waiting period for purchasing a handgun.[73] The Ninth Circuit has upheld Brady Bill provisions following challenges to required background checks by sheriffs in Arizona and Montana.[74] (See Chapter 4 for the text of the Brady Bill.)

Federal legislation, however, has not been the driving force behind gun control. Tens of thousands of gun control ordinances exist at local and state levels. In recent years, many states have followed Florida's 1987 lead and have passed laws that allow most citizens to carry concealed weapons, usually providing they are licensed, fingerprinted, have completed safety training courses, or some combination of these.[75] Only eight states forbid citizens to carry concealed weapons.[76] Opponents of the new relaxed weapons laws fear more people carrying guns will mean more opportunity for bloodshed. Supporters think people now have more power to protect themselves from violent criminals.

Several questions commonly arise in gun control debates. Can legislation control guns? Do gun control laws violate the Second Amendment right to bear arms? How do we stop criminals from obtaining weapons illegally? Why not impose stiffer mandatory sentences for people who misuse guns? Why have the thousands of local gun control ordinances failed to stem the tide of gun use?

People who support gun control laws assert that new ordinances will keep lethal guns off the streets and out of the hands of people who might use them to kill. They also point to accidental deaths that occur on hunting outings or when children play with loaded guns.

Directly opposed to these laws is the National Rifle Association, one of the largest political action groups in the United States and a vocal opponent of restrictive gun control laws all over the country. "Guns don't kill people, people do," a common slogan, fairly accurately describes the philosophy of gun control opponents. Criminals, they assert, would find other weapons if they did not have access to guns. Further, many criminals obtain their weapons through illegal channels on the black market, and gun control laws will only serve to keep weapons out of the hands of law-abiding citizens. Citizens should have the right to protect themselves, and gun control laws violate the Second Amendment right to bear arms.

Opposition to gun control laws and other federal restrictions, along with the fiery 1993 siege of the Branch Davidian compound in Waco, Texas, have spurred an increase in citizen militia groups around the United States. One writer has stated, "Opposition to gun control is the catalyst that spawned growing support for the militias."[77]

Most advocates find themselves somewhere in between the extremes of banning all guns and allowing guns to be freely sold and traded. Licensing requirements, waiting periods, criminal background checks, and other restrictions make it more difficult for criminals to obtain guns by legal means while ensuring that law-abiding citizens have access to them.

Notes

1. Herbert Hoover, "Inaugural Address," in *Public Papers of the Presidents* (Washington, DC: U.S. Government Printing Office, 1974), p. 2.

2. "Crime in the United States—1992," *FBI Law Enforcement Bulletin* 62, no. 11 (November 1993), p. 24.

3. Ibid.

4. Federal Bureau of Investigation, *Uniform Crime Reports* (Washington, DC: U.S. Department of Justice, 1992). Statistics reflect crimes reported to law enforcement agencies.

5. Otto G. Obermaier, "Revamping the Criminal Law Patchwork," *New Jersey Law Journal* (5 December 1994), p. 25.

6. Gordon Witkin, "Cops under Fire," *U.S. News and World Report* (3 December 1990), p. 32.

7. Federal Bureau of Investigation, *Uniform Crime Reports,* 1963, 1980, and 1993.

8. Michel Marriott, "Young, Angry, and Lethal; Watch Out: Aging Thugs Will Be Replaced by Younger, More Violent Criminals," *Newsweek* (26 December 1994), p. 122.

9. Federal Bureau of Investigation, *Uniform Crime Reports,* 1963 and 1990.

10. Jay Robert Nash, *Encyclopedia of World Crime* (Wilmette, IL: Crimebooks, 1990), vol. 5, p. 461.

11. Charles McClain, "Criminal Law Reform: Historical Development in the United States," *Encyclopedia of Crime and Justice* (New York: Free Press, 1983), p. 510.

12. Ibid.

13. Federal Bureau of Investigation, *Uniform Crime Reports*, 1963.

14. President's Commission on Law Enforcement and Administration of Justice, "The Challenge of Crime in a Free Society: A Report" (Washington, DC: U.S. Government Printing Office, 1967).

15. Louis B. Schwartz, "Criminal Law Reform: Current Issues in the United States," *Encyclopedia of Crime and Justice*, pp. 514–515.

16. Obermaier, "Revamping the Criminal Law Patchwork," p. 25.

17. Ibid.

18. Task Force on Organized Crime, The President's Commission on Law Enforcement and Administration of Justice, *Task Force Report: Organized Crime* (Washington, DC: U.S. Government Printing Office, 1967), p. 1.

19. Francis A. J. Ianni and Elizabeth Reuss-Ianni, "Organized Crime: Overview," *Encyclopedia of Crime and Justice*, pp. 1094–1106.

20. Bonnie Angelo, "Wanted: A New Godfather," *Time* (13 April 1992), p. 30.

21. The act is part of the Violent Crime Control and Law Enforcement Act of 1994.

22. Bureau of Justice Statistics, *Drugs, Crime, and the Justice System: A National Report* (Washington, DC: U.S. Government Printing Office, 1992), p. 3.

23. Ibid.

24. Ibid.

25. Ibid.

26. Ibid.

27. David Whitman, "A Potent Brew: Booze and Crime," *U.S. News and World Report* (31 May 1993), p. 57.

28. Bureau of Justice Statistics, *Drugs, Crime, and the Justice System: A National Report*, p. 3.

29. John McCormick, "The 'Disciples' of Drugs—And Death: The Feds Take Aim at a Weird Chicago Street Gang That Has Grown into a Vicious National Network," *Newsweek* (5 February 1996), p. 56.

30. Grover Norquist, "Making Crime Pay," *American Spectator* 26, no. 5 (May 1993), p. 44.

31. Charles Colson, "Begging for Tyranny," *Christianity Today* 38, no. 3 (7 March 1994), p. 80.

32. Barbara Dority, "Anti-Crime Hysteria," *Humanist* 54, no. 1 (January–February 1994), p. 37.

33. Katie Hafner, "Kevin Mitnick, Unplugged," *Esquire* 124, no. 2 (August 1995), p. 80.

34. Ibid.

35. Desmond Rowland and James Bailey, *Law Enforcement Handbook* (New York: Facts on File, 1983), pp. 256–266.

36. Hafner, "Kevin Mitnick, Unplugged," p. 80.

37. Rowland and Bailey, *Law Enforcement Handbook*, pp. 256–266.

38. Ibid.

39. "Doctor Found Guilty in Fertility Case," *New York Times* (5 March 1995), p. A14.

40. Richter H. Moore Jr., "Wiseguys: Smarter Criminals and Smarter Crime in the 21st Century," *Futurist* 28, no. 5 (September–October 1994), p. 33.

41. David Whitman, "The Untold Story of the L.A. Riot," *U.S. News and World Report* (31 May 1993), p. 34.

42. "Millionaire of the Week," *Time* (2 May 1994), p. 13.

43. Nancy Gibbs, "Oh My God, They're Killing Themselves!" *Time* (3 May 1993), p. 26.

44. Sifakis, "Campbell, Bertram: Wrong Man," *Encyclopedia of American Crime*, pp. 117–118.

45. Ibid., p. 708.

46. John J. Fay, *The Police Dictionary and Encyclopedia* (Springfield, IL: Charles C. Thomas, 1988), p. 361.

47. One hundred and third Congress, Violent Crime Control and Law Enforcement Act of 1994, Title XXI.

48. Barry Wise, "Catching Crooks with Computers," *American City and County* 110, no. 6 (May 1995), p. 54.

49. Ibid.

50. George Witkin and Katia Hetter, "High-Tech Crime Solving," *U.S. News and World Report* (11 July 1994), p. 30.

51. Ibid.

52. Jerold H. Israel, "Grand Jury," *Encyclopedia of Crime and Justice*, p. 810.

53. Federal Bureau of Investigation, *Uniform Crime Reports*, 1963 and 1993.

54. Margaret K. Rosenheim, "Juvenile Justice: Organization and Process," *Encyclopedia of Crime and Justice,* p. 973.

55. Ibid., p. 383.

56. Federal Bureau of Investigation, *Uniform Crime Reports,* 1993.

57. Bruce Bower, "Criminal Intellects: Researchers Look at Why Lawbreakers Often Brandish Low IQs," *Science News* 147, no. 15 (15 April 1995), p. 232.

58. Moore, "Wiseguys: Smarter Criminals and Smarter Crime in the 21st Century," p. 33.

59. Federal Bureau of Investigation, *Uniform Crime Reports,* 1992.

60. Cited in Sifakis, "Anatomy and Crime," *Encyclopedia of American Crime,* p. 23.

61. James A. Gondles Jr., "Genetic Research: How Far Is Too Far?" *Corrections Today* 56, no. 2 (April 1994), p. 8.

62. President Bill Clinton, "Proclamation 6551—National Crime Victims' Rights Week, 1993," *Weekly Compilation of Presidential Documents* 29, no. 17 (3 May 1993), p. 708.

63. Evan Stark, *Everything You Need To Know about Street Gangs* (New York: Rosen Publishing Group, 1992), p. 13.

64. H. Range Hutson, Deirdre Anglin, Demetrios N. Kyriacou, Joel Hart, and Kevin Spears, "The Epidemic of Gang-Related Homicides In Los Angeles County from 1979 through 1994," *Journal of the American Medical Association* 274, no. 13 (4 October 1995), p. 1031.

65. Ibid.

66. Stark, *Everything You Need To Know about Street Gangs,* p. 25.

67. Walter B. Miller, "Youth Gangs and Groups," *Encyclopedia of Crime and Justice,* pp. 1671–1679.

68. Ibid.

69. Stark, *Everything You Need To Know about Street Gangs,* 1992, p. 16.

70. Gordon Witkin, "Enlisting the Feds in the War on Gangs," *U.S. News and World Report* (6 March 1995), p. 38.

71. Federal Bureau of Investigation, *Uniform Crime Reports,* 1990–1993.

72. James Lindgren and Franklin E. Zimring, "Regulation of Guns," *Encyclopedia of Crime and Justice,* p. 840.

73. One hundred and third Congress, Brady Handgun Violence Prevention Act, 1993.

74. Julie Brienza, "Ninth Circuit Upholds Tenets of Brady Act," *Trial* 31, no. 12 (December 1995), p. 63.

75. Denise Griffin, "Up in Arms over Guns," *State Legislatures* 21, no. 9 (October–November 1995), p. 32.

76. Ibid.

77. Mike Tharp, "The Rise of Citizen Militias: In Montana and Other States, Fury at Gun Control and Government Sparks a Call to Arms," *U.S. News and World Report* (15 August 1994), p. 34.

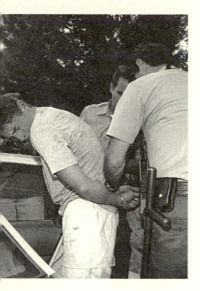

Chronology

E very aspect of crime has increased during the twentieth century. The relatively
small U.S. crime problem was controlled
largely by local law enforcement in the
early 1900s. As time progressed, the number
of offenses grew, as did the involvement of
the federal government. A significant amount
of federal legislation has turned crimes formerly handled by the states into federal offenses and expanded the powers of federal
investigation agencies, such as the FBI.

Within this larger trend, some smaller
ones can be observed. In the 1960s, the U.S.
Supreme Court began to issue rulings designed to protect defendants' rights, and
legislation was enacted that sought to reduce crime by improving social circumstances. In the 1980s and 1990s, another
trend—that of protecting victims' rights—
emerged. New crimes associated with sophisticated technology have increased
rapidly during this time.

The chronology presented here highlights some of the key developments in
these trends and describes individuals and
cases that have played a role in them.

Early 1900s	Large numbers of immigrants, mainly from Eastern Europe, arrive in the United States. Ethnic gangs and Mafia

47

Early
1900s
cont.
organizations form among Irish, Jewish, Italian, and other groups. Authorities have already identified the first Italian Mafia members who have caused serious trouble in the United States at the turn of the century in New Orleans.

1900 William McKinley is elected president.

1904 Theodore Roosevelt is elected president.

1908 William Howard Taft is elected president.

1910 The Mann Act, a federal law, outlaws the transport of females in interstate or foreign commerce for prostitution and other immoral purposes.

President Taft appoints Edward D. White to serve as chief justice of the Supreme Court.

1912 Woodrow Wilson is elected president.

1913 Earnest A. Hooton joins the faculty at Harvard University. This anthropologist's controversial studies attempt to find biological links between criminals and the crimes they commit. Hooton conducts a massive study of more than 17,000 criminals in ten states. Criminals, he would argue in essence, can be categorized by race and physical characteristics, based on which they can be expected to commit certain kinds of crimes. Hooton is a forerunner of later geneticists who attempt to link crime with genetic makeup.

1914 In *Weeks v. United States*, Justice William R. Day pleads with states to stop admitting illegally obtained evidence into the courtroom. At this time, illegal searches and seizures and forced confessions are commonplace. Police departments are known to use techniques called the "third degree" to extract confessions from suspects.

1916 The case of Charles E. Stielow, accused of shooting a farmer and his wife, brings the science of ballistics to prominence. Charles E. Waite uses microphotography to prove that the bullets used in the crime could not have come from Stielow's gun, and Stielow is acquitted.

1917   The Bolshevik Revolution in Russia overthrows that country's centuries-old monarchy. Revolutionary leader Vladimir I. Lenin orders his soldiers to execute the ruling family of the Romanov dynasty. The revolution sparks fear of a "red menace" in the United States. A young J. Edgar Hoover is assigned to investigate potential Communists and subversive movements.

Post–   Local crime commissions begin to form in major cities,
World   including Chicago, Baltimore, Kansas City, Cleveland,
War I   and Los Angeles.

1919   The United States Supreme Court upholds convictions of five people accused of inciting opposition to World War I.

Forensics expert Edward Oscar Heinrich forms a scientifically advanced crime detection lab in San Francisco. Heinrich is proficient in several aspects of science, and his expertise is ultimately called upon to help solve many crimes.

Attorney General A. Mitchell Palmer creates the General Intelligence Division inside the Justice Department to investigate radicals after a series of bombings. Palmer appoints J. Edgar Hoover to head the new agency.

Congress passes the Volstead Act to support the Eighteenth Amendment. The act outlaws the manufacture, sale, consumption, and distribution of alcoholic beverages.

1920s   International Association of Chiefs of Police (IACP) convenes a Committee on Uniform Records to develop a national crime statistics program. Early form of the *Uniform Crime Reports* results. The committee proposes standard definitions for crimes, and a common language emerges among the nation's police departments.

The American Law Institute—an organization of legal experts, lawyers, and judges—begins work on a Model Penal Code. Ironically, the proposed code's impact

1920
cont.

would not be felt until the 1950s, when it would spur debate and subsequently influence many states to revise their criminal codes.

1920

The Eighteenth Amendment to the U.S. Constitution takes effect, prohibiting the manufacture and sale of alcoholic beverages. The amendment ushers in the era known as Prohibition, which lasts until the end of 1933. During this thirteen-year period, the illegal bootlegging businesses of Al "Scarface" Capone and other gangsters flourish.

Warren G. Harding is elected president.

1921

President Warren G. Harding appoints William H. Taft chief justice of the United States Supreme Court.

William Marston of Fordham University publishes an article that states his belief that telling lies affects a person's blood pressure. California police chief August Vollmer and his sergeant later test a lie detector apparatus made from a blood pressure machine. They find it is successful in separating lies from the truth.

1924

Twenty-nine-year-old J. Edgar Hoover, who has earned a reputation in the Department of Justice for his efficiency and dedication, is named to head the Bureau of Investigation. The bureau has about 200 agents, some of whom are corrupt and inefficient. Hoover is ordered to clean up the agency.

Calvin Coolidge is elected president.

1925

The National Crime Commission is organized in New York City. Members include Elbert H. Gary of U.S. Steel, Franklin D. Roosevelt, and the future Chief Justice Charles Evans Hughes.

1926

The lie detector machine is improved. It can now combine blood pressure, pulse, breathing rate, and sweat readings. The machine has problems in the future. Some suspects figure out how to fool the machine by thinking about other things when they answer potentially incriminating questions or by taking mild drugs such as aspirin beforehand. Some innocent people become nervous when hooked up to the machine and appear to be guilty.

1928   Herbert Hoover is elected president. In his inaugural address (in *Public Papers of the Presidents*, 1974), dedicated largely to the issue of crime, Hoover states:

> To reestablish the vigor and effectiveness of law enforcement we must critically consider the entire Federal machinery of justice, the redistribution of its functions, the simplification of its procedure, the provision of additional special tribunals, the better selection of juries, and the more effective organization of our agencies of investigation and prosecution that justice may be sure and that it may be swift. While the authority of the Federal Government extends to but part of our vast system of national, State, and local justice, yet the standards which the Federal Government establishes have the most profound influence upon the whole structure.

Eliot Ness is charged with assembling a small force to combat the influence of Al Capone's bootlegging operations in Chicago. At this time, police corruption and bribe taking are rampant. Ness combs the files of hundreds of law enforcement officers in search of agents who can be trusted. He chooses nine officers who have flawless records and are experts in marksmanship, wiretapping, and other activities essential to fighting Capone. Ness dubs the ten-man force "the Untouchables."

1929   President Hoover selects 11 members to serve on the National Commission on Law Observance and Enforcement. George W. Wickersham, attorney general under President Taft, serves as chair. The commission is assigned to investigate law enforcement problems associated with Prohibition but soon expands its inquiry to include the entire criminal justice system.

Author John Landesco releases a thorough investigation of Mafia activity entitled *Organized Crime in Chicago*.

1930   Congress passes a bill to create a division within the Bureau of Investigation (later the Federal Bureau of Investigation) to gather statistics from law enforcement agencies across the country. In August, the first *Uniform Crime Reports* (UCR) is published using data from about 400 agencies. UCR becomes one of the two most important sources of national crime statistics.

Charles Evans Hughes is appointed by President Herbert Hoover to the chief justice's seat on the United States Supreme Court.

1931   The Wickersham Commission issues a report on defects in the criminal justice system and calls for major reforms in law enforcement and in the judicial system. It finds that an increased number of cases is burdening the court system, recommends more funding for law enforcement, and advocates prison reform and the expansion of federal efforts to control crime. Few reforms are implemented, and the report's suggestions are largely ignored.

1932   In *Powell v. Alabama*, the United States Supreme Court overturns the convictions of nine black youths convicted on rape charges without legal counsel.

Franklin Delano Roosevelt is elected president.

The son of famed aviator Charles Lindbergh is kidnapped from his home. The kidnapping eventually develops into a murder case and prompts federal antikidnapping legislation.

1933   The Securities Act of 1933, a federal law, requires all securities to be registered and information to be provided on all issuers of securities.

The Bureau of Investigation is renamed the Federal Bureau of Investigation (FBI). By this time, Hoover has molded the agency into an effective crime-fighting organization.

J. Edgar Hoover declares war on "public enemies."

The Twenty-First Amendment nullifies the Eighteenth Amendment, ending the Prohibition era. Mafia gangs that prospered during Prohibition continue gambling, racketeering, and loan-sharking enterprises.

1934   Congress passes the Federal Bank Robbery Act, making bank robbery a federal crime. The aim of the bill is to give federal law enforcement agencies authority and jurisdiction in bank robbery cases.

1935   Former Untouchables leader Eliot Ness becomes public safety director of an administration in Cleveland. He is charged with ridding the city of the Mayfield Road Mob and its gambling, prostitution, and bootlegging operations.

1936   Congress passes the Federal Kidnapping Act, which makes kidnapping a federal offense. The law stems from the 1932 kidnapping of aviator Charles Lindbergh's son.

Frank J. Wilson, whose agents had previously infiltrated Al Capone's bootlegging operation in Chicago, becomes head of the Secret Service. He pursues producers of counterfeit currency.

1937   Chicago dentist Edward A. Ryan writes an article for the *Journal of Criminal Law and Criminology* that suggests that the Department of Justice should use dental records as a means of identifying people. Ryan argues that peculiarities in each individual's teeth are an effective means of identification and might help investigators to identify bodies when other methods fail.

1938   The Federal Food, Drug, and Cosmetic Act passes to attempt to combat fraud and deception in food, drug, and cosmetic markets.

1939   Harvard anthropologist Earnest A. Hooton publishes the first volume of *The American Criminal* trilogy entitled *The Native White Criminal of Native White Parentage.* Hooton has tried to prove in his controversial studies that links exist between a person's physical makeup and the crimes he or she commits.

1940   Congress passes the Smith Act, designed to punish those who advocate the overthrow of the government by force, sedition, or treason. This act is passed with the threat of U.S. involvement in World War II looming.

1941   President Franklin Delano Roosevelt appoints Harlan F. Stone chief justice of the United States Supreme Court.

1942   The United States Supreme Court, in *Betts v. Brady*, rules that state courts are not necessarily required to provide legal counsel to defendants. States are, however, required to appoint counsel for a defendant whose case is complicated or whose mental capacity would not allow a fair trial.

1945   President Roosevelt dies in office. Vice President Harry S. Truman becomes president.

1946   President Truman appoints Frederick M. Vinson chief justice of the United States Supreme Court.

1947   The United States Supreme Court rules in *Adamson v. California* to uphold the conviction of a California man who claimed the state infringed upon his right against self-incrimination. The case is destined to stand as legal precedent until the 1964 *Malloy v. Hogan* decision. Justice Hugo Black writes a strong dissenting opinion.

1948   Harry S. Truman is elected president.

1950   Organized crime begins once again to gain national attention. Congress forms the Special Committee to Investigate Organized Crime in Interstate Commerce, chaired by Tennessee Senator Estes Kefauver. Months of hearings, research, and testimony from more than 800 witnesses lead the committee to conclude that illegal gambling is widespread and lucrative but that it is not organized on a national level. A report issued by the committee warns of Mafia organizations that have risen to prominence through bootlegging, rackets, gambling, and violence—especially in Chicago and New York.

        A number of state commissions are also formed to investigate organized crime.

1951   Congress passes the Hobbs Act, which forbids the use of theft, extortion, and violence to interfere with interstate commerce.

         The United States Supreme Court in *Dennis v. Hopper* upholds the convictions of Communists charged with violating the Smith Act.

1952   The Travel Act makes it a federal violation for a person to travel or to use interstate and foreign commerce to commit a crime. The act is amended twice, in 1961 and 1976.

         Dwight D. Eisenhower is elected president.

1953   President Eisenhower appoints Earl Warren chief justice of the United States Supreme Court, ushering in an era of legal decisions aimed at preserving defendants' rights. Warren had served as the Republican governor of California and had run as a candidate for vice president in 1948. Warren Court decisions would prove to be much further to the left than Eisenhower expected, and its rulings would extend several federal constitutional rights to the states.

1954   The Washington, D.C., Court of Appeals creates the Durham Rule, which requires that expert witnesses must show that a defendant using the insanity defense is mentally diseased. The Durham Rule is a major departure from the M'Naghten Rule, used until this time, which only required that jurors had to determine whether a mental disease rendered a defendant unaware of the crime while he or she was committing it.

1955   The United Nations adopts Standard Minimum Rules for the Treatment of Prisoners.

1956   A United States Supreme Court ruling in *Griffin v. Illinois* requires states to provide convicted felons with transcripts of their case's court proceedings, even if the defendant cannot pay for these transcripts.

1957   The United States Supreme Court hands down a landmark ruling in *Jencks v. United States* that requires the

1957
cont. government to allow a defendant's attorneys access to pretrial documents. Following the Court's lead, Congress passes the Jencks Act, which stipulates that a criminal defendant being prosecuted in a federal court must be allowed to see the prosecution's documents.

In another precedent-setting case, *Mallory v. United States,* the Court overturns a conviction on the grounds that the defendant was not taken promptly to a magistrate after his arrest. This case, along with *McNabb v. United States,* establishes the McNabb-Mallory Rule, which states that an arrestee must be taken to a magistrate quickly or any incriminating statements he or she makes will not be admissible in court.

1958 The United States Supreme Court in *Tropp v. Dulles* encourages punishment for crimes that reflects the "dignity of man" and "evolving standards of decency."

1959 In *Spano v. New York,* the Court rules that a defendant has a right not to be questioned without an attorney present once he or she has been indicted for a crime.

Early
1960s Large increases in crime figures help to put crime permanently on the national policy agenda. *Uniform Crime Reports* shows several statistical increases from 1958 to 1963: total crime rate up by 30 percent, violent crime rate up 12 percent, and property crime rate up 32 percent.

1960s The Office of Law Enforcement Assistance (OLEA) is formed, with Courtney Evans, a 25-year veteran of the FBI, as its head.

Riots and sit-ins by civil rights advocates, opponents of the Vietnam War, and other political demonstrators raise concerns about public order.

1960 John F. Kennedy is elected president.

1961 Congress passes the Racketeer Influenced Corrupt Organizations Act (RICO), which outlaws racketeering in interstate and foreign commerce. The act also contains provisions aimed at curbing bribery of government officials. It is amended in 1970.

A United States Supreme Court ruling in *Mapp v. Ohio* applies the Exclusionary Rule to all states. The rule states that all evidence gathered through illegal search and seizure or in violation of the Fourth Amendment is inadmissible in court. The rule comes under judicial fire in the early 1980s.

1962   In *Robinson v. California,* the United States Supreme Court invalidates a California statute that makes addiction to narcotics a misdemeanor crime. The Court says the statute amounts to "cruel and unusual punishment" and violates the Eighth and Fourteenth Amendments.

1963   The United States Supreme Court ruling in *Gideon v. Wainwright* strengthens a defendant's right to legal counsel. The decision reverses a state conviction because the state did not provide an attorney for an impoverished defendant.

President Kennedy is assassinated in Dallas, Texas. Vice President Lyndon B. Johnson takes the presidential oath of office.

President Johnson asks Chief Justice Earl Warren to chair a commission to investigate Kennedy's assassination. The commission interviews about 550 witnesses over a ten-month period and concludes that Lee Harvey Oswald acted as a lone assassin. It also finds that Oswald's murderer, Jack Ruby, acted alone and criticizes the FBI and the Secret Service for failing to protect the president. Critics say the commission has failed to seriously consider the possibility of a conspiracy. A 1970s House probe into the Warren Commission's investigation finds some of these charges valid.

1964   With the *Malloy v. Hogan* ruling, the United States Supreme Court says the right against self-incrimination, guaranteed by the Fifth Amendment, applies to the states.

The Court hands down another important ruling in *Massiah v. United States.* After a defendant had obtained counsel, been charged, entered a plea, and obtained release on bail, he got into a car with a friend who had

1964
cont.

participated in the same crime. Federal agents had re-cruited the friend to serve as an informer and had bugged his car. The agents had subsequently obtained several incriminating statements from the defendant through the wiretaps. On appeal, the Court overturns his conviction and establishes this legal precedent: if a defendant has been formally charged, he or she has the right to have an attorney present unless he or she know-ingly relinquishes that right, and law enforcement offi-cers are prohibited from trying to obtain incriminating statements under other conditions.

In a case involving black students who staged a sit-in on corporate-owned restaurant property, the Court rules in *Bell v. Maryland* that corporations do not have the same legal status as individuals and are sometimes required to deal with people with whom they do not want to have contact.

President Johnson is officially elected.

The United States Supreme Court, in *Escobedo v. Illinois,* overturns a conviction that resulted from the defen-dant's statements to police after officers did not allow him to have an attorney present.

1965

The Law Enforcement Assistance Act establishes OLEA and a $20.6 million grant program for research and de-velopment. The money is used to fund more than 350 projects.

1966

Congress creates the National Commission on Reform of Federal Criminal Law, chaired by former governor of California Edmund "Pat" Brown. The task of the Brown Commission, as it becomes popularly known, is to or-ganize the federal criminal laws and statutes scattered throughout the United States Code.

The United States Supreme Court hands down a land-mark ruling on obtaining confessions in *Miranda v. Ari-zona.* It sets several standards for a usable, legitimate confession. Police officers must inform a person they ar-rest that (1) he or she has the right to remain silent; (2)

anything he or she says can and will be used against him or her; (3) he or she has the right to have a lawyer present during any questioning; and (4) if he or she cannot afford to hire a lawyer, the court will appoint one. From this time on, new arrestees would be read their "Miranda rights."

1967   President Lyndon Johnson's Task Force on Organized Crime issues thorough reports attempting to outline the scope of the national organized crime problem and proposing strategies for fighting the problem. The task force cites several problems it believes have impeded effective efforts against criminal organizations in the past: difficulty in obtaining proof of their existence, insufficient resources, lack of coordination among law enforcement personnel, and lack of commitment to fighting the problem. To help cope with organized crime, the commission recommends expanding the wiretapping and surveillance authority of law enforcement agencies, forming special organized crime units in city police departments, and increasing protection for potential witnesses.

President Johnson forms the Commission on Law Enforcement and Administration of Justice, chaired by Attorney General Nicholas Katzenbach. The commission releases a report entitled *The Challenge of Crime in a Free Society.* It also proposes the victimization report, or a method of compiling crime statistics based on individual reports of victimization, deemed by some to be a more accurate method of collecting crime statistics. Another of the commission's reports, "Crime and Its Impact, an Assessment," looks into crime trends; the economic impact of crime, offenders, and victims; white-collar crime; statistics; riots; and other aspects of crime.

The National Commission on the Causes and Prevention of Violence is formed.

More than 100 cities nationwide experience inner-city riots. The National Guard is activated in some cases.

President Johnson appoints the first black Supreme Court Justice, Thurgood Marshall.

1967
cont.
Two important state court decisions, *Adderly v. Wainwright* in Florida and *Hill v. Nelson* in California, effectively abolish the death penalty in those states. All death row inmates are given a stay of execution.

The United States Supreme Court hands down a decision in *See v. Seattle* that protects commercial property from being inspected without a warrant.

Frank Rizzo becomes the police commissioner in Philadelphia. Rizzo's police department acquires a national reputation for its tough law-and-order approach to fighting crime, but allegations of police abuses also surface.

The Court rules in *Katz v. United States* that Fourth Amendment rights extend to electronic surveillance even if there is no physical intrusion into a person's property. The Court says people have a reasonable expectation of privacy that the government must not infringe upon without complying with Fourth Amendment restrictions.

1968
President Johnson signs into law a large piece of legislation known as the Omnibus Crime Control and Safe Streets Act of 1968. The new law creates state councils to administer funding for crime prevention programs and makes some changes in criminal procedure. Particularly noteworthy are relaxed standards for admitting confessions into court.

The Law Enforcement Assistance Administration (LEAA) is formed inside the Department of Justice.

The Kerner Commission is formed to look into the causes of public disturbances during the 1960s. It produces three studies that examine the roles of demonstrators and racial attitudes at the time.

Congress passes the Gun Control Act of 1968, the most significant federal attempt to regulate firearms to date. The act aims to reduce gun sales to criminals and other high-risk groups, curb firearms traffic, and slow the importation of firearms.

In *Terry v. Ohio*, the United States Supreme Court says police may stop and search a suspect if they have reason to believe he or she is armed and dangerous. The decision creates a "reasonable suspicion" standard to apply to cases in which an officer must act quickly. Such searches would become known as "Terry Searches." The ruling is a departure from the "defendants' rights" trend of the Warren Court.

James Q. Wilson releases *Varieties of Police Behavior: The Management of Law and Order in Eight Communities*, which outlines basic types of police departments: the watchman, the legalistic, and the service department. Wilson argues that the service department is the most effective because it gains the cooperation of the community it serves.

The United States Supreme Court rules in *Witherspoon v. Illinois* that defendants cannot be sentenced to die if people who oppose the death penalty are intentionally excluded from the jury.

President Johnson forms the National Commission on Reform of Criminal Laws. The commission's work lasts into the Nixon administration. It submits a report to the president recommending the abolition of the insanity defense, mandatory sentencing for certain crimes, and other strict proposals.

The Jury Selection and Service Act outlaws discrimination in selecting jury members for federal cases.

Richard M. Nixon is elected president.

1969   The National Commission on the Causes and Prevention of Violence convenes. It releases a 15-volume report that urges the government to invest more heavily in efforts to prevent crime and criticizes existing police structures and attitudes.

In *Johnson v. Avery*, the United States Supreme Court says that a state cannot prohibit an inmate from representing other prisoners in court unless it provides another attorney for the prisoner.

1969 President Richard Nixon appoints Warren E. Burger
cont. chief justice of the Supreme Court.

1970 The Comprehensive Drug Abuse Prevention and Control Act becomes law. A "no-knock" provision allows police to execute a warrant on the arrestee's premises without knocking. The provision sparks criticism and is repealed in 1974.

The Organized Crime Control Act outlaws the use of profits from organized crime to run a legitimate business in interstate commerce. It also establishes more stringent gambling laws and increases sentences for dangerous criminals.

An Arkansas court rules in favor of inmates from two prisons in that state who equated poor prison conditions with "cruel and unusual punishment." The court orders the state to take steps toward improving the conditions.

The United States Supreme Court says in *Colonnade Catering Corporation v. United States* that Congress can force carefully regulated businesses to submit to inspections without a warrant.

1972 The United States Supreme Court rules in *Adams v. Williams* that police are permitted to frisk a suspect based on a tip from a known informer.

Longtime director of the Federal Bureau of Investigation J. Edgar Hoover dies of a heart attack. As his legacy, Hoover leaves a large, world-renowned investigatory agency that he built from the shambles of corruption and inefficiency.

In *Argersinger v. Hamlin*, the United States Supreme Court says defendants have the right to a lawyer during all legal proceedings and mandates states to provide counsel to defendants who cannot afford a private lawyer.

The Court rules in *Furman v. Georgia* that the death penalty as written in state laws amounts to "cruel and unusual punishment." The decision strikes down all state death penalty laws.

The Court also rules in *Branburg v. Hayes* that courts can hold reporters in contempt if they refuse to reveal a source relevant to a grand jury's criminal investigation.

In *United States v. United States District Court,* the high court says the government cannot wiretap citizens for the sake of national security without judicial approval.

1973 President Richard Nixon signs the Crime Control Act of 1973.

The LEAA, an agency under the Department of Justice, begins the ongoing National Crime Panel Survey. The statistics are gathered by interviewing households and businesses across the country.

The United States Supreme Court says in *United States v. Russell* that a defendant who is already involved in an illegal enterprise has not been entrapped. The decision gives undercover law enforcement agents more flexibility in pursuing criminals.

The National Advisory Commission on Criminal Justice Standards and Goals convenes. The commission produces six reports aimed at forming national criminal justice standards.

1974 The Juvenile Justice and Delinquency Prevention Act of 1974 establishes the Office of Juvenile Justice and Delinquency Prevention (OJJDP).

The Speedy Trial Act is passed to establish prosecutorial time limits in federal criminal cases.

The United States Supreme Court attacks the Exclusionary Rule in *United States v. Calandra.* The Court calls for a cost-benefit analysis for discerning police misconduct in determining whether to admit evidence into a trial.

1974
cont.

In *Nixon v. United States,* the Court says the president cannot withhold evidence from a criminal trial under the right of executive privilege.

Mired in scandal and facing possible impeachment, President Nixon resigns. Vice President Gerald Ford is sworn in as president on August 9.

1975

Congressional investigations of the FBI reveal abuses in J. Edgar Hoover's career that include spying on personal enemies not even suspected of crimes.

1976

In *Commonwealth v. O'Neal,* the Massachusetts Supreme Court forbids the death penalty for a murderer who commits a murder in the process of rape.

Gregg v. Georgia, an important United States Supreme Court case, affirms new state death penalty laws rewritten as a result of the *Furman v. Georgia* decision. By this time, 35 states have new death penalty laws on their books. The Georgia law involved in this case requires consideration of both aggravating and mitigating circumstances in decisions to apply the death penalty.

The Court rules in *Nebraska Press Association v. Stuart* that judges cannot forbid press coverage of high-profile trials unless the coverage threatens the defendant's right to a fair trial.

In *Stone v. Powell,* the Court expresses its opinion that the Exclusionary Rule costs too much and produces too much contention between state and federal courts when defendants attempt to have evidence barred from their trials. The Court says the rule causes more trouble than it is worth for the small effect it has on police behavior.

President Gerald Ford signs the Crime Control Act of 1976, which funds the Law Enforcement Assistance Administration for another three years.

James E. Carter is elected president.

1977

The Foreign Corrupt Practices Act makes it illegal to bribe foreign officials.

The United States Supreme Court rules in *Coker v. Georgia* that the death penalty cannot be used to punish rape and can only be used to punish homicide.

A federal court bans a television station in Texas from airing a planned broadcast of an execution in *Gannett v. Estelle*.

1978   A 13-year-old boy kills a seminary student in New York. The law requires that he be tried in family court, and he receives the maximum—an 18-month renewable sentence. Critics complain about the lax punishment for violent juvenile defendants, and the state passes a law allowing juveniles to be tried as adults.

1979   The United States Supreme Court upholds the state parole process in Nebraska in *Greenholtz v. Inmates of the Nebraska Penal Correction Complex*. The parole process does not require that the parole board show inmates the evidence considered when making parole decisions.

1980   The Civil Rights of Institutionalized Persons Act allows the attorney general of the United States to intervene on behalf of prisoners in state institutions if he or she determines that they are imprisoned under inadequate conditions.

The Parental Kidnapping Prevention Act is passed to combat the kidnapping of minors by parents who do not have legal custody of their children.

Ronald W. Reagan is elected president.

1981   John Hinckley Jr. unsuccessfully attempts to assassinate President Reagan. Sarah Brady, the wife of James Brady—who was also a victim in Hinckley's attack—begins to lobby for tougher federal gun control laws as a result of the shooting.

President Reagan appoints the first woman, Sandra Day O'Connor, to the United States Supreme Court.

1982   Congress passes the Victim and Witness Protection Act of 1982.

1982   Congress defunds LEAA, thus ending its 14-year
cont.   existence.

1983   In *Illinois v. Gates,* the United States Supreme Court
        deals another blow to the Exclusionary Rule. It relaxes
        the "probable cause" standard for warrants and releases
        police from the obligation to show that an anonymous
        tip came from an informant.

        An Illinois judge operates a Repeat Offenders Court to
        speed up the process of trying and sentencing repeat of-
        fenders. The judge has ordered the prosecution to work
        more quickly in cases involving repeat offenders. The court
        has a high conviction rate, shorter trial lengths, and less
        plea bargaining than regular courts. The judge establishes
        the court because he is irritated by the high volume of re-
        peat offenders who came into his courtroom and by the fre-
        quent instances of plea bargaining that brought them right
        back. Offenders nickname the judge "Father Time" because
        he is known for imposing lengthy sentences.

        Michigan v. Long, another United States Supreme Court
        ruling, stipulates that a defendant can be convicted for
        possession of drugs even if the illegal substances are
        found during a search for weapons. In other words,
        governments can prosecute for crimes the defendant
        was not initially suspected of committing if evidence
        obtained during another search points to an offense.

1984   Congress passes the Victims of Crime Act of 1984. If the
        legal focus of the 1960s was on defendants' rights, the
        focus of the 1980s and 1990s is on victims' rights.

        The Comprehensive Crime Control Act of 1984 allocates
        $69 million for training and technical aid to law en-
        forcement and relaxes standards and requirements for
        using wiretaps.

        The Sentencing Reform Act of 1984 creates the United
        States Sentencing Commission and establishes federal
        sentencing guidelines.

        In *New York v. Quarles,* the United States Supreme Court
        reverses a decision by the New York Court of Appeals

that prohibited introducing information in court that a suspect had given to police before being read his Miranda rights. The court creates a "public safety exception" to the requirements of the *Miranda v. Arizona* decision that allows police to ask questions in perilous situations before a suspect is read his or her rights.

In its continuing assault on the Exclusionary Rule, the Court creates a "good faith" exception in *United States v. Leon*, which says that evidence obtained by police who execute a faulty warrant is admissible in court if the officers believe the warrant is valid.

The United Nations holds a Crime Congress in Milan. For the first time in UN history it makes victims' rights part of the agenda. The congress produces the *Declaration of Basic Principles of Justice for Victims of Crime and Abuse of Power*.

The National Institute of Justice is established under the Department of Justice. The agency's duties focus primarily on conducting research, establishing criminal justice programs and methods, and disseminating information.

1986   President Ronald Reagan appoints William H. Rehnquist chief justice of the United States Supreme Court.

1987   The Computer Security Act of 1987 requires federal government agencies to upgrade computer security and instructs the National Bureau of Standards to develop guidelines for government computer and telecommunications networks.

Florida relaxes its law governing concealed weapons, setting off a string of similar laws in other states that permit citizens to carry concealed handguns, usually provided they are licensed and trained.

Former Philadelphia police commissioner and mayor Frank Rizzo decides to run for mayor once again. He is defeated by Wilson Goode.

A New York jury acquits Bernard Goetz of attempted murder charges. When four black youths approached

1987
cont.

him and harassed him for money in 1985, Goetz pulled out a gun and shot them. None of the youths died. A nationwide controversy erupts, with critics fearing a rise in vigilantism and supporters praising Goetz for defending himself against an increasingly violent tide of criminals.

1988   George Bush is elected president.

1989   In a ruling on *Penry v. Lynaugh,* the United States Supreme Court upholds the death sentence of a mentally impaired man convicted of murder. The Court says the death penalty can be applied to both mentally impaired people and 16-year-olds. The decision is part of a 1980s trend in the Court toward stricter punishment and away from the defendants' rights focus of the Warren Court.

Massachusetts Governor Michael Dukakis signs a bill placing restrictions on driver's licenses for those convicted of drug offenses. Adult offenders may lose their licenses for up to five years; juveniles may have to wait until their twenty-first birthday to obtain a license.

A United States District Court rules that the Illinois death penalty is unconstitutional. The law has never been used.

Texas Governor Bill Clements approves a massive overhaul of the state's criminal justice system.

The Federal Bureau of Investigation begins accepting data for its new computerized National Incident-Based Reporting System (NIBRS). The new system will take a few years to implement, but when fully functioning it will allow law enforcement agencies to obtain necessary data quickly. The system improves upon the *Uniform Crime Reports* by recording and processing more data about each crime.

A series of accidental shootings prompts Florida to enact a new law that requires adults to keep loaded guns away from children. Offenders face a $5,000 fine and five years in prison. Other new crime laws in Florida institute mandatory revocation of driver's licenses for drunk driving suspects who refuse to take Breathalyzer tests, mandatory drug screening for some corrections personnel, and a mandatory minimum three-year sentence for a person convicted of selling drugs near schools.

Ohio Governor Richard Celeste approves new laws that expand the Ohio Victims Compensation Program, allowing victims of drunk drivers to file compensation claims against them. The Ohio bill is one of innumerable new laws that, unlike the defendants' rights spirit of the 1960s, reflect a legal tendency toward victims' rights.

The U.S. military invades Panama and arrests Panama's leader Manuel Noriega, who officials allege is involved in international drug smuggling.

A private company in the Dallas, Texas, area, Westcott Communications, establishes the Law Enforcement Television Network. Programming is geared especially toward law enforcement and is available only to law enforcement agencies by subscription. The network broadcasts 24 hours a day, although only two or three programming hours are original. Programs instruct police in new techniques and training methods and keep them posted on recent crime news.

Members of a Los Angeles narcotics team are suspended on allegations that they stole thousands of dollars confiscated in drug raids.

The General Assembly in Virginia passes a gun control law that establishes a toll-free number allowing police to conduct criminal background checks on people who want to purchase guns.

Missouri executes its first convicted murderer since the mid-1960s.

1990   Congress passes the Crime Control Act of 1990, which provides additional funding for law enforcement and

1990
cont.
corrections and creates new penalties for drug offenses, bank fraud, and child abuse.

Massachusetts Governor Michael Dukakis signs bills aimed at strengthening state laws to protect victims of domestic abuse and to allow the public greater access to criminal records.

The California Supreme Court unanimously kills a part of Proposition 115 that limits defendants' rights under the state constitution.

Washington, D.C., mayor Marion Barry is captured on video smoking crack in an FBI undercover operation. A jury later finds Barry guilty of a misdemeanor drug possession charge.

1991
City officials in Modesto, California, ban cruising and loitering on the city's main street in an effort to cut down on vandalism and street crime.

Georgia Governor Zell Miller signs a bill that allows circulation of pictures of repeat drunk driving offenders in state newspapers.

Several states now have "rape shield" laws designed to prevent public identification of rape victims. These laws have raised questions about conflicts with the First Amendment. A Circuit Court refuses to review a Florida rape shield law.

In a unanimous decision, the United States Supreme Court strikes down New York's "Son of Sam" law in *Simon and Schuster v. Members of the New York Crime Victims Board.* The law requires that criminals who profit from their crimes by writing about them must give the proceeds to a crime victims board. It and similar laws in 41 other states have the dual aims of prohibiting criminals from profiting from their crimes and of compensating their victims. The Court says the New York law is too broad.

With his video camera, an onlooker captures LAPD officers beating motorist Rodney King. The tape plays on

the evening news around the United States, and an out-
cry against the injustices of police brutality prompts officials to bring charges against the arresting officers.

Missouri Governor John Ashcroft signs a controversial bill
into law that requires people convicted of sexual and violent crimes to give a blood sample for a state genetic bank.

Texas Governor Ann Richards signs bills that require
convicted capital murderers to spend at least 35 years in
prison before they become eligible for parole and to
allow the state to prosecute cases of spousal rape.

An Illinois law goes into effect that expands the public's
right to view criminal conviction records through the
state police. The law is expected to make it easier for potential employers to check the backgrounds of people
they wish to hire.

1992   The FBI successfully prosecutes New York Gambino
family crime boss John Gotti on 13 charges of murder,
gambling, racketeering, and tax fraud. Gotti had escaped three previous indictments since 1986 and had
earned the nickname "Teflon Don."

U.S. News and World Report estimates that crime costs
businesses at least $120 billion per year in losses, legal
expenses, and security costs. Losses are passed on to
consumers, who pay more for goods and services.

A Gallup poll finds that 89 percent of Americans fear
crime is worsening nationwide.

The United Nations asks for a new commission to deal
with crime prevention and criminal justice. It recommends that the current Committee on Crime Prevention
and Control be dissolved.

An act of Congress instructs the National Crime Information Center to establish a National Stolen Auto Part
Information System to contain the identification numbers of stolen passenger motor vehicles and their parts.

Connecticut passes an antistalking bill.

1992   In *Jacobson v. United States*, the United States Supreme
cont.   Court throws out the conviction of a man who received
        child pornography in the mail on the grounds that he
        was entrapped. Jacobson had ordered a sexually explicit
        magazine before Congress passed an act prohibiting the
        receipt by mail of this type of child pornography. The
        Postal Inspection Service targeted the man in a sting op-
        eration and heavily encouraged him to order newly ille-
        gal material the Court says he was not predisposed to
        order. The case sets boundaries, although not stringent
        ones, on the 1973 *United States v. Russell* decision.

        The Court rules in *White v. Illinois* that statements made
        to a mother, authorities, and hospital personnel by a
        child who was a victim of sexual assault are admissible
        in court even though the child was available for trial.

        In *Doggett v. United States*, the United States Supreme
        Court throws out the conviction of a man tried on drug
        charges whose trial took place more than eight years
        after his indictment, on the grounds that the govern-
        ment violated his right to a speedy trial. The man had
        fled the country and subsequently reentered the United
        States, but officials did not find him for several years.
        The Court faults the government for not actively pursu-
        ing him.

        The United States Supreme Court, in *United States v.
        Felix*, upholds the conviction of a man who was tried in
        two different states on similar federal charges. The man
        had committed very similar drug offenses in both Okla-
        homa and Missouri, and the Court finds that they are
        two different sets of offenses regardless of their similar-
        ity. The Court also finds that evidence from the man's
        Missouri trial that was introduced in his Oklahoma trial
        does not violate double jeopardy rights.

        A new law in Louisiana, the Children's Code, mandates
        that juvenile defendants must be incarcerated with
        adults if they have been charged as adults.

        A federal disclosure law requires colleges and universi-
        ties to provide the public with annual information on

the extent of crime on their campuses. Before this ruling, some campuses released the information voluntarily.

A Los Angeles jury acquits the officers involved in the Rodney King beating, sparking deadly riots in the city. Los Angeles courts arraign more than 13,000 people in connection with the uprisings. Later, the federal government brings charges of civil rights abuses against the officers, raising questions about double jeopardy. The officers are ultimately convicted.

William J. Clinton is elected president.

Chief Justice of the Supreme Court William Rehnquist criticizes Congress for continuing to make offenses formerly handled by states federal crimes.

1993   Congress passes the Brady Handgun Violence Prevention Act, known as the Brady Bill, which establishes a national waiting period for purchasing a handgun and a national instant criminal background check system.

Maryland institutes a measure providing constitutional protection to crime victims.

The murder of James Jordan, father of famed basketball star Michael Jordan, is part of the reason the North Carolina legislature calls a special session on crime.

New York City institutes an automated teller machine security law.

Initiative 593, passed in Washington state, mandates a life sentence for people convicted of a third violent crime.

The United States Supreme Court rules in *United States Department of Justice et al. v. Landano* that information the FBI gathers during an investigation is not always confidential. The defendant had filed a request for information pertaining to his case under the Freedom of Information Act and said he thought the information might prove his innocence.

1993   With the authorization of Attorney General Janet Reno,
cont.   agents from the Bureau of Alcohol, Tobacco, and Firearms and the Federal Bureau of Investigation storm the
Branch Davidian compound in Waco, Texas, with tanks
and tear gas. The compound goes up in flames, killing
cult members inside—some of whom are children. Authorities had wanted only to arrest the cult's leader,
David Koresh, on suspicion that he was abusing children and illegally stockpiling weapons.

1994   President Bill Clinton signs the Violent Crime Control
and Law Enforcement Act of 1994, the largest piece of
anticrime legislation in U.S. history. The $30 billion bill
aims to put 100,000 new police officers on the streets of
the United States and contains a number of smaller acts:
the Jacob Wetterling Crimes against Children and Sexually Violent Offender Registration Act, the Safe Homes
for Women Act of 1994, the Equal Justice for Women in
the Courts Act of 1994, the Public Safety Partnership
and Community Policing Act of 1994, and many others.
The bill expands the death penalty to more than 50 federal crimes and bans several types of assault weapons.
Critics, including Supreme Court Justice Sandra Day
O'Connor, complain that the bill introduces too many
new federal offenses that will clog an already overburdened federal court system. The creation of new federal
offenses will allow federal agencies to investigate
crimes formerly handled exclusively by state agencies.

Missouri passes a truth-in-sentencing law designed to
keep convicted felons in prison for longer periods of
time. Under the law, criminals found guilty of second-
degree murder are obligated to serve 85 percent of a
mandatory 30-year sentence before they are eligible for
parole. Until now, second-degree murder convicts in the
state could apply for parole almost immediately.

The *National Journal of Law* reports that the percentage of
Americans who fear for their safety—64 percent—has
almost doubled since 1989.

The city of Chicago bans the sale of most kinds of handgun ammunition.

Dallas, Texas, passes an ordinance that establishes a nighttime curfew for the city's youth. The ordinance is aimed at curbing growing gang warfare and juvenile crime problems.

California Governor Pete Wilson signs a "three-strikes" bill into law. The bill mandates a term of life in prison, without parole for at least 25 years, for any person convicted of his or her third felony if he or she has two prior convictions for violent crimes. Thirty other states have similar laws under consideration this year. Georgia passes a "two-strikes" law.

With the lieutenant governor's tie-breaking vote, Virginia narrowly defeats a bill that would allow relatives of murder victims to watch the murderer's execution. Similar proposals have surfaced in other states.

In *Sandoval v. California* and *Victor v. Nebraska,* the United States Supreme Court upholds two murder convictions and says there is nothing wrong with jury instruction that includes moral certainty. The Court declines to extend its authority to what it calls state matters.

Governor William Weld signs a bill in Massachusetts that allows school principals to exclude from classrooms students accused of committing violent crimes.

With its ruling *NOW v. Scheidler,* the Court extends statutes of RICO, originally drafted to combat organized crime, to antiabortion protestors.

1995   The nationally televised murder trial of former football star O. J. Simpson brings unprecedented media coverage to a criminal trial. A lengthy discussion of the merits and drawbacks of blood DNA evidence linking Simpson to the murders raises questions about the use of new forensics technology. Controversial allegations of mishandling evidence and other police abuses bring more trouble to the Los Angeles Police Department, which is still reeling from the Rodney King beating case in 1991.

1995
cont.

The U.S. House of Representatives, now with a Republican majority, launches an attack on last year's massive crime bill. At the core of the charge is a proposal to replace President Clinton's plan to put 100,000 new officers on the streets with a plan to give $10 billion in block grants to cities.

With the help of a computer security expert in California, agents arrest one of the FBI's most wanted computer hackers, Kevin Mitnick, in Raleigh, North Carolina. Mitnick was wanted for breaking into corporate computer systems, and agents find more than 20,000 stolen credit card numbers in his possession. The arrest raises concerns about new breeds of criminals that are arising with the advent of sophisticated technology.

Missouri Governor Mel Carnahan signs a bill into law that permits the state to try children of any age as adults for murder, robbery, rape, and other crimes.

Texas Governor George W. Bush signs bills designed to shorten the time between the convictions and executions of convicted murderers, get tough on juvenile crime, and require repeat offenders to spend more time in prison.

An Oakland Circuit Court judge strikes down an anti-stalking law in Michigan.

Georgia Governor Zell Miller signs bills to provide crime victims with information about their attackers and to limit the amount of time convicted murderers have to appeal their death sentences.

The town of Silverton, Oregon, passes an ordinance that holds parents responsible when their children break the law. Similar ordinances are under consideration elsewhere in the United States, and they stem from growing concern about the increase in juvenile crime.

New York reinstitutes the death penalty.

The bombing of the Alfred P. Murrah Federal Building in Oklahoma City, Oklahoma, results in 168 deaths. Authorities arrest two suspects, Timothy McVeigh and

Terry Nichols, who allegedly have connections with citizen militias that are angry over increased government intrusion into their lives, gun control laws, and the decision to invade the Branch Davidian compound in Waco, Texas. The FBI and other officials ask for legislation from Congress that would expand federal power to investigate groups that threaten to employ domestic terrorism.

A law in Illinois requires school bus drivers to be fingerprinted and to have criminal background checks.

All but three states have enacted laws that comply with a Department of Education rule that holds that students who bring weapons to school must be suspended.

The Jefferson Parish, Louisiana, council passes an ordinance permitting neighborhoods to erect gates around their boundaries. Other U.S. localities consider similar ordinances.

1996   The United States Supreme Court agrees to review the sentences of the Los Angeles Police Department officers convicted of beating Rodney King in 1991.

Federal prosecutors pursue a prison inmate named Larry Hoover. Agents allege that Hoover controls a 50,000-member cultish gang called the "Gangster Disciples," which has members in 35 states, from his cell in Dixon, Illinois.

President Bill Clinton's remarks on crime in the annual State of the Union Address reflect the current national approach toward fighting crime. The president said:

> Our fourth great challenge is to take our streets back from crime and gangs and drugs. At last we have begun to find a way to reduce crime, forming community partnerships with local police forces to catch criminals and prevent crime.
> This strategy, called community policing, is clearly working. Violent crime is coming down all across America. In New York City, murders are down 25 percent; in St. Louis, 18 percent; and in Seattle, 32 percent. But we still have a long way to go before our streets are safe and our people are free from fear. The

1996
cont.

Crime Bill of 1994 is critical to the success of community policing. It provides funds for 100,000 new police in communities of all sizes. We are already a third of the way there, and I challenge the Congress to finish the job. Let us stick with a strategy that is working and keep the crime rate coming down. Community policing also requires bonds of trust between citizens and police. I ask all Americans to respect and support our law enforcement officers, and to our police I say, our children need you as role models and heroes. Don't let them down.

The Brady Bill has already stopped 44,000 people with criminal records from buying guns. The assault weapons ban is keeping 19 kinds of assault weapons out of the hands of violent gangs. I challenge the Congress to keep those laws on the books.

Our next step in the fight against crime is to take on gangs the way we once took on the mob. I am directing the FBI and other investigative agencies to target gangs that involve juveniles and violent crime and to seek authority to prosecute as adults teenagers who maim and kill like adults. And I challenge local housing authorities and tenant associations: Criminal gang members and drug dealers are destroying the lives of decent tenants. From now on, the rule for residents who commit crime and peddle drugs should be, one strike and you're out.

I challenge every State to match Federal policy to assure that serious violent criminals serve at least 85 percent of their sentence. More police and punishment are important, but they are not enough. We have got to keep more of our young people out of trouble with prevention strategies not dictated by Washington but developed in communities. I challenge all of our communities, all of our adults, to give our children futures to say yes to, and I challenge Congress not to abandon the Crime Bill's support of these grassroots prevention efforts.

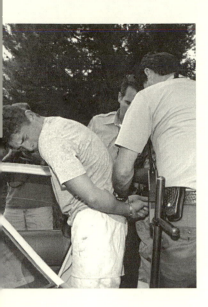

Biographical Sketches

M any sociologists, investigators, and law enforcement agents have dedicated their lives to careers they believe will lessen crime problems in some way, and politicians have tried to formulate policy to stem the tide of crime. The amount of information and the number of people involved in these efforts at the end of the twentieth century have grown exponentially since the early 1900s; thus, it is difficult to isolate any few people who have had the most influence. The biographies in this chapter, therefore, generally focus on people who have attempted to use new approaches to curb crime.

Sol Sheldon Glueck (1896–1980) and Eleanor Touroff Glueck (1898–1972)

Sol Sheldon Glueck and Eleanor Touroff Glueck were married in 1922 and joined the staff at Harvard University. There, they conducted in-depth studies of juvenile delinquency, juvenile corrections, and other aspects of criminology.

In one famous study, *500 Criminal Careers*, published in 1930, the Gluecks studied the criminal activity over a five-year period of 500 young men who had served sentences in the Massachusetts Reformatory. The study presented extensive data on the former inmates. The Gluecks found that

- The educational level of the offender's parents had little relation to his criminal status after his release from the Reformatory.
- Offenders who had originally left home before age 14 were more likely to remain delinquents than those who left home after age 14.
- Among all offenders, those who were first known to be delinquent before age 11 were the least likely to reform. Those who were first identified as delinquents between ages 14 and 16 were the most likely to reform.
- Those delinquents who had intelligence levels classified as "normal" were almost three times as likely to reform as those whose intelligence was classified as "borderline" or "moron or imbecile."

The Gluecks continued to study the criminal activity of the same former inmates for many years. The first follow-up to *500 Criminal Careers* was entitled *Later Criminal Careers* (published in 1937); it examined the same young men for an additional five-year period.

In the follow-up study, the Gluecks connected criminal behavior with unhappy family lives. Of the men who did not engage in criminal activity during the ten years following their release, 96 percent had successful family relationships, whereas only 9.6 percent of those who were classified as "serious offenders" succeeded in their family relationships.

In addition to juvenile delinquency, the couple studied juvenile justice and reform. *One Thousand Juvenile Delinquents: Their Treatment by Court and Clinic* (1934) focused on the Boston Juvenile Court.

During their lengthy careers, the Gluecks conducted many follow-up studies, kept thorough case histories, and conducted follow-up research. Their work is still studied today. Among the books one or both authored are *500 Criminal Careers, Criminal Careers in Retrospect, Five Hundred Delinquent Women, Later Criminal Careers, Family Environment and Delinquency, Toward a Typology of Juvenile Offenders,* and *One Thousand Juvenile Delinquents: Their Treatment by Court and Clinic.*

Edward Oscar Heinrich
(1881–1953)

Born in Clintonville, Wisconsin, this prominent forensics expert was on the cutting edge of his era. In 1919, 13 years before the Federal Bureau of Investigation's laboratory came into existence, Heinrich set up his own crime detection center in San Francisco. Heinrich employed scientific investigatory techniques that were not widely used in crime solving at the time.

Heinrich was a scientist of all trades—geology, physics, biochemistry, handwriting analysis, ballistics, and ink and paper analysis. His widely varied expertise contributed to his success. In addition to working at his crime lab, he lectured on criminology at the University of California at Berkeley.

Heinrich conducted investigations with the premise that criminals always leave clues at the scene of the crime. He helped other investigators determine whether deaths had resulted from murders, suicides, or accidents and often proved their first inclinations to be wrong. He was called upon in 1916 to investigate an explosion, presented evidence in the famed Fatty Arbuckle murder case, and supplied his services to police around the United States.

Heinrich conducted his work in an era when forensic science was rapidly advancing. In 1916, the trial of accused murderer Charles Stielow ushered in the science of ballistics. New York investigator Charles E. Waite cleared Stielow by scientifically proving with the use of microphotography that the deadly bullets could not have come from his gun. Ballistics evidence soon came into widespread use, and it was one of Heinrich's areas of proficiency.

One of Heinrich's crowning achievements was solving a 1923 bombing and robbery that had resulted in four deaths. The perpetrator had left at the scene a detonator with batteries, a Colt revolver, a pair of overalls, and some shoe covers. The crime baffled investigators for weeks before they called Heinrich. From the items listed, he was able to piece together a picture of the suspect and determine where he lived. A brown hair on the overalls indicated his hair color, the wear on his overalls showed he was left-handed, stains on the overalls came from fir trees in the Pacific Northwest, and a worn mail receipt treated with iodine vapor pointed to Oregon. The man in question and his two brothers were arrested after more than three years in hiding.

Although investigation techniques have become far more sophisticated since Heinrich's time, his contributions to criminal investigation were widely appreciated among investigators during his lifetime. He was still working in his crime lab when death ended his successful 45-year career in 1953.

Earnest A. Hooton (1887–1954)

Earnest A. Hooton was a Harvard anthropologist who conducted controversial studies in an attempt to prove biological links between criminals and their crimes. He was born in Clemonsville, Wisconsin, and studied at the University of Wisconsin. He was a Rhodes scholar and went on to study at Oxford. In 1913, he joined the faculty at Harvard University and remained there until his death.

As an anthropologist, Hooton studied fossil remains of early humans and compared people with early primates. His other interest was exploring links between biology and crime. Prior to Hooton's studies, other scientists—most notably the Italian Cesare Lombroso (1836–1909)—had investigated potential connections between physical attributes and criminal behavior. Lombroso asserted that criminals tend to have long arms, sloping foreheads, and primitive brains.

Hooton conducted a massive study involving more than 17,000 criminal subjects in ten states. He divided the subjects into racial categories and then subclassified them according to physical characteristics. "Old Americans," he said, were people born to white American parents. "Pure Nordics" had blue eyes, light hair, and long heads. The former, Hooton argued, were more likely to commit rape than other groups. Pure Nordics committed crimes like forgery or fraud.

Critics of Hooton's work accused him of fixing the results of his study. Some alleged he purposely used large, physically superior men in his control group to prove his hypothesis that criminals were physically inferior. Others said the height differentials Hooton identified among criminals were too insignificant to prove his assertions. Many also charged that his study did not explain the vast majority of these groups that were law-abiding citizens.

Hooton's work preceded the studies of modern scientists who look for genetic factors that may lead people to commit crime. His study focused on outward physical characteristics, but modern researchers have taken his work a step further with investigations of genetic material. For example, some researchers argue that an extra Y chromosome appears at a disproportionately high rate in criminals. Opponents of biological and genetic research in connection with crime fear it can lead to selective breeding and to the abortion of "unfit" fetuses that have suspect genes.

Hooton's works include *Crimes and the Man, Man's Poor Relations, Twilight of Man,* and *Young Man, You Are Normal.* Hooton died of a heart attack in 1954.

J. Edgar Hoover (1895–1972)

Perhaps no man in law enforcement was both as revered and as hated as the longtime director of the Federal Bureau of Investigation J. Edgar Hoover. Hoover was born in Washington, D.C., in 1895, the youngest of three children. As a child Hoover was shy, introverted, and studious, and he excelled in his studies. From a very young age, he displayed dedication to his work. In 1913, he entered George Washington University, where he earned a law degree. He graduated with honors and received a master's degree in 1917.

Although he did not fight in World War I, he served as a major in the Army Reserves. His big break came when he was hired by the Department of Justice to work in the office of John Lord O'Brien, then in charge of war-related work under Attorney General Thomas W. Gregory. During the war, large numbers of foreigners were arrested on suspicion of espionage. Hoover worked in O'Brien's office sorting through the cases and trying to separate the spies from innocent immigrants.

In 1919, Attorney General A. Mitchell Palmer promoted Hoover to the top position in the newly created General Intelligence Division, formed to combat a recent string of bombings. The attorney general instructed Hoover to investigate subversive political movements believed to be responsible for the terrorist attacks. The "red menace" in the United States following the 1917 Bolshevik Revolution in Russia proved to be the catalyst Hoover needed to jump-start his career. He read up on theories of communism and was thoroughly dedicated to investigating potential Communists. Hoover kept files on about 450,000 suspected radicals and organized raids on aliens.

In 1924, at age 29, Hoover was appointed to the position he retained until his death—head of the Bureau of Investigation. At that time, the agency was small, poorly organized, and rife with corruption. Hoover was assigned to clean it up—a job that suited him well. The condition of the agency was appalling to Hoover, who was meticulous, strong willed, and efficient. Hoover purged corrupt and improperly trained agents from the bureau and hired new recruits with law or accounting backgrounds. He successfully acquired funds to establish a fingerprint division, a training academy, a ballistics division, and a forensics division. He also expanded field offices and encouraged improvements in detection.

In 1933, Hoover launched a war on outlaw criminals he called "public enemies"—notorious figures such as Pretty Boy Floyd, John Herbert Dillinger, and Alvin Karpis. From time to time, he chose a "public enemy number one."

Hoover's war had its opponents. Senator Kenneth D. McKellar questioned Hoover's competence to head the bureau and observed that he had never personally arrested anyone. Hoover responded by arresting one of his public enemies, Alvin Karpis, after agents had tracked him down. He made sure the press was nearby to publicize the arrest but was embarrassed when it turned out that none of his agents had brought handcuffs.

Hoover demanded organization and required employees to document their activities. His fame grew when bureau agents arrested some of the nation's most wanted outlaws. Hollywood producers contacted him when they made movies about crimes the bureau was involved with. Hoover wrote a number of books throughout his career, including *J. Edgar Hoover on Communism, Juvenile Delinquency, Masters of Deceit: The Story of Communism,* and *A Study of Communism.*

By the 1940s, the small 200-member bureau had expanded to thousands of employees and acquired a new name, the Federal Bureau of Investigation (FBI). Agents were armed and trained. With World War II the danger of spies and another "red scare" returned, and Hoover began to root out corruption as diligently as before. He organized informer networks and relentlessly investigated suspected Communists during the postwar period. During the war, his staff grew to 5,000. One day after the Japanese attacked Pearl Harbor, the bureau had nearly 2,000 people arrested—Hoover's list was ready before the attack.

Until the Kennedy administration, Hoover enjoyed a virtually free reign atop the FBI. When President John F. Kennedy was elected, however, a particular source of enmity emerged. Robert Kennedy, attorney general in his brother's administration, ordered Hoover to assign more agents to civil rights and

organized crime cases, both of which had become political issues that were important to the president's public image.
Hoover resented this new encroachment on his authority but
followed the order sufficiently to somewhat appease Kennedy.

Hoover would not publicly acknowledge the extent of organized crime and preferred to expend the FBI's resources on suspected subversives. In his defense, the bureau's jurisdiction was
limited with regard to organized crime syndicates that did not
operate in more than one city.

Hoover was arbitrary and capricious, hiring and firing as he
wished and developing obsessions with trailing particular individuals. He kept records on the Kennedys, whom he thoroughly
disliked. He was particularly obsessed with civil rights leader
Martin Luther King Jr., and he had King followed and bugged
his telephones. President Lyndon Johnson reportedly enjoyed
daily gossip sheets Hoover provided that contained information
on the affairs of politicians in Washington.

Few careers receive as intense a mix of criticism and praise
as did Hoover's. On the one hand, he took a tiny, corrupt Bureau of Investigation and single-handedly transformed it into a
large and famed investigatory agency. Under his direction, the
agency tracked down and apprehended many wanted criminals. During World War II, the FBI apprehended a number of
genuine foreign spies. On the other hand, Hoover's office
served as a platform for his personal vendettas, even more so
toward the end of his career. He kept tabs on all of his personal
political enemies, as well as on the political opponents of people
with whom he hoped to ingratiate himself. His targets were as
diverse as Martin Luther King Jr., the Kennedys, Communist
party members, and the Ku Klux Klan. Some were not suspected of any illegal activity.

Hoover never married and had little social life. Throughout
his career, he remained thoroughly dedicated to his duties at the
FBI and rarely left his home and his office. He was both widely
respected and widely suspected. On May 1, 1972, he was still
the head of the FBI when he died of a heart attack, ending a 48-
year career served under eight presidents.

Lyndon B. Johnson (1908–1973)

Lyndon Baines Johnson served as the thirty-sixth president of
the United States from 1963 to 1969. He was vice president to

John F. Kennedy when Kennedy was shot in November 1963. Johnson became president after the assassination and was officially elected in 1964.

Johnson was born in central Texas, the oldest of five children. He graduated from high school in 1924. He did not attend college until 1927, when he enrolled at Southwest Texas State Teachers College. He became involved in campus politics and debating, and he excelled in both areas. Johnson started a political group called the White Stars that took over campus politics, and he served as editor of the college paper.

When a Texas Democrat named Richard M. Kleberg won election to the U.S. House of Representatives in 1931, Johnson got his first political break. He had campaigned for Kleberg, and the newly elected member of Congress took the 23-year-old to Washington, D.C., as his secretary. In 1935, President Franklin Delano Roosevelt appointed Johnson head of the National Youth Administration in Texas. Two years later, the aspiring politician ran for Congress and won. Johnson remained very supportive of Roosevelt's New Deal programs and became one of the popular president's personal friends.

In 1948, Johnson was elected to the U.S. Senate. Three years later, he was elected the Democratic whip. By 1955, he had become the Senate majority leader. In 1960, Johnson became a Democratic candidate for president, but John F. Kennedy won the nomination. Kennedy invited him to run as vice president, and Johnson accepted. In 1963, he became president upon Kennedy's death.

During his years as president, Johnson became mired in all sorts of problems. The Vietnam War was becoming increasingly unpopular at home, and the Cold War with the Soviet Union was heating up abroad. Large increases in crime statistics during this time caused Johnson to consider criminal activity to be another of his problems.

Prior to the Johnson administration, relatively little federal crime control legislation had been passed. Congress passed new laws periodically that federalized offenses formerly handled by cities and states. Such laws were usually spurred by a particular high-profile crime, such as the Lindbergh kidnapping in 1932, which led to the passage of federal antikidnapping legislation. All the same, the authority to deal with crime rested largely with local and state governments.

The Johnson administration brought crime permanently to the national political agenda—a fact not everybody welcomed.

State and local law enforcement agencies complained about the increasing extent of federal involvement in fighting crime.

Johnson rejected the law-and-order approach to crime espoused by police leaders like Philadelphia's Frank Rizzo. In step with the changing political atmosphere of the 1960s, Johnson believed poor economic and social circumstances were responsible for much of the crime problem. He tried to formulate programs to mitigate these circumstances.

Johnson formed commissions to investigate organized crime, the criminal justice system, and criminal law reform. The most famous of these groups, the Commission on Law Enforcement and Administration of Justice, produced a lengthy report entitled *The Challenge of Crime in a Free Society* in 1967. The report prompted Congress to pass a major crime bill, the Omnibus Crime Control and Safe Streets Act of 1968, which created councils to administer funding for crime prevention programs and relaxed standards for obtaining confessions.

Some argue that Johnson brought national attention to problems too long ignored. Regardless of Johnson's intent, his legacy consists of a large and uncoordinated body of federal anticrime legislation. Richard Nixon immediately began to attack Johnson's prevention-oriented crime control strategy when he was elected and called for a law-and-order approach. Nearly every president elected since Johnson has made a serious effort to pass crime control legislation in some form. Since the 1960s, it has been essential for a national politician to appear to be tough on crime.

Arthur Koehler (1885–1967)

The name Arthur Koehler brought fear to many arson suspects when the famous "wood detective" was active in criminal investigation. Koehler had a lifelong fascination with wood that began in his childhood. He worked with the U.S. Forest Service for 36 years until his retirement in 1948. During much of that time, he also served as the chief wood identification expert at the Forest Products Laboratory in Madison, Wisconsin.

Koehler's most noteworthy case was the kidnapping of aviator Charles Lindbergh's son in 1932. Not expecting much, investigators asked Koehler to trace the wood used to make the kidnapper's ladder. Eighteen months later, Koehler had found the lumberyard that had sold the wood, the forest from which it had been taken, and the mill that had processed it. Although

Koehler's evidence did not initially lead to the capture of the murderer, it later proved to be instrumental in convicting him. After his arrest, Koehler linked one of suspect Bruno Richard Hauptmann's tools to the ladder and a ladder rail to his home.

Koehler was involved in solving a number of other crimes. He matched wood pieces from a Wisconsin farmer's shop to pieces of elm from a deadly bomb. When a man stole high-quality logs from a forest, Koehler traced them back to their stumps. His evidence was used to convict other bombers and arsonists.

Eliot Ness (1902–1957)

Eliot Ness is perhaps best known for his leadership of the ten-man group that waged war against Al Capone's bootlegging operations during the Prohibition era in Chicago. The group, known as "the Untouchables," acquired a reputation for its toughness and incorruptibility in an era when police corruption was widespread and bribe taking was very common.

Ness graduated from the University of Chicago and in 1928, at age 26, was charged with putting together a small unit of men to battle Capone's organization. Rampant police corruption allowed Capone's underground to flourish during that time, so Ness's task of assembling a unit of honest and able officers was not an easy one. After poring through hundreds of law enforcement personnel files, Ness picked out nine additional men who became his partners. They were chosen for both their skills and their honesty. Ness called them "Untouchables" because the Mafia could not sway them with bribes or deter them with threats.

It was the Internal Revenue Service rather than the Untouchables that eventually brought down Al Capone, but Ness's force caused many headaches for the underworld king. His officers conducted raids on illegal distilleries. Ness alerted the press before a raid, and the media coverage both pleased the group's leader and helped to break down the public perception that Mafia gangs were invincible.

Ness moved on to another post in the Department of Justice and continued investigating Prohibition-related illegal activity. In 1935, he became director of a reform administration in Cleveland, Ohio. Again he faced a powerful gang in the city, known as the Mayfield Road Mob, and again he faced widespread police corruption that allowed the gang to flourish. Gambling, prostitution, and bootlegging held strong influence in the city. As before, Ness proved to be up to the task. He fired and transferred corrupt police officers and survived several attempts to kill him. When he left the administration after six years, he and his officers had succeeded in driving the Mayfield Road Mob out of town.

During World War II, Ness served as the federal director of the Office of Defense's Division of Social Protection. He opened a private practice after the war. He wrote a book called *The Untouchables*. Eliot Ness died at the relatively young age of 54 in 1957.

Frank Rizzo (1920–1991)

Frank Rizzo, the son of a policeman, was born to Italian immigrants in Philadelphia in 1920. He grew up in an ethnic neighborhood in south Philadelphia. In 1943, he joined the Philadelphia Police Department. Rizzo was large and tough and was feared around the city. He became the police commissioner in 1967. Under Rizzo's leadership, the department acquired a reputation as one of the toughest and best in the country. He took a stringent law-and-order approach to fighting crime and for many years enjoyed widespread public support.

Rizzo became famous for his outspokenness and tough talk and for his tough approach to urban unrest that manifested itself in groups like the Black Panthers. He targeted inner-city crime, and his officers were widely feared by the city's criminal population. In one famous raid, his officers invaded the Black Panthers' headquarters and confiscated the group's firearms stockpile a month before it planned to conduct a "revolutionary people's convention." Officers also targeted strip joints and shady coffeehouses.

Rizzo became a Democratic mayor of Philadelphia in 1971 and continued to exert strong influence over the police department in his new position. He was reelected in 1975, and he was so popular that he tried to have the two-term limitation removed so he could run again.

About this time, serious allegations of brutality in the police department began to emerge. Officers had forcibly extracted confessions from innocent people, and Rizzo continued to ignore the abuses. In one extreme case, an innocent mentally impaired man was convicted of murder after the police had forced him to confess.

Two reporters, Jonathan Neumann and William Marimow, from the *Philadelphia Inquirer* halted Rizzo's political career with a series of investigatory articles into the Philadelphia police department. A source close to the police department known as "Deep Nightstick" provided them with much of their information. Neumann and Marimow found that courts had thrown out illegally obtained confessions in at least 80 cases, but no investigation had ever followed. The "Deep Nightstick" articles resulted in the convictions of several officers, the end of Rizzo's political career for a time, and a Pulitzer Prize for the journalists.

In 1987, Rizzo once again ran for mayor of Philadelphia but lost to the man who became the city's first black mayor, Wilson Goode. After his narrow loss, Rizzo became a radio talk show host until 1991, when he decided to run for mayor again. Rizzo secured the Republican nomination, but he died of a heart attack at age 70 on July 16, 1991, just before the November elections.

Earl Warren (1891–1974)

Earl Warren is best known for his tenure as chief justice of the United States Supreme Court. He was born in Los Angeles, California, and obtained a law degree from the University of California. He served as his state's attorney general from 1939 to 1943 and as its governor between 1943 and 1953. Warren ran in the vice president's spot in 1948.

President Dwight D. Eisenhower appointed Warren chief justice of the Supreme Court in 1953 as a reward for his help during the election. Eisenhower had appointed a Republican, but Warren soon acquired a reputation as a liberal justice. Known as the Warren Court during his 1953–1969 tenure, the Court handed down a series of rulings designed to expand the rights of criminal defendants. The other significant action of the Warren Court was the extension of many constitutional rights to the states.

Some of the most significant rulings handed down during Warren's leadership are summarized here.

- *Griffin v. Illinois* (1956). The Court required states to give a felony defendant transcripts of his or her court proceedings regardless of whether the defendant could pay for them. This ruling was especially valuable to defendants who were appealing convictions.

- *Jencks v. United States* (1957). The government must permit a defendant's lawyers to see pretrial reports. The ruling in this case reduces courtroom surprises and allows future defendants' attorneys to better prepare for the prosecution's attack.
- *Mallory v. United States* (1957). A person who is arrested must be taken promptly to a magistrate who decides whether the evidence against him or her merits a charge. In combination with the 1943 *McNabb v. United States* ruling, this case established the McNabb-Mallory Rule, which stipulates that an arrestee must be taken swiftly to a magistrate or any incriminating statements the suspect makes will be inadmissible in court.
- *Spano v. New York* (1959). Once a defendant has been indicted, he or she has the right to refuse to answer questions in the absence of an attorney.
- *Mapp v. Ohio* (1961). This case extended the Exclusionary Rule to all states. The rule forbids any evidence to be introduced in the courtroom that is obtained by illegal search and seizure, or in violation of the Fourth Amendment. The rule came under judicial attack in the 1970s and 1980s.
- *Robinson v. California* (1962). This decision invalidated a California statute that made narcotics addiction a misdemeanor crime. The court said drug addiction is a disease and held that making it a crime amounted to "cruel and unusual punishment."
- *Gideon v. Wainwright* (1963). The Court overturned the conviction of a felony defendant who was not provided with a lawyer when he could not afford one. The court said the state therefore violated the Sixth Amendment right of a defendant "to have the assistance of counsel for his defense."
- *Escobedo v. Illinois* (1964). The Court ruled that a suspect's statements are not admissible in court when a defendant is denied permission to have counsel present.
- *Malloy v. Hogan* (1964). This decision overturned the 1947 *Adamson v. California* ruling. The Court applied the Fifth Amendment right against self-incrimination to all states.
- *Massiah v. United States* (1964). In this decision, the Court held that a defendant who is formally charged has the

right to have an attorney present unless he or she knowingly relinquishes that right. Agents had captured incriminating statements from the defendant on tape after he had already been charged and released on bail.

- *Miranda v. Arizona* (1966). In perhaps the most famous decision of this era, the Court overturned a rape conviction on the grounds that the suspect had not been advised of his legal rights. Suspects are now read their "Miranda rights" upon arrest, which basically state: "You have the right to remain silent. Anything you say can and will be used against you in a court of law. You have the right to an attorney. If you cannot afford one, one will be appointed for you."
- *Katz v. United States* (1967). The Court extended the Fourth Amendment to electronic surveillance, even if no physical intrusion occurs into someone's property.
- *See v. Seattle* (1967). The Court threw out the conviction of a warehouse owner who had refused to admit a fire inspector to his premises. It said that commercial property cannot be forcibly inspected without a warrant.
- *Witherspoon v. Illinois* (1968). Defendants cannot be sentenced to death by a jury from which people who voice opposition to the death penalty have been excluded.

When President John F. Kennedy was assassinated in 1963, newly sworn-in President Johnson asked Warren to chair a commission that would investigate the shooting. Warren accepted the task, and his commission interviewed over 500 witnesses during a ten-month period. It produced the *Warren Report*, which concluded that assassin Lee Harvey Oswald had acted alone, as had Jack Ruby, the man who shot Oswald. The report also criticized the Federal Bureau of Investigation and the Secret Service. Critics charged that the commission failed to thoroughly investigate the possibility of a conspiracy. A U.S. House of Representatives investigation in the 1970s reconsidered the evidence and concluded that the possibility of a conspiracy did exist.

Warren tried to resign from the Court in 1968, but in part because of a Senate filibuster that prevented a vote on the nomination of a successor, he remained in the chief justice's seat until 1969. Succeeding courts have shown a conservative backlash and have placed limitations on many of the Warren Court's decisions, including *Miranda v. Arizona* and *Mapp v. Ohio*.

Frank J. Wilson (1887–1970)

Before he became head of the Secret Service in 1936, Frank J. Wilson already had one major credit to his name: he had brought down Chicago bootlegging king Al Capone. Wilson was assigned to infiltrate the Capone organization by his superior at the Internal Revenue Service's enforcement branch, who had decided to pursue Capone for income tax evasion.

The Mafia boss owned nothing in his own name and had not filed taxes for a few years, so agents had to infiltrate his organization to obtain the necessary information, which they eventually succeeded in doing. Capone put a contract out on Wilson's life but eventually called off the killing. Al Capone was later convicted and sent to prison.

Wilson also gained notoriety for his involvement in the 1932 kidnapping and murder case of aviator Charles Lindbergh's son by insisting that investigators record the serial numbers on the ransom money. The bills turned up in several areas around the Bronx, leading investigators to suspect a local man. When Bruno Richard Hauptmann used some of the money at a gas station, police tracked him down and found more of the currency at his home.

In 1936, Wilson became head of the Secret Service, where he launched a largely successful war against counterfeit currency. He is also credited with reforming presidential security policy. Wilson retired from the Secret Service in 1947. He wrote a book with Beth Day entitled *Special Agent*. He died in 1970.

James Q. Wilson (1931–)

A professor of management and public policy at the University of California at Los Angeles, James Q. Wilson has studied and written about crime for more than 30 years. His academic colleagues consider him to be conservative, largely because of his assertion that crime results from individual behavior rather than from surrounding circumstances.

In 1968, Wilson published *Varieties of Police Behavior: The Management of Law and Order in Eight Communities*, which outlined three different types of police departments. The watchman department has weak leadership, low morale, and poor discipline and is generally regarded as inept. A legalistic department is efficiently run, with strong leaders and strict discipline. The third type, the service department, is not as organized as the legalistic department but is also not inept. It differs from the other two forms in that it maintains good relations with the community. Wilson argued that the service types are the most effective in solving crimes because they encourage the surrounding community to cooperate.

Wilson, who has been called a "deterrence pragmatist," has argued that a person's awareness that punishment will result from the commission of a crime is an effective deterrent. In *The Moral Sense,* published in 1993, Wilson maintained that cultures do not shape human morality but that morality comes from human nature, which spans all cultures. The book centers on what Wilson defined as moral sentiments: duty, fairness, sympathy, and self-control. In another book (co-written with Richard J. Herrnstein), *Crime and Human Nature,* published in 1985, Wilson argued that evil is inherent in every individual. In law-abiding citizens, evil is sufficiently controlled by good, but that restraint fails in criminals. When criminals think the benefits of committing a crime exceed the drawbacks, they commit crimes.

Wilson has served on panels and presidential commissions and has written numerous books and countless articles. His books include *Crime, Crime and Public Policy, Crime and Human Nature, The Moral Sense, Thinking about Crime, On Character: Essays,* and *Varieties of Police Behavior: The Management of Law and Order in Eight Communities.*

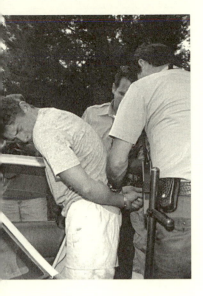

Facts, Statistics, and Documents

Facts and Statistics

The figures in this chapter are intended to illustrate several different trends. First, overall crime levels in the 1990s are significantly higher than levels in 1963. The figures then trace yearly changes in the number of murders, burglaries, forcible rapes, and several other crimes between 1985 and 1993. The second major point these figures reveal is that juvenile crimes are becoming more violent, and children are committing crimes at very young ages. Some other aspects of criminal activity are also revealed in these statistics: the types of weapons used to commit crimes, the relationship of murder victims to their murderers, the number of offenses police clear with arrests, the relationship of drugs to criminal activity, and types of criminal activity in each state. It is important to keep in mind that most of these statistics reflect only crimes that have been reported to the police.

The Federal Bureau of Investigation (FBI) provides the most comprehensive national crime statistics available. Each year, the agency compiles the *Uniform Crime Reports* (UCR) from crimes reported to law enforcement agencies nationwide. The main weak-

95

ness of these statistics is that many crimes go unreported, so the numbers do not reflect all of the crimes that are committed.

The Bureau of Justice Statistics conducts the *National Crime Survey* (NCS), which relies on ongoing interviews with households across the United States for its data. Because murder victims cannot respond to the survey, the NCS does not provide homicide data.

Both data sources lack good statistics on offenses that are part of organized criminal activity. These offenses are sometimes described as "victimless crimes." Both buyers and sellers of illegal goods are usually willing participants, and those who are not refrain from reporting offenses to the police for fear of reprisals by the organization.

Most of the data in this chapter come from the more thorough *Uniform Crime Reports*. Some frequently used terms and definitions as used in UCR data are given here. All definitions are taken from the 1993 edition of UCR.

It should be noted that in some cases definitions have changed over the years. For example, "motor vehicle theft" was formerly called "auto theft." "Larceny-theft" is now one category; in 1963 it was divided into "$50 and over" and "under $50."

Common Terms

Aggravated Assault An unlawful attack by one person upon another for the purpose of inflicting severe or aggravated bodily injury. This type of assault is usually accompanied by the use of a weapon or by means likely to produce death or great bodily harm. Simple assaults are excluded.

Other Assaults (simple) Assaults and attempted assaults where no weapon is used and which do not result in serious or aggravated injury to the victim.

Arson Any willful or malicious burning or attempt to burn—with or without intent to defraud—a dwelling house, public building, motor vehicle or aircraft, personal property of another, etc.

Burglary: The unlawful entry of a structure to commit a felony or a theft. Attempted forcible entry is included.

Criminal Homicide (a) Murder and nonnegligent manslaughter: the willful (nonnegligent) killing of one human being by another. Deaths caused by negligence, attempts to kill, assaults to kill, suicides, accidental deaths, and justifiable homicides are excluded. Justifiable homicides are limited to (1) the killing of a felon by a law enforcement officer in the line of duty, and (2) the killing of a felon by a private citizen. (b) Manslaughter by negligence: the killing of another person through gross negligence. Traffic fatalities are excluded. Although manslaughter by negligence is a Part I crime, it is not excluded in the Crime Index.

Drug Abuse Violations State and local offenses relating to the unlawful possession, sale, use, growing, and manufacturing of narcotic drugs.

Embezzlement Misappropriation or misapplication of money or property entrusted to one's care, custody, or control.

Forcible Rape The carnal knowledge of a female forcibly and against her will. Included are rapes by force and attempts or assaults to rape. Statutory offenses (no force used, victim under age of consent) are excluded.

Forgery and Counterfeiting Making, altering, uttering, or possessing, with intent to defraud, anything false in the semblance of that which is true. Attempts are included.

Fraud Fraudulent conversion and obtaining money or property by false pretenses. Included are confidence games and bad checks, except forgery and counterfeiting.

Gambling Promoting, permitting, or engaging in illegal gambling. (This definition is taken from *Uniform Crime Reports*, 1963.)

Larceny-Theft The unlawful taking, carrying, leading, or riding away of property from the possession or constructive possession of another.

Motor Vehicle Theft The theft or attempted theft of a motor vehicle. Does not include motorboats, construction equipment, airplanes, or farming equipment.

Prostitution and Commercialized Vice Sex offenses of a commercialized nature, such as prostitution, keeping a bawdy house, procuring, or transporting women for immoral purposes. Attempts are included.

Robbery Taking or attempting to take anything of value from the care, custody, or control of a person or persons by force or threat of force or violence, and/or by putting the victim in fear.

Sex Offenses Statutory rape and offenses against chastity, common decency, morals, and the like. Attempts are included; forcible rape, prostitution, and commercialized vice are excluded.

Stolen Property—Buying, Receiving, Possessing Buying, receiving, and possessing stolen property, including attempts.

Vandalism Willful or malicious destruction, injury, disfigurement, or defacement of any public or private property, real or personal, without consent of the owner or persons having custody or control.

Weapons—Carrying, Possessing, etc. All violations of regulations or statutes controlling the carrying, using, possessing, furnishing, and manufacturing of deadly weapons or silencers. Attempts are included.

General Trends

Although the FBI began collecting crime statistics in 1930, reporting methods improved dramatically in the early 1960s when crime became a permanent issue at the national level. Figures 4.1–4.11 illustrate some general trends in crime from 1963 to 1993, with emphasis on the years 1985–1993.

In 1963, UCR reported one murder every hour, a forcible rape every 32 minutes, and an auto theft each minute in the United States. In 1993—30 years later—*Uniform Crime Reports* (1993) indicated that the frequency had risen to a murder every 28 minutes, a forcible rape every 6 minutes, and a motor vehicle theft every 29 seconds. Year-to-year statistics will show slight rises and falls, but when the statistics are viewed over the long term, they show significant rises.

For example, according to *Uniform Crime Reports* (1963, 1993), New York state had a crime index rate of 5,551.3 offenses per 100,000 inhabitants in 1993, up from 1,289.7 per 100,000 residents in 1963—a more than fourfold increase. The national index rates for robbery, burglary, and larceny-theft more than doubled in that time period, according to *Uniform Crime Reports* (1963, 1993).

Crime rates rose and fell by slight increments between 1985 and 1993, but they remained far above 1963 levels. Aggravated assaults, for example, fell slightly between 1992 and 1993, but with more than 400 offenses per 100,000 inhabitants in both years (compared with 78.4 in 1963), according to *Uniform Crime Reports* (1963, 1992, 1993), the small dip hardly seems significant.

State Crime Data

Tables 4.1 and 4.2 list states in ascending order according to crime rate in 1963 and 1993. The first column lists the state, the second its crime rate per 100,000 inhabitants, and the third the total number of murders committed in that state during that year. West Virginia had the lowest crime rate in 1993; the District of Columbia had the highest. In 1963, Mississippi had the lowest overall crime rate, and Nevada had the highest rate.

Juvenile Offenses

In recent years, the frequency of juvenile crime has increased more dramatically than the crime rate as a whole. In 1990, about 14 percent of those arrested for murder or nonnegligent manslaughter were under age 18, and about 1.5 percent were under age 15. In 1985, the percentages were about 8 percent for those under age 18 and 1 percent for those under age 15. In 1963, the percentage of murders committed by juveniles was about 8 percent.

Juveniles under age 15 were arrested in connection with 5.3 percent of all reported offenses in 1990, and those under age 18 accounted for 15.6 percent. Figures 4.12–4.19 illustrate trends in juvenile arrest rates for various offenses.

Offenses Cleared by Arrest

How much crime goes unpunished? As discussed earlier, not all crimes are reported to the police. Of those that are reported, a staggering number remain unsolved.

Violent crimes such as murder and forcible rape are solved more often than are property crimes. In 1993, 34 percent of murder and nonnegligent manslaughter offenses and 47 percent of forcible rapes remained uncleared by arrest, whereas 87 percent of burglaries, 80 percent of larceny-theft offenses, and 86 percent of motor vehicle thefts remained uncleared.

As Figures 4.20 and 4.21 illustrate, the percentage of crimes that go unsolved has risen with the frequency of offenses, although that percentage remained relatively steady between 1985 and 1993.

Drugs and Crime

The correlation between drug use and crime is relatively high. The BJS reported that 30 percent of jail inmates in 1983 and 27 percent of inmates in 1989 had committed their offenses under the influence of a drug. Among prison inmates, the percentage rose from 25 percent in 1974 to 35 percent in 1986.

According to a National Institute of Justice Survey conducted in 1990, the percentages of people shown in Table 4.3 were under the influence of drugs when arrested for their offense.

Weapons Used in Murder/Nonnegligent Manslaughter

Figures 4.22 and 4.23 list the weapons used to commit murder in 1963 and in 1990 and 1993. "Personal weapons" include pushing. The 1990s statistics break weapons down into more specific categories than do the 1960s data, but one fact is obvious from both decades: firearms are used to commit most murders.

Victim-Offender Relationships

It is often said that many victims know their attackers, rapists, or murderers, and statistics support this assertion. Figure 4.24 shows the relationships between victims and their murderers. Almost half knew the person who killed them.

Tables and Figures

Tables

Table 4.1 State Crime Rates in Ascending Order, 1963

State[a]	Crime Rate Per 100,000 Inhabitants	Total Murders
Mississippi	393.2	164
North Dakota	472.9	13
West Virginia	473.7	95
New Hampshire	531.1	20
Maine	545.8	19
Iowa	577.0	35
South Dakota	585.7	9
Wisconsin	594.7	70
Arkansas	648.2	137
Nebraska	663.6	29
Vermont	668.2	2
Pennsylvania	767.2	265
Kansas	782.6	57
Idaho	787.4	18
North Carolina	789.6	370
Ohio	839.9	306
Alabama	848.8	340
Minnesota	864.0	41
Wyoming	895.6	12
Virginia	926.2	249
Kentucky	926.4	172
Connecticut	974.5	47
Louisiana	990.6	235
Tennessee	1,014.0	239
Oklahoma	1,076.2	129
Indiana	1,089.2	129
South Carolina	1,095.1	249
Georgia	1,106.3	390
Washington	1,114.7	76
Utah	1,125.4	24
Montana	1,128.3	14
Massachusetts	1,137.1	101
Oregon	1,142.7	55
Rhode Island	1,219.1	12
Maryland	1,225.9	207

(continues)

Table 4.1 *continued*

State[a]	Crime Rate Per 100,000 Inhabitants	Total Murders
Delaware	1,228.7	22
Texas	1,234.3	757
New Jersey	1,234.4	181
New York	1,289.7	669
Alaska	1,291.1	16
New Mexico	1,313.7	55
Michigan	1,348.6	268
Hawaii	1,357.0	12
Missouri	1,387.0	223
Colorado	1,534.5	94
Florida	1,592.4	463
Illinois	1,640.0	523
Arizona	1,935.3	93
California	2,164.2	673
Nevada	2,990.1	29

[a]The District of Columbia was not included in state rankings at this time. The number of murders reflects only those murders for which full information was provided.
Source: Uniform Crime Reports, 1963.

Table 4.2 State Crime Rates in Ascending Order, 1993

State	Crime Rate Per 100,000 Inhabitants	Total Murders[a]
West Virginia	2,532.6	125
North Dakota	2,820.3	11
New Hampshire	2,905.0	20
South Dakota	2,958.2	18
Maine	3,153.9	7
Pennsylvania	3,271.4	804
Kentucky	3,529.7	236
Idaho	3,845.1	31
Iowa	3,846.4	45
Vermont	3,972.4	12
Wisconsin	4,054.1	222
Virginia	4,115.5	539
Nebraska	4,117.1	28
Wyoming	4,163.0	16
Minnesota	4,386.2	131

(continues)

Table 4.2 *continued*

State	Crime Rate Per 100,000 Inhabitants	Total Murders[a]
Mississippi	4,418.3	218
Indiana	4,465.1	357
Ohio	4,485.3	599
Rhode Island	4,499.0	39
Connecticut	4,650.4	206
Montana	4,790.0	b
New Jersey	4,800.8	418
Arkansas	4,810.7	244
Delaware	4,872.1	20
Alabama	4,878.8	473
Massachusetts	4,893.9	210
Kansas	4,975.3	b
Missouri	5,095.4	546
Utah	5,237.4	58
Tennessee	5,239.5	450
Oklahoma	5,294.3	272
Michigan	5,452.5	922
Colorado	5,526.8	206
New York	5,551.3	2,415
Alaska	5,567.9	54
Illinois	5,617.9	b
North Carolina	5,652.3	771
Oregon	5,765.6	143
South Carolina	5,903.4	375
Washington	5,952.3	264
Maryland	6,106.5	632
Nevada	6,180.1	129
Georgia	6,193.0	750
New Mexico	6,266.1	95
Hawaii	6,277.0	43
Texas	6,439.1	2,142
California	6,456.9	4,094
Louisiana	6,846.6	721
Arizona	7,431.7	330
Florida	8,351.0	1,223
District of Columbia	11,761.1	417

[a]The number of murders reflects only those murders for which full information was provided.
[b]No data were available.
Source: Uniform Crime Reports, 1993.

Table 4.3 Percentage of Arrestees Testing Positive for Drug Use, 1990

	Sex of Arrestee	
Category of Arrest	Males	Females
Drug Sale/Possession	79	81
Burglary	68	58
Robbery	66	66
Larceny-Theft	64	59
Stolen Vehicle	60	65
Stolen Property	59	59
Homicide	52	49
Fraud/Forgery	50	55
Prostitution	49	81
Assault	48	50

Sources: Based on urinalysis results from 19,883 male and 7,947 female arrestees. National Institute of Justice Drug Use Forecasting Program unpublished data, 1990; Bureau of Justice Statistics.

Figures

Figure 4.1 Rate of Crime Index Offenses in the United States per 100,000 Inhabitants, 1963 and 1993

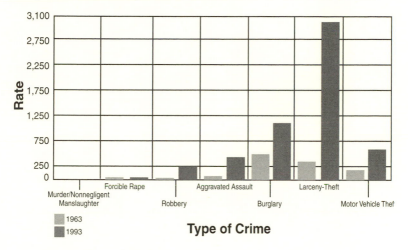

Source: Uniform Crime Reports, 1963, 1993.

Figure 4.2 Rate of Crime Index Offenses in the United States per 100,000 Inhabitants, 1980 and 1993

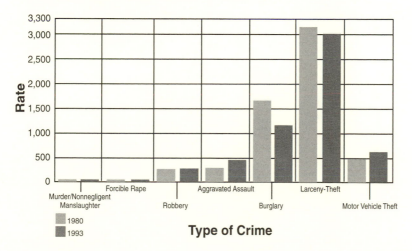

Source: Uniform Crime Reports, 1980, 1993.

Figure 4.3   Total Crime Index Offenses in the United States, 1963 (percent)

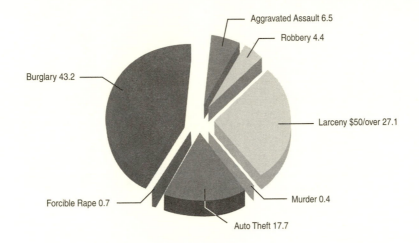

Source: Uniform Crime Reports, 1963.

Figure 4.4   Total Crime Index Offenses in the United States, 1993 (percent)

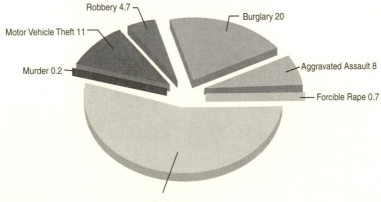

Source: Uniform Crime Reports, 1993.

Figure 4.5 Rate of Murder/Nonnegligent Manslaughter in the United States per 100,000 Inhabitants, 1985–1993

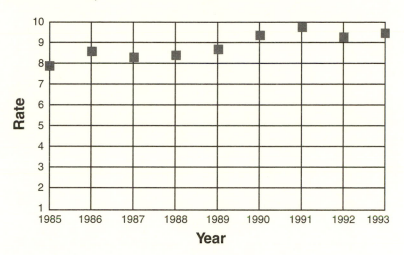

Source: Uniform Crime Reports, 1985–1993.

Figure 4.6 Rate of Forcible Rape in the United States per 100,000 Inhabitants, 1985–1993

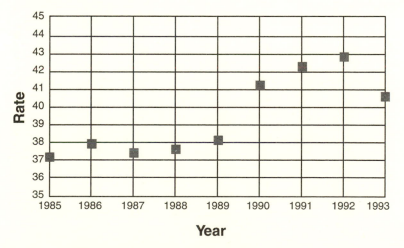

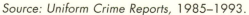

Source: Uniform Crime Reports, 1985–1993.

Figure 4.7 Rate of Robbery in the United States per 100,000 Inhabitants, 1985–1993

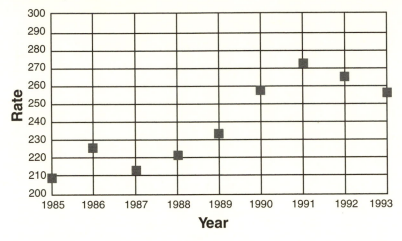

Source: Uniform Crime Reports, 1985–1993.

Figure 4.8 Rate of Aggravated Assault in the United States per 100,000 Inhabitants, 1985–1993

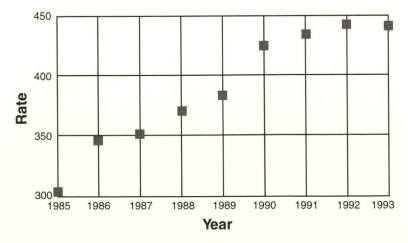

Source: Uniform Crime Reports, 1985–1993.

Figure 4.9 Rate of Burglary in the United States per 100,000 Inhabitants, 1985–1993

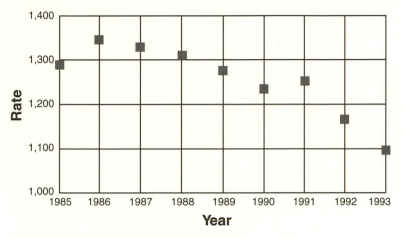

Source: Uniform Crime Reports, 1985–1993.

Figure 4.10 Rate of Larceny-Theft in the United States per 100,000 Inhabitants, 1985–1993

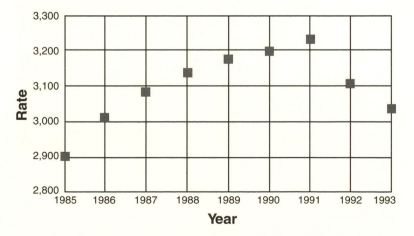

Source: Uniform Crime Reports, 1985–1993.

Figure 4.11 Rate of Motor Vehicle Theft in the United States per 100,000 Inhabitants, 1985–1993

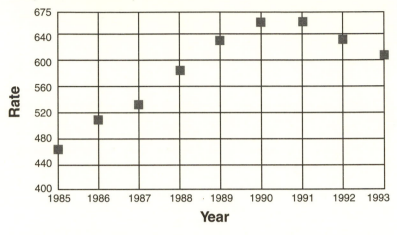

Source: Uniform Crime Reports, 1985–1993.

Figure 4.12 Arrestees in the United States under Ages 15 and 18, 1963 and 1993

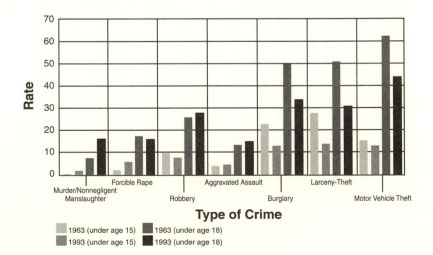

Source: Uniform Crime Reports, 1963, 1993.

Figure 4.13 Number of Juvenile Arrests for Murder/Nonnegligent Manslaughter in the United States, 1985 and 1990

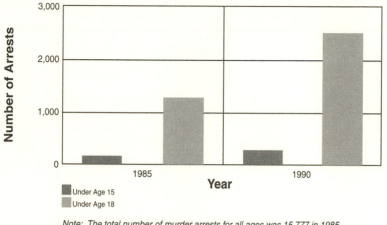

Note: The total number of murder arrests for all ages was 15,777 in 1985
and 18,298 in 1990.

Source: Uniform Crime Reports, 1985, 1990.

Figure 4.14 Number of Juvenile Arrests for Forcible Rape in the United States, 1985 and 1990

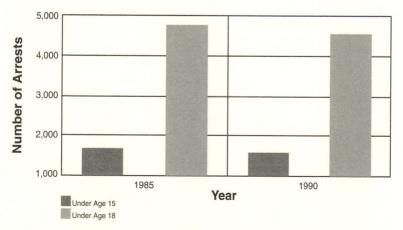

Note: The total number of forcible rape arrests for all ages was 31,934 in 1985
and 30,966 in 1990.

Source: Uniform Crime Reports, 1985, 1990.

Figure 4.15 Number of Juvenile Arrests for Robbery in the United States, 1985 and 1990

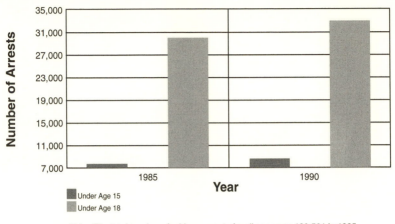

Note: The total number of robbery arrests for all ages was 120,501 in 1985 and 136,300 in 1990.

Source: Uniform Crime Reports, 1985, 1990.

Figure 4.16 Number of Juvenile Arrests for Aggravated Assault in the United States, 1985 and 1990

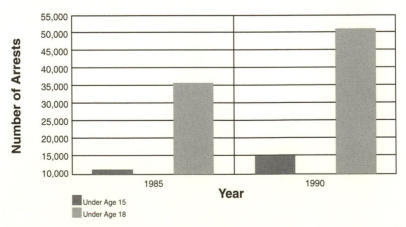

Note: The total number of aggravated assault arrests for all ages was 263,120 in 1985 and 376,917 in 1990.

Source: Uniform Crime Reports, 1985, 1990.

Figure 4.17   Number of Juvenile Arrests for Burglary in the United States, 1985 and 1990

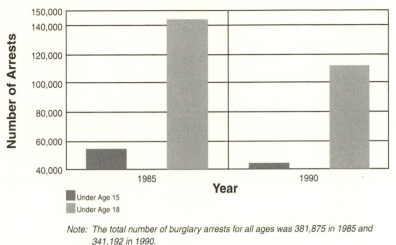

Note: The total number of burglary arrests for all ages was 381,875 in 1985 and
       341,192 in 1990.

Source: Uniform Crime Reports, 1985, 1990.

Figure 4.18   Number of Juvenile Arrests for Larceny-Theft in the United States, 1985 and 1990

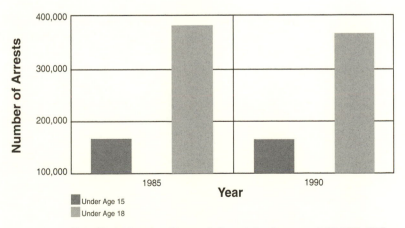

Note: The total number of larceny-theft arrests for all ages was 1,179,066 in 1985
       and 1,241,236 in 1990.

Source: Uniform Crime Reports, 1985, 1990.

Figure 4.19 Number of Juvenile Arrests for Motor Vehicle Theft in the United States, 1985 and 1990

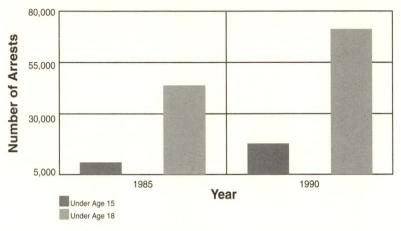

Note: The total number of motor vehicle theft arrests for all ages was 115,621 in 1985 and 168,338 in 1990.

Source: Uniform Crime Reports, 1985, 1990.

Figure 4.20 Offenses Cleared by Arrest, 1963 and 1993 (percent)

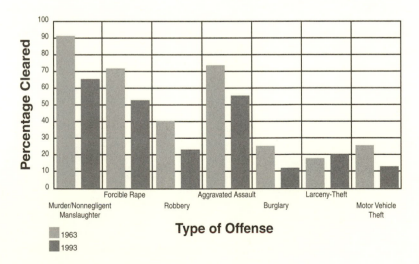

Source: Uniform Crime Reports, 1963, 1993.

Figure 4.21 Offenses Cleared by Arrest, 1985 (percent)

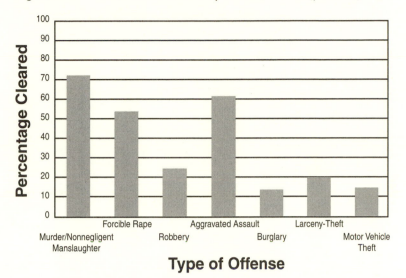

Source: Uniform Crime Reports, 1985.

Figure 4.22 Murder Weapons Used, 1963

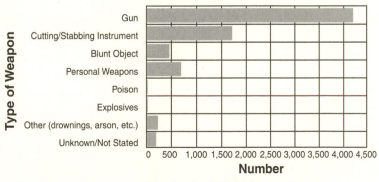

Note: Based on 7,549 murders.

Source: Uniform Crime Reports, 1963.

Figure 4.23 Murder Weapons Used, 1990 and 1993

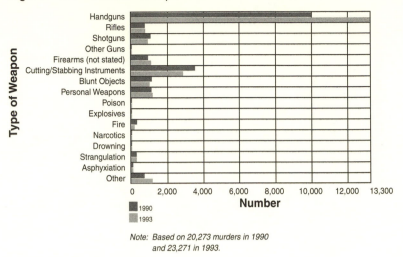

Note: Based on 20,273 murders in 1990
and 23,271 in 1993.

Source: Uniform Crime Reports, 1993.

Figure 4.24 Relationship of Murder Victim to Offender in the United States, 1993

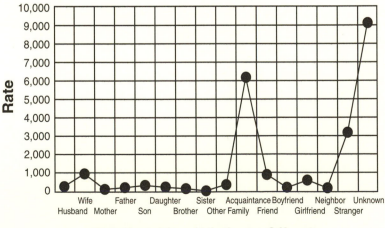

Note: Based on 23,271 murders.

Source: Uniform Crime Reports, 1993.

Documents

The Violent Crime Control and Law Enforcement Act of 1994 is the largest and most comprehensive crime bill to become law in U.S. history. President Bill Clinton signed it on September 13, 1994, making it Public Law 103-322. The act amended many of the crime provisions in the United States Code. Although many conservatives have complained that the bill does not go far enough in punishing criminals, as of June 1996 the Republican Congress had not tried to overturn it. Following is an abridged version of the crime bill, as well as a portion of Title I of the Brady Handgun Violence Prevention Act passed in early 1993.

Violent Crime Control and Law Enforcement Act of 1994 (excerpts*)

AN ACT
To control and prevent crime.

Section 1. Short Title.
This Act may be cited as the "Violent Crime Control and Law Enforcement Act of 1994".

TITLE I—Public Safety and Policing

Sec. 10001. Short Title.
This title may be cited as the "Public Safety Partnership and Community Policing Act of 1994".

Sec. 10002. Purposes.
The purposes of this title are to—
(1) substantially increase the number of law enforcement officers interacting directly with members of the community ("cops on the beat");
(2) provide additional and more effective training of law enforcement officers to enhance their problem solving, service, and other skills needed in interacting with members of the community;

---

*The following pages contain excerpts from the act, excerpted in order; omissions are *not* indicated in any way.

(3) encourage the development and implementation of innovative programs to permit members of the community to assist State, Indian tribal government, and local law enforcement agencies in the prevention of crime in the community; and

(4) encourage the development of new technologies to assist State, Indian tribal government, and local law enforcement agencies in reorienting the emphasis of their activities from reacting to crime to preventing crime, by establishing a program of grants and assistance in furtherance of these objectives, including the authorization for a period of 6 years of grants for the hiring and rehiring of additional career law enforcement officers.

Sec. 10003. Community Policing; "Cops on the Beat".

(a) In general.—Title I of the Omnibus Crime Control and Safe Streets Act of 1968 (42 U.S.C. 3711 et seq.) is amended—

(3) by inserting after part P the following new part:

"Part Q—Public Safety and Community Policing; 'Cops on the Beat'

"Sec. 1701. Authority To Make Public Safety and Community Policing Grants.

"(a) Grant Authorization.—The Attorney General may make grants to States, units of local government, Indian tribal governments, other public and private entities, and multi-jurisdictional or regional consortia thereof to increase police presence, to expand and improve cooperative efforts between law enforcement agencies and members of the community to address crime and disorder problems, and otherwise to enhance public safety.

TITLE II—Prisons
Subtitle A—Violent Offender Incarceration and Truth in Sentencing Incentive Grants

Sec. 20101. Grants for Correctional Facilities.

(a) Grant Authorization.—The Attorney General may make grants to individual States and to States organized as multi-State compacts to construct, develop, expand, modify, operate, or improve correctional facilities, including boot camp facilities and other alternative correctional facilities that can free conventional prison space for the confinement of violent offenders, to ensure that prison cell space is available for the confinement of violent offenders and to implement truth in sentencing laws for sentencing violent offenders.

Subtitle B—Punishment for Young Offenders

Sec. 20201. Certain Punishment for Young Offenders.

(a) In General.—Title I of the Omnibus Crime Control and Safe Streets Act of 1968 (42 U.S.C. 3711 et seq.), as amended by section 10003(a), is amended—

(3) by inserting after part Q the following new part:

"Part R—Certain Punishment for Young Offenders

"Sec. 1801. Grant Authorization.

"(a) In General.—The Attorney General may make grants under this part to States, for the use by States and units of local government, for the purpose of developing alternative methods of punishment for young offenders to traditional forms of incarceration and probation.

Subtitle D—Miscellaneous Provisions

Sec. 20405. Crediting of "GOOD TIME".

Section 3624 of title 18, United States Code, is amended—

(4) in subsection (b)—

(B) by inserting after the first sentence the following:

"A prisoner who is serving a term of imprisonment of more than 1 year for a crime of violence, other than a term of imprisonment for the duration of the prisoner's life, may receive credit toward the service of the prisoner's sentence, beyond the time served, of up to 54 days at the end of each year of the prisoner's term of imprisonment, beginning at the end of the first year of the term, subject to determination by the Bureau of Prisons that, during that year, the prisoner has displayed exemplary compliance with such institutional disciplinary regulations.".

Sec. 20412. Education Requirement for Early Release.

Section 3624(b) of title 18, United States Code, is amended—

(3) by adding at the end the following:

"(2) Credit toward a prisoner's service of sentence shall not be vested unless the prisoner has earned or is making satisfactory progress toward a high school diploma or an equivalent degree.

"(3) The Attorney General shall ensure that the Bureau of Prisons has in effect an optional General Educational Development program for inmates who have not earned a high school diploma or its equivalent.

"(4) Exemptions to the General Educational Development requirement may be made as deemed appropriate by the Director of the Federal Bureau of Prisons.".

Sec. 20413. Conversion of Closed Military Installations into Federal Prison Facilities.

(a) Study of Suitable Bases.—The Secretary of Defense and the Attorney General shall jointly conduct a study of all military installations selected before the date of enactment of this Act to be closed pursuant to a base closure law for the purpose of evaluating the suitability of any of these installations, or portions of these installations, for conversion into Federal prison facilities. As part of the study, the Secretary and the Attorney General shall identify the military installations so evaluated that are most suitable for conversion into Federal prison facilities.

Sec. 20418. Correctional Job Training and Placement.

(a) Purpose.—It is the purpose of this section to encourage and support job training programs, and job placement programs, that provide services to incarcerated persons or ex-offenders.

(c) Establishment of Office.—

(1) In general.—The Attorney General shall establish within the Department of Justice an Office of Correctional Job Training and Placement. The Office shall be headed by a Director, who shall be appointed by the Attorney General.

TITLE III—Crime Prevention
Subtitle A—Ounce of Prevention Council

Sec. 30101. Ounce of Prevention Council.

(a) Establishment.—

(1) In general.—There is established an Ounce of Prevention Council (referred to in this title as the "Council"), the members of which—

(A) shall include the Attorney General, the Secretary of Education, the Secretary of Health and Human Services, the Secretary of Housing and Urban Development, the Secretary of Labor, the Secretary of Agriculture, the Secretary of the Treasury, the Secretary of the Interior, and the Director of the Office of National Drug Control Policy; and

(B) may include other officials of the executive branch as directed by the President.

(c) Administrative Responsibilities and Powers.—In addition to the program coordination provided in subsection (b), the

Council shall be responsible for such functions as coordinated planning, development of a comprehensive crime prevention program catalogue, provision of assistance to communities and community-based organizations seeking information regarding crime prevention programs and integrated program service delivery, and development of strategies for program integration and grant simplification. The Council shall have the authority to audit the expenditure of funds received by grantees under programs administered by or coordinated through the Council. In consultation with the Council, the Chair may issue regulations and guidelines to carry out this subtitle and programs administered by or coordinated through the Council.

Sec. 30102. Ounce of Prevention Grant Program.
(a) In General.—The Council may make grants for—

(1) summer and after-school (including weekend and holiday) education and recreation programs;

(2) mentoring, tutoring, and other programs involving participation by adult role models (such as D.A.R.E. America);

(3) programs assisting and promoting employability and job placement; and

(4) prevention and treatment programs to reduce substance abuse, child abuse, and adolescent pregnancy, including outreach programs for at-risk families.

Subtitle B—Local Crime Prevention Block Grant Program

Sec. 30201. Payments To Local Governments.
(2) Use.—Amounts paid to a unit of general local government under this section shall be used by that unit for carrying out one or more of the following purposes:

(A) Education, training, research, prevention, diversion treatment, and rehabilitation programs to prevent juvenile violence, juvenile gangs, and the use and sale of illegal drugs by juveniles.

(B) Programs to prevent crimes against the elderly based on the concepts of the Triad model.

(C) Programs that prevent young children from becoming gang involved, including the award of grants or contracts to community-based service providers that have a proven track record of providing services to children ages 5 to 18.

(D) Saturation jobs programs, offered either separately or in conjunction with the services provided for under the Youth Fair Chance Program, that provide employment opportunities leading to permanent unsubsidized employment for disadvantaged young adults 16 through 25 years of age.

(E) Midnight sports league programs that shall require each player in the league to attend employment counseling, job training, and other educational classes provided under the program, which shall be held in conjunction with league sports games at or near the site of the games.

(F) Supervised sports and recreation programs, including Olympic Youth Development Centers established in cooperation with the United States Olympic Committee, that are offered—

(i) after school and on weekends and holidays, during the school year; and

(ii) as daily (or weeklong) full-day programs (to the extent available resources permit) or as part-day programs, during the summer months.

(G) Prevention and enforcement programs to reduce—

(i) the formation or continuation of juvenile gangs; and

(ii) the use and sale of illegal drugs by juveniles.

(H) Youth anticrime councils to give intermediate and secondary school students a structured forum through which to work with community organizations, law enforcement officials, government and media representatives, and school administrators and faculty to address issues regarding youth and violence.

(I) Award of grants or contracts to the Boys and Girls Clubs of America, a national nonprofit youth organization, to establish Boys and Girls Clubs in public housing.

(J) Supervised visitation centers for children who have been removed from their parents and placed outside the home as a result of abuse or neglect or other risk of harm to them and for children whose parents are separated or divorced and the children are at risk because—

(i) there is documented sexual, physical, or emotional abuse as determined by a court of competent jurisdiction;

(ii) there is suspected or elevated risk of sexual, physical, or emotional abuse, or there have been threats of parental abduction of the child;

(iii) due to domestic violence, there is an ongoing risk of harm to a parent or child;

(iv) a parent is impaired because of substance abuse or mental illness;

(v) there are allegations that a child is at risk for any of the reasons stated in clauses (i), (ii), (iii), and (iv), pending an investigation of the allegations; or

(vi) other circumstances, as determined by a court of competent jurisdiction, point to the existence of such a risk.

(K) Family Outreach Teams which provide a youth worker, a parent worker, and a school-parent organizer to provide training in outreach, mentoring, community organizing, and peer counseling and mentoring to locally recruited volunteers in a particular area.

(L) To establish corridors of safety for senior citizens by increasing the numbers, presence, and watchfulness of law enforcement officers, community groups, and business owners and employees.

(M) Teams or units involving both specially trained law enforcement professionals and child or family services professionals that on a 24-hour basis respond to or deal with violent incidents in which a child is involved as a perpetrator, witness, or victim.

(N) Dwelling units to law enforcement officers without charge or at a substantially reduced rent for the purpose of providing greater security for residents of high crime areas.

Subtitle C—Model Intensive Grant Programs

Sec. 30301. Grant Authorization.
(a) Establishment.—
(1) In general.—The Attorney General may award grants to not more than 15 chronic high intensive crime areas to develop comprehensive model crime prevention programs that—

(A) involve and utilize a broad spectrum of community resources, including nonprofit community organizations, law enforcement organizations, and appropriate State and Federal agencies, including the State educational agencies;

(B) attempt to relieve conditions that encourage crime; and

(C) provide meaningful and lasting alternatives to involvement in crime.

Subtitle D—Family and Community Endeavor Schools Grant Program

Sec. 30401. Community Schools Youth Services and Supervision Grant Program.
(d) Program Requirements.—

(1) Location.—A community-based organization that receives a grant under this section to assist in carrying out such a program shall ensure that the program is carried out—

(A) when appropriate, in the facilities of a public school during nonschool hours; or

(B) in another appropriate local facility in a State or Indian country, such as a college or university, a local or State park or recreation center, church, or military base, that is—

(i) in a location that is easily accessible to children in the community; and

(ii) in compliance with all applicable local ordinances.

(2) Use of funds.—Such community-based organization—

(A) shall use funds made available through the grant to provide, to children in the eligible community, services and activities that—

(i) shall include supervised sports programs, and extracurricular and academic programs, that are offered—

(I) after school and on weekends and holidays, during the school year; and

(II) as daily full-day programs (to the extent available resources permit) or as part-day programs, during the summer months;

(B) in providing such extracurricular and academic programs, shall provide programs such as curriculum-based supervised educational, workforce preparation, entrepreneurship, cultural, health programs, social activities, arts and crafts programs, dance programs, tutorial and mentoring programs, and other related activities;

(C) may use—

(i) such funds for minor renovation of facilities that are in existence prior to the operation of the program and that are necessary for the operation of the program for which the organization receives the grant, purchase of sporting and recreational equipment and supplies, reasonable costs for the transportation of participants in the program, hiring of staff, provision of meals for such participants, provision of health services consisting of an initial basic physical examination, provision of first aid and nutrition guidance, family counselling, parental training, and substance abuse treatment where appropriate; and

(D) may not use such funds to provide sectarian worship or sectarian instruction.

Sec. 30402. Family and Community Endeavor Schools Grant Program.

(a) Short Title.—This section may be cited as the "Family and Community Endeavor Schools Act".

(b) Purpose.—It is the purpose of this section to improve the overall development of at-risk children who reside in eligible communities as defined in subsection (l)(3).

(d) Program Requirements.—

(1) Improvement programs.—A local entity that receives funds under this section shall develop or expand programs that are designed to improve academic and social development by instituting a collaborative structure that trains and coordinates the efforts of teachers, administrators, social workers, guidance counselors, parents, and school volunteers to provide concurrent social services for at-risk students at selected public schools in eligible communities.

(2) Optional activities.—A local entity that receives funds under this section may develop a variety of programs to serve the comprehensive needs of students, including—

(A) homework assistance and after-school programs, including educational, social, and athletic activities;

(B) nutrition services;

(C) mentoring programs;

(D) family counseling; and

(E) parental training programs.

Subtitle G—Assistance for Delinquent and At-Risk Youth

Sec. 30701. Grant Authority.

(a) Grants.—

(1) In general.—In order to prevent the commission of crimes or delinquent acts by juveniles, the Attorney General may make grants to public or private nonprofit organizations to support the development and operation of projects to provide residential services to youth, aged 11 to 19, who—

(A) have dropped out of school;

(B) have come into contact with the juvenile justice system; or

(C) are at risk of dropping out of school or coming into contact with the juvenile justice system.

(3) Services.—Such services shall include activities designed to—

(A) increase the self-esteem of such youth;

(B) assist such youth in making healthy and responsible choices;

(C) improve the academic performance of such youth pursuant to a plan jointly developed by the applicant and the school which each such youth attends or should attend; and

(D) provide such youth with vocational and life skills.

Subtitle H—Police Recruitment

Sec. 30801. Grant Authority.

(a) Grants.—

(1) In general.—The Attorney General may make grants to qualified community organizations to assist in meeting the costs of qualified programs which are designed to recruit and retain applicants to police departments.

Subtitle K—National Community Economic Partnership

Sec. 31101. Short Title.

This subtitle may be cited as the "National Community Economic Partnership Act of 1994".

Chapter 1—Community Economic Partnership Investment Funds

Sec. 31111. Purpose.

It is the purpose of this chapter to increase private investment in distressed local communities and to build and expand the capacity of local institutions to better serve the economic needs of local residents through the provision of financial and technical assistance to community development corporations.

Sec. 31112. Provision of Assistance.

(a) Authority.—The Secretary of Health and Human Services (referred to in this subtitle as the "Secretary") may, in accordance with this chapter, provide nonrefundable lines of credit to community development corporations for the establishment, maintenance, or expansion of revolving loan funds to be utilized to finance projects intended to provide business and employment opportunities for low-income, unemployed, or underemployed individuals and to improve the quality of life in urban and rural areas.

Chapter 2—Emerging Community Development Corporations

Sec. 31121. Community Development Corporation Improvement Grants.

(a) Purpose.—It is the purpose of this section to provide assistance to community development corporations to upgrade the management and operating capacity of such corporations and to enhance the resources available to enable such corporations to increase their community economic development activities.

(b) Skill Enhancement Grants.—

(1) In general.—The Secretary shall award grants to community development corporations to enable such corporations to attain or enhance the business management and development skills of the individuals that manage such corporations to enable such corporations to seek the public and private resources necessary to develop community economic development projects.

(c) Operating Grants.—

(1) In general.—The Secretary shall award grants to community development corporations to enable such corporations to support an administrative capacity for the planning, development, and management of low-income community economic development projects.

Sec. 31122. Emerging Community Development Corporation Revolving Loan Funds.

(a) Authority.—The Secretary may award grants to emerging community development corporations to enable such corporations to establish, maintain, or expand revolving loan funds, to make or guarantee loans, or to make capital investments in new or expanding local businesses.

Subtitle O—Urban Recreation and At-Risk Youth

Sec. 31501. Purpose of Assistance.

Section 1003 of the Urban Park and Recreation Recovery Act of 1978 is amended by adding the following at the end: "It is further the purpose of this title to improve recreation facilities and expand recreation services in urban areas with a high incidence of crime and to help deter crime through the expansion of recreation opportunities for at-risk youth. It is the further purpose of this section to increase the security of urban parks and to promote collaboration between local agencies involved in parks and recreation, law enforcement, youth social services, and [the] juvenile justice system.".

Subtitle Q—Community-Based Justice Grants for Prosecutors

Sec. 31701. Grant Authorization.
(a) In General.—The Attorney General may make grants to State, Indian tribal, or local prosecutors for the purpose of supporting the creation or expansion of community-based justice programs.

Subtitle S—Family Unity Demonstration Project

Sec. 31901. Short Title.
This subtitle may be cited as the "Family Unity Demonstration Project Act".

Sec. 31902. Purpose.
The purpose of this subtitle is to evaluate the effectiveness of certain demonstration projects in helping to—

(1) alleviate the harm to children and primary caretaker parents caused by separation due to the incarceration of the parents;

(2) reduce recidivism rates of prisoners by encouraging strong and supportive family relationships; and

(3) explore the cost effectiveness of community correctional facilities.

Chapter 1—Grants To States

Sec. 31911. Authority To Make Grants.
(a) General Authority.—The Attorney General may make grants, on a competitive basis, to States to carry out in accordance with this subtitle family unity demonstration projects that enable eligible offenders to live in community correctional facilities with their children.

Chapter 2—Family Unity Demonstration Project for Federal Prisoners

Sec. 31921. Authority of the Attorney General.
(a) In General.—With the funds available to carry out this subtitle for the benefit of Federal prisoners, the Attorney General, acting through the Director of the Bureau of Prisons, shall select eligible prisoners to live in community correctional facilities with their children.

Subtitle T—Substance Abuse Treatment in Federal Prisons

Sec. 32001. Substance Abuse Treatment in Federal Prisons.
Section 3621 of title 18, United States Code, is amended—
(2) by adding at the end the following new subsection:
"(e) Substance Abuse Treatment.—
"(1) Phase-in.—In order to carry out the requirement of the last sentence of subsection (b) of this section, that every prisoner with a substance abuse problem have the opportunity to participate in appropriate substance abuse treatment, the Bureau of Prisons shall, subject to the availability of appropriations, provide residential substance abuse treatment (and make arrangements for appropriate aftercare)—
"(A) for not less than 50 percent of eligible prisoners by the end of fiscal year 1995, with priority for such treatment accorded based on an eligible prisoner's proximity to release date;
"(B) for not less than 75 percent of eligible prisoners by the end of fiscal year 1996, with priority for such treatment accorded based on an eligible prisoner's proximity to release date; and
"(C) for all eligible prisoners by the end of fiscal year 1997 and thereafter, with priority for such treatment accorded based on an eligible prisoner's proximity to release date.
"(2) Incentive for prisoners' successful completion of treatment program.—
"(A) Generally.—Any prisoner who, in the judgment of the Director of the Bureau of Prisons, has successfully completed a program of residential substance abuse treatment provided under paragraph (1) of this subsection, shall remain in the custody of the Bureau under such conditions as the Bureau deems appropriate. If the conditions of confinement are different from those the prisoner would have experienced absent the successful completion of the treatment, the Bureau shall periodically test the prisoner for substance abuse and discontinue such conditions on determining that substance abuse has recurred.

Subtitle U—Residential Substance Abuse Treatment for State Prisoners

Sec. 32101. Residential Substance Abuse Treatment for State Prisoners.
(a) Residential Substance Abuse Treatment for Prisoners.—
Title I of the Omnibus Crime Control and Safe Streets Act of

1968 (42 U.S.C. 3711 et seq.), as amended by section 20201(a), is amended—

(3) by inserting after part R the following new part:

"Part S—Residential Substance Abuse Treatment for State Prisoners

"Sec. 1901. Grant Authorization.

"(a) The Attorney General may make grants under this part to States, for use by States and units of local government for the purpose of developing and implementing residential substance abuse treatment programs within State correctional facilities, as well as within local correctional and detention facilities in which inmates are incarcerated for a period of time sufficient to permit substance abuse treatment.

Subtitle X—Gang Resistance Education and Training

Sec. 32401. Gang Resistance Education and Training Projects.

(a) Establishment of Projects.—

(1) In general.—The Secretary of the Treasury shall establish not less than 50 Gang Resistance Education and Training (GREAT) projects, to be located in communities across the country, in addition to the number of projects currently funded.

TITLE IV—Violence Against Women

Sec. 40001. Short Title.

This title may be cited as the "Violence Against Women Act of 1994".

Subtitle A—Safe Streets for Women

Sec. 40101. Short Title.

This subtitle may be cited as the "Safe Streets for Women Act of 1994".

Chapter 1—Federal Penalties for Sex Crimes

Sec. 40111. Repeat Offenders.

(a) In General.—Chapter 109A of title 18, United States Code, is amended by adding at the end the following new section:

"**Sec. 2247. Repeat offenders.**

"Any person who violates a provision of this chapter, after one or more prior convictions for an offense punishable under this chapter, or after one or more prior convictions under the laws of any State relating to aggravated sexual abuse, sexual abuse, or abusive sexual contact have become final, is punishable by a term of imprisonment up to twice that otherwise authorized.".

(b) Amendment of Sentencing Guidelines.—The Sentencing Commission shall implement the amendment made by subsection (a) by promulgating amendments, if appropriate, in the sentencing guidelines applicable to chapter 109A offenses.

Sec. 40112. Federal Penalties.

(a) Amendment of Sentencing Guidelines.—Pursuant to its authority under section 994(p) of title 28, United States Code, the United States Sentencing Commission shall review and amend, where necessary, its sentencing guidelines on aggravated sexual abuse under section 2241 of title 18, United States Code, or sexual abuse under section 2242 of title 18, United States Code, as follows:

(1) The Commission shall review and promulgate amendments to the guidelines, if appropriate, to enhance penalties if more than 1 offender is involved in the offense.

(2) The Commission shall review and promulgate amendments to the guidelines, if appropriate, to reduce unwarranted disparities between the sentences for sex offenders who are known to the victim and sentences for sex offenders who are not known to the victim.

(3) The Commission shall review and promulgate amendments to the guidelines to enhance penalties, if appropriate, to render Federal penalties on Federal territory commensurate with penalties for similar offenses in the States.

(4) The Commission shall review and promulgate amendments to the guidelines, if appropriate, to account for the general problem of recidivism in cases of sex offenses, the severity of the offense, and its devastating effects on survivors.

Sec. 40113. Mandatory Restitution for Sex Crimes.

(a) Sexual Abuse.—

(1) In general.—Chapter 109A of title 18, United States Code, is amended by adding at the end the following new section:

"Sec. 2248. Mandatory restitution

"(a) In General.—Notwithstanding section 3663, and in addition to any other civil or criminal penalty authorized by law, the court shall order restitution for any offense under this chapter.

"(b) Scope and Nature of Order.—

"(1) Directions.—The order of restitution under this section shall direct that—

"(A) the defendant pay to the victim (through the appropriate court mechanism) the full amount of the victim's losses as determined by the court, pursuant to paragraph (3); and

"(B) the United States Attorney enforce the restitution order by all available and reasonable means.

"(2) Enforcement by victim.—An order of restitution also may be enforced by a victim named in the order to receive the restitution in the same manner as a judgment in a civil action.

(b) Sexual Exploitation and Other Abuse of Children.—

(1) In general.—Chapter 110 of title 18, United States Code, is amended by adding at the end the following new section:

"Sec. 2259. Mandatory restitution

"(a) In General.—Notwithstanding section 3663, and in addition to any other civil or criminal penalty authorized by law, the court shall order restitution for any offense under this chapter.

"(b) Scope and Nature of Order.—

"(1) Directions.—The order of restitution under this section shall direct that—

"(A) the defendant pay to the victim (through the appropriate court mechanism) the full amount of the victim's losses as determined by the court, pursuant to paragraph (3); and

"(B) the United States Attorney enforce the restitution order by all available and reasonable means.

"(2) Enforcement by victim.—An order of restitution may also be enforced by a victim named in the order to receive the restitution in the same manner as a judgment in a civil action.

Chapter 2—Law Enforcement and Prosecution Grants To Reduce Violent Crimes Against Women

Sec. 40121. Grants To Combat Violent Crimes against Women.

(a) In General.—Title I of the Omnibus Crime Control and Safe Streets Act of 1968 (42 U.S.C. 3711 et seq.), as amended by section 32101(a), is amended—

(3) by inserting after part S the following new part:

"Part T—Grants To Combat Violent Crimes against Women

"Sec. 2001. Purpose of the Program and Grants.
"(a) General Program Purpose.—The purpose of this part is to assist States, Indian tribal governments, and units of local government to develop and strengthen effective law enforcement and prosecution strategies to combat violent crimes against women, and to develop and strengthen victim services in cases involving violent crimes against women.

Chapter 5—Assistance To Victims of Sexual Assault

Sec. 40151. Education and Prevention Grants To Reduce Sexual Assaults against Women.
Part A of title XIX of the Public Health and Human Services Act (42 U.S.C. 300w et seq.) is amended by adding at the end the following new section:

"Sec. 1910A. Use of Allotments for Rape Prevention Education.
"(a) Permitted Use.—Notwithstanding section 1904(a)(1), amounts transferred by the State for use under this part may be used for rape prevention and education programs conducted by rape crisis centers or similar nongovernmental nonprofit entities for—
"(1) educational seminars;
"(2) the operation of hotlines;
"(3) training programs for professionals;
"(4) the preparation of informational materials; and
"(5) other efforts to increase awareness of the facts about, or to help prevent, sexual assault, including efforts to increase awareness in underserved racial, ethnic, and language minority communities.
"(b) Targeting of Education Programs.—States providing grant monies must ensure that at least 25 percent of the monies are devoted to education programs targeted for middle school, junior high school, and high school students.

Sec. 40155. Education and Prevention Grants To Reduce Sexual Abuse of Runaway, Homeless, and Street Youth.
Part A of the Runaway and Homeless Youth Act (42 U.S.C. 5711 et seq.) is amended—

(2) by inserting after section 315 the following new section:
"Grants for Prevention of Sexual Abuse and Exploitation

"Sec. 316. (a) In General.—The Secretary shall make grants under this section to private, nonprofit agencies for street-based outreach and education, including treatment, counseling, provision of information, and referral for runaway, homeless, and street youth who have been subjected to or are at risk of being subjected to sexual abuse.

Subtitle B—Safe Homes for Women

Sec. 40201. Short Title.
This title may be cited as the "Safe Homes for Women Act of 1994".

Chapter 1—National Domestic Violence Hotline

Sec. 40211. Grant for a National Domestic Violence Hotline.
The Family Violence Prevention and Services Act (42 U.S.C. 10401 et seq.) is amended by adding at the end the following new section:

"Sec. 316. National Domestic Violence Hotline Grant.
"(a) In General.—The Secretary may award a grant to a private, nonprofit entity to provide for the operation of a national, toll-free telephone hotline to provide information and assistance to victims of domestic violence.

"Part U—Grants To Encourage Arrest Policies

"Sec. 2101. Grants.
"(a) Purpose.—The purpose of this part is to encourage States, Indian tribal governments, and units of local government to treat domestic violence as a serious violation of criminal law.
"(b) Grant Authority.—The Attorney General may make grants to eligible States, Indian tribal governments, or units of local government for the following purposes:
"(1) To implement mandatory arrest or proarrest programs and policies in police departments, including mandatory arrest programs and policies for protection order violations.

"(2) To develop policies and training in police departments to improve tracking of cases involving domestic violence.

"(3) To centralize and coordinate police enforcement, prosecution, or judicial responsibility for domestic violence cases in groups or units of police officers, prosecutors, or judges.

"(4) To coordinate computer tracking systems to ensure communication between police, prosecutors, and both criminal and family courts.

"(5) To strengthen legal advocacy service programs for victims of domestic violence.

"(6) To educate judges in criminal and other courts about domestic violence and to improve judicial handling of such cases.

Chapter 6—Community Programs on Domestic Violence

Sec. 40261. Establishment of Community Programs on Domestic Violence.

The Family Violence Prevention and Services Act (42 U.S.C. 10401 et seq.), as amended by section 40251, is amended by adding at the end the following new section:

"Sec. 318. Demonstration Grants for Community Initiatives.

"(a) In General.—The Secretary shall provide grants to nonprofit private organizations to establish projects in local communities involving many sectors of each community to coordinate intervention and prevention of domestic violence.

Chapter 9—Data and Research

Sec. 40291. Research Agenda.

(a) Request for Contract.—The Attorney General shall request the National Academy of Sciences, through its National Research Council, to enter into a contract to develop a research agenda to increase the understanding and control of violence against women, including rape and domestic violence. In furtherance of the contract, the National Academy shall convene a panel of nationally recognized experts on violence against women, in the fields of law, medicine, criminal justice, and direct services to victims and experts on domestic violence in diverse, ethnic, social, and language minority communities and the social sciences. In setting the agenda, the Academy shall focus primarily on preventive, educative, social, and legal strategies, including addressing the needs of underserved populations.

Sec. 40292. State Databases.

(a) In General.—The Attorney General shall study and report to the States and to Congress on how the States may collect centralized databases on the incidence of sexual and domestic violence offenses within a State.

Chapter 10—Rural Domestic Violence and Child Abuse Enforcement

Sec. 40295. Rural Domestic Violence and Child Abuse Enforcement Assistance.

(a) Grants.—The Attorney General may make grants to States, Indian tribal governments, and local governments of rural States, and to other public or private entities of rural States—

(1) to implement, expand, and establish cooperative efforts and projects between law enforcement officers, prosecutors, victim advocacy groups, and other related parties to investigate and prosecute incidents of domestic violence and child abuse;

(2) to provide treatment and counseling to victims of domestic violence and child abuse; and

(3) to work in cooperation with the community to develop education and prevention strategies directed toward such issues.

Subtitle C—Civil Rights for Women

Sec. 40301. Short Title.

This subtitle may be cited as the "Civil Rights Remedies for Gender-Motivated Violence Act".

Sec. 40302. Civil Rights.

(a) Purpose.—Pursuant to the affirmative power of Congress to enact this subtitle under section 5 of the Fourteenth Amendment to the Constitution, as well as under section 8 of Article I of the Constitution, it is the purpose of this subtitle to protect the civil rights of victims of gender motivated violence and to promote public safety, health, and activities affecting interstate commerce by establishing a Federal civil rights cause of action for victims of crimes of violence motivated by gender.

Subtitle D—Equal Justice for Women in the Courts Act

Sec. 40401. Short Title.
This subtitle may be cited as the "Equal Justice for Women in the Courts Act of 1994".

Chapter 1—Education and Training for Judges and Court Personnel in State Courts

Sec. 40411. Grants Authorized.
The State Justice Institute may award grants for the purpose of developing, testing, presenting, and disseminating model programs to be used by States (as defined in section 202 of the State Justice Institute Act of 1984 (42 U.S.C. 10701)) in training judges and court personnel in the laws of the States and by Indian tribes in training tribal judges and court personnel in the laws of the tribes on rape, sexual assault, domestic violence, and other crimes of violence motivated by the victim's gender.

Chapter 2—Education and Training for Judges and Court Personnel in Federal Courts

Sec. 40421. Authorizations of Circuit Studies; Education and Training Grants.
(a) Studies.—In order to gain a better understanding of the nature and the extent of gender bias in the Federal courts, the circuit judicial councils are encouraged to conduct studies of the instances, if any, of gender bias in their respective circuits and to implement recommended reforms.

Subtitle E—Violence against Women Act Improvements

Sec. 40503. Payment of Cost of Testing for Sexually Transmitted Diseases.
(a) For Victims in Sex Offense Cases.—Section 503(c)(7) of the Victims' Rights and Restitution Act of 1990 (42 U.S.C. 10607(c)(7)) is amended by adding at the end the following: "The Attorney General shall provide for the payment of the cost of up to 2 anonymous and confidential tests of the victim for sexually transmitted diseases, including HIV, gonorrhea, herpes, chlamydia, and syphilis, during the 12 months following sexual assaults that pose a risk of transmission, and the cost of a counseling

session by a medically trained professional on the accuracy of such tests and the risk of transmission of sexually transmitted diseases to the victim as the result of the assault. A victim may waive anonymity and confidentiality of any tests paid for under this section.".

Sec. 40504. Extension and Strengthening of Restitution.
Section 3663(b) of title 18, United States Code, is amended—
(4) by inserting after paragraph (3) the following new paragraph:
"(4) in any case, reimburse the victim for lost income and necessary child care, transportation, and other expenses related to participation in the investigation or prosecution of the offense or attendance at proceedings related to the offense; and".

Sec. 40505. Enforcement of Restitution Orders through Suspension of Federal Benefits.
Section 3663 of title 18, United States Code, is amended by adding at the end the following new subsection:
"(i)(1) A Federal agency shall immediately suspend all Federal benefits provided by the agency to the defendant, and shall terminate the defendant's eligibility for Federal benefits administered by that agency, upon receipt of a certified copy of a written judicial finding that the defendant is delinquent in making restitution in accordance with any schedule of payments or any requirement of immediate payment imposed under this section.

Sec. 40506. National Baseline Study on Campus Sexual Assault.
(a) Study.—The Attorney General, in consultation with the Secretary of Education, shall provide for a national baseline study to examine the scope of the problem of campus sexual assaults and the effectiveness of institutional and legal policies in addressing such crimes and protecting victims. The Attorney General may utilize the Bureau of Justice Statistics, the National Institute of Justice, and the Office for Victims of Crime in carrying out this section.

Subtitle F—National Stalker and Domestic Violence Reduction

Sec. 40601. Authorizing Access To Federal Criminal Information Databases.
(a) Access and Entry.—Section 534 of title 28, United States Code, is amended by adding at the end the following:

"(e)(1) Information from national crime information databases consisting of identification records, criminal history records, protection orders, and wanted person records may be disseminated to civil or criminal courts for use in domestic violence or stalking cases. Nothing in this subsection shall be construed to permit access to such records for any other purpose.

"(2) Federal and State criminal justice agencies authorized to enter information into criminal information databases may include—

"(A) arrests, convictions, and arrest warrants for stalking or domestic violence or for violations of protection orders for the protection of parties from stalking or domestic violence; and

"(B) protection orders for the protection of persons from stalking or domestic violence, provided such orders are subject to periodic verification.

Sec. 40602. Grant Program.

(a) In General.—The Attorney General is authorized to provide grants to States and units of local government to improve processes for entering data regarding stalking and domestic violence into local, State, and national crime information databases.

Sec. 40609. Inclusion in National Incident-Based Reporting System.

Not later than 2 years after the date of enactment of this Act, the Attorney General, in accordance with the States, shall compile data regarding domestic violence and intimidation (including stalking) as part of the National Incident-Based Reporting System (NIBRS).

TITLE V—Drug Courts

Sec. 50001. Drug Courts.

(a) In General.—Title I of the Omnibus Crime Control and Safe Streets Act of 1968 (42 U.S.C. 3711 et seq.), as amended by section 40231(a), is amended—

(3) by inserting after part U the following new part:

"Part V—Drug Courts

"Sec. 2201. Grant Authority.

"The Attorney General may make grants to States, State courts, local courts, units of local government, and Indian tribal governments, acting directly or through agreements with other public or private entities, for programs that involve—

"(1) continuing judicial supervision over offenders with substance abuse problems who are not violent offenders; and

"(2) the integrated administration of other sanctions and services, which shall include—

"(A) mandatory periodic testing for the use of controlled substances or other addictive substances during any period of supervised release or probation for each participant;

"(B) substance abuse treatment for each participant;

"(C) diversion, probation, or other supervised release involving the possibility of prosecution, confinement, or incarceration based on noncompliance with program requirements or failure to show satisfactory progress; and

"(D) programmatic, offender management, and aftercare services such as relapse prevention, health care, education, vocational training, job placement, housing placement, and child care or other family support services for each participant who requires such services.

TITLE VI—Death Penalty

Sec. 60001. Short Title.

This title may be cited as the "Federal Death Penalty Act of 1994".

Sec. 60002. Constitutional Procedures for the Imposition of the Sentence of Death.

(a) In General.—Part II of title 18, United States Code, is amended by inserting after chapter 227 the following new chapter:

"Chapter 228—Death Sentence

"Sec. 3591. Sentence of death

"(a) A defendant who has been found guilty of—

"(1) an offense described in section 794 or section 2381; or

"(2) any other offense for which a sentence of death is provided, if the defendant, as determined beyond a reasonable doubt at the hearing under section 3593—

"(A) intentionally killed the victim;

"(B) intentionally inflicted serious bodily injury that resulted in the death of the victim;

"(C) intentionally participated in an act, contemplating that the life of a person would be taken or intending that lethal force would be used in connection with a person, other than one of the participants in the offense, and the victim died as a direct result of the act; or

"(D) intentionally and specifically engaged in an act of violence, knowing that the act created a grave risk of death to a person, other than one of the participants in the offense, such that participation in the act constituted a reckless disregard for human life and the victim died as a direct result of the act, shall be sentenced to death if, after consideration of the factors set forth in section 3592 in the course of a hearing held pursuant to section 3593, it is determined that imposition of a sentence of death is justified, except that no person may be sentenced to death who was less than 18 years of age at the time of the offense.

"(b) A defendant who has been found guilty of—

"(1) an offense referred to in section 408(c)(1) of the Controlled Substances Act (21 U.S.C. 848(c)(1)), committed as part of a continuing criminal enterprise offense under the conditions described in subsection (b) of that section which involved not less than twice the quantity of controlled substance described in subsection (b)(2)(A) or twice the gross receipts described in subsection (b)(2)(B); or

"(2) an offense referred to in section 408(c)(1) of the Controlled Substances Act (21 U.S.C. 848(c)(1)), committed as part of a continuing criminal enterprise offense under that section, where the defendant is a principal administrator, organizer, or leader of such an enterprise, and the defendant, in order to obstruct the investigation or prosecution of the enterprise or an offense involved in the enterprise, attempts to kill or knowingly directs, advises, authorizes, or assists another to attempt to kill any public officer, juror, witness, or members of the family or household of such a person, shall be sentenced to death if, after consideration of the factors set forth in section 3592 in the course of a hearing held pursuant to section 3593, it is determined that imposition of a sentence of death is justified, except that no person may be sentenced to death who was less than 18 years of age at the time of the offense.

"Sec. 3592. Mitigating and aggravating factors to be considered in determining whether a sentence of death is justified

"(a) Mitigating Factors

"(1) Impaired capacity.

"(2) Duress.

"(3) Minor participation.

"(4) Equally culpable defendants.

"(5) No prior criminal record.

"(6) Disturbance.

"(7) Victim's consent.

"(8) Other factors.

"(b) Aggravating Factors for Espionage and Treason.—In determining whether a sentence of death is justified for an offense described in section 3591(a)(1), the jury, or if there is no jury, the court, shall consider each of the following aggravating factors for which notice has been given and determine which, if any, exist:

"(1) Prior espionage or treason offense.

"(2) Grave risk to national security.

"(3) Grave risk of death.

"(c) Aggravating Factors for Homicide.—In determining whether a sentence of death is justified for an offense described in section 3591(a)(2), the jury, or if there is no jury, the court, shall consider each of the following aggravating factors for which notice has been given and determine which, if any, exist:

"(1) Death during commission of another crime.

"(2) Previous conviction of violent felony involving firearm.

"(3) Previous conviction of offense for which a sentence of death or life imprisonment was authorized.

"(4) Previous conviction of other serious offenses.

"(5) Grave risk of death to additional persons.

"(6) Heinous, cruel, or depraved manner of committing offense.

"(7) Procurement of offense by payment.

"(8) Pecuniary gain.

"(9) Substantial planning and premeditation.

"(10) Conviction for two felony drug offenses.

"(11) Vulnerability of victim.

"(12) Conviction for serious federal drug offenses.

"(13) Continuing criminal enterprise involving drug sales to minors.

"(14) High public officials.

"(15) Prior conviction of sexual assault or child molestation.

"(d) Aggravating Factors for Drug Offense Death Penalty.— In determining whether a sentence of death is justified for an offense described in section 3591(b), the jury, or if there is no jury, the court, shall consider each of the following aggravating factors for which notice has been given and determine which, if any, exist:

"(1) Previous conviction of offense for which a sentence of death or life imprisonment was authorized.

"(2) Previous conviction of other serious offenses.

"(3) Previous serious drug felony conviction.

"(4) Use of firearm.

"(5) Distribution to persons under 21.

"(6) Distribution near schools.

"(7) Using minors in trafficking.

"(8) Lethal adulterant.

"Sec. 3595. Review of a sentence of death

"(a) Appeal.—In a case in which a sentence of death is imposed, the sentence shall be subject to review by the court of appeals upon appeal by the defendant. Notice of appeal must be filed within the time specified for the filing of a notice of appeal. An appeal under this section may be consolidated with an appeal of the judgment of conviction and shall have priority over all other cases.

Sec. 60011. Death Penalty for Sexual Exploitation of Children.

Section 2251(d) of title 18, United States Code, is amended by adding at the end the following: "Whoever, in the course of an offense under this section, engages in conduct that results in the death of a person, shall be punished by death or imprisoned for any term of years or for life.".

TITLE VII—Mandatory Life Imprisonment for Persons Convicted of Certain Felonies

Sec. 70001. Mandatory Life Imprisonment for Persons Convicted of Certain Felonies.

Section 3559 of title 18, United States Code, is amended—

(2) by adding the following new subsection at the end:

"(c) Imprisonment of Certain Violent Felons.—

"(1) Mandatory life imprisonment.—Notwithstanding any other provision of law, a person who is convicted in a court of the United States of a serious violent felony shall be sentenced to life imprisonment if—

"(A) the person has been convicted (and those convictions have become final) on separate prior occasions in a court of the United States or of a State of—

"(i) 2 or more serious violent felonies; or

"(ii) one or more serious violent felonies and one or more serious drug offenses; and

"(B) each serious violent felony or serious drug offense used as a basis for sentencing under this subsection, other than the first, was committed after the defendant's conviction of the preceding serious violent felony or serious drug offense.

TITLE VIII—Applicability of Mandatory Minimum Penalties in Certain Cases

Sec. 80001. Limitation on Applicability of Mandatory Minimum Penalties in Certain Cases.

(a) In General.—Section 3553 of title 18, United States Code, is amended by adding at the end the following new subsection:

"(f) Limitation on Applicability of Statutory Minimums in Certain Cases.—Notwithstanding any other provision of law, in the case of an offense under section 401, 404, or 406 of the Controlled Substances Act (21 U.S.C. 841, 844, 846) or section 1010 or 1013 of the Controlled Substances Import and Export Act (21 U.S.C. 961, 963), the court shall impose a sentence pursuant to guidelines promulgated by the United States Sentencing Commission under section 994 of title 28 without regard to any statutory minimum sentence, if the court finds at sentencing, after the Government has been afforded the opportunity to make a recommendation, that—

"(1) the defendant does not have more than 1 criminal history point, as determined under the sentencing guidelines;

"(2) the defendant did not use violence or credible threats of violence or possess a firearm or other dangerous weapon (or induce another participant to do so) in connection with the offense;

"(3) the offense did not result in death or serious bodily injury to any person;

"(4) the defendant was not an organizer, leader, manager, or supervisor of others in the offense, as determined under the sentencing guidelines and was not engaged in a continuing criminal enterprise, as defined in 21 U.S.C. 848; and

"(5) not later than the time of the sentencing hearing, the defendant has truthfully provided to the Government all information and evidence the defendant has concerning the offense or offenses that were part of the same course of conduct or of a common scheme or plan, but the fact that the defendant has no relevant or useful other information to provide or that the Government is already aware of the information shall not preclude a determination by the court that the defendant has complied with this requirement.

TITLE IX—Drug Control

Sec. 90102. Increased Penalties for Drug-Dealing in "Drug-Free" Zones.
Pursuant to its authority under section 994 of title 28, United States Code, the United States Sentencing Commission shall amend its sentencing guidelines to provide an appropriate enhancement for a defendant convicted of violating section 419 of the Controlled Substances Act (21 U.S.C. 860).

Sec. 90103. Enhanced Penalties for Illegal Drug Use in Federal Prisons and for Smuggling Drugs into Federal Prisons.
(a) Declaration of Policy.—It is the policy of the Federal Government that the use or distribution of illegal drugs in the Nation's Federal prisons will not be tolerated and that such crimes shall be prosecuted to the fullest extent of the law.

Sec. 90107. Violent Crime and Drug Emergency Areas.
(b) Declaration of Violent Crime and Drug Emergency Areas.—If a major violent crime or drug-related emergency exists throughout a State or a part of a State, the President may declare the State or part of a State to be a violent crime or drug emergency area and may take appropriate actions authorized by this section.

(c) Procedure.—

(1) In general.—A request for a declaration designating an area to be a violent crime or drug emergency area shall be made, in writing, by the chief executive officer of a State or local government, respectively (or in the case of the District of Columbia, the mayor), and shall be forwarded to the Attorney General in such form as the Attorney General may by regulation require. One or more cities, counties, States, or the District of Columbia may submit a joint request for designation as a major violent crime or drug emergency area under this subsection.

TITLE X—Drunk Driving Provisions

Sec. 100001. Short Title.
This title may be cited as the "Drunk Driving Child Protection Act of 1994".

Sec. 100002. State Laws Applied in Areas of Federal Jurisdiction.
Section 13(b) of title 18, United States Code, is amended—
(2) by adding at the end the following new paragraph:
"(2)(A) In addition to any term of imprisonment provided for operating a motor vehicle under the influence of a drug or alcohol imposed under the law of a State, territory, possession, or district, the punishment for such an offense under this section shall include an additional term of imprisonment of not more than 1 year, or if serious bodily injury of a minor is caused, not more than 5 years, or if death of a minor is caused, not more than 10 years, and an additional fine of not more than $1,000, or both, if—
"(i) a minor (other than the offender) was present in the motor vehicle when the offense was committed; and
"(ii) the law of the State, territory, possession, or district in which the offense occurred does not provide an additional term of imprisonment under the circumstances described in clause (i).

TITLE XI—Firearms
Subtitle A—Assault Weapons

Sec. 110101. Short Title.
This subtitle may be cited as the "Public Safety and Recreational Firearms Use Protection Act".

Sec. 110102. Restriction on Manufacture, Transfer, and Possession of Certain Semiautomatic Assault Weapons.
(a) Restriction.—Section 922 of title 18, United States Code, is amended by adding at the end the following new subsection:
(v)(1) It shall be unlawful for a person to manufacture, transfer, or possess a semiautomatic assault weapon.
(2) Paragraph (1) shall not apply to the possession or transfer of any semiautomatic assault weapon otherwise lawfully possessed under Federal law on the date of the enactment of this subsection.
(3) Paragraph (1) shall not apply to—
"(A) any of the firearms, or replicas or duplicates of the firearms, specified in Appendix A to this section, as such firearms were manufactured on October 1, 1993;
"(B) any firearm that—
"(i) is manually operated by bolt, pump, lever, or slide action;
"(ii) has been rendered permanently inoperable; or

"(iii) is an antique firearm;

"(C) any semiautomatic rifle that cannot accept a detachable magazine that holds more than 5 rounds of ammunition; or

"(D) any semiautomatic shotgun that cannot hold more than 5 rounds of ammunition in a fixed or detachable magazine.

The fact that a firearm is not listed in Appendix A shall not be construed to mean that paragraph (1) applies to such firearm. No firearm exempted by this subsection may be deleted from Appendix A so long as this subsection is in effect.

"(4) Paragraph (1) shall not apply to—

"(A) the manufacture for, transfer to, or possession by the United States or a department or agency of the United States or a State or a department, agency, or political subdivision of a State, or a transfer to or possession by a law enforcement officer employed by such an entity for purposes of law enforcement (whether on or off duty);

"(B) the transfer to a licensee under title I of the Atomic Energy Act of 1954 for purposes of establishing and maintaining an on-site physical protection system and security organization required by Federal law, or possession by an employee or contractor of such licensee on-site for such purposes or off-site for purposes of licensee-authorized training or transportation of nuclear materials;

"(C) the possession, by an individual who is retired from service with a law enforcement agency and is not otherwise prohibited from receiving a firearm, of a semiautomatic assault weapon transferred to the individual by the agency upon such retirement; or

"(D) the manufacture, transfer, or possession of a semiautomatic assault weapon by a licensed manufacturer or licensed importer for the purposes of testing or experimentation authorized by the Secretary.".

Sec. 110103. Ban of Large Capacity Ammunition Feeding Devices.

(a) Prohibition.—Section 922 of title 18, United States Code, as amended by section 110102(a), is amended by adding at the end the following new subsection:

"(w)(1) Except as provided in paragraph (2), it shall be unlawful for a person to transfer or possess a large capacity ammunition feeding device.

"(2) Paragraph (1) shall not apply to the possession or transfer of any large capacity ammunition feeding device otherwise lawfully possessed on or before the date of the enactment of this subsection.

"(3) This subsection shall not apply to—

"(A) the manufacture for, transfer to, or possession by the United States or a department or agency of the United States or a State or a department, agency, or political subdivision of a State, or a transfer to or possession by a law enforcement officer employed by such an entity for purposes of law enforcement (whether on or off duty);

"(B) the transfer to a licensee under title I of the Atomic Energy Act of 1954 for purposes of establishing and maintaining an on-site physical protection system and security organization required by Federal law, or possession by an employee or contractor of such licensee on-site for such purposes or off-site for purposes of licensee-authorized training or transportation of nuclear materials;

"(C) the possession, by an individual who is retired from service with a law enforcement agency and is not otherwise prohibited from receiving ammunition, of a large capacity ammunition feeding device transferred to the individual by the agency upon such retirement; or

"(D) the manufacture, transfer, or possession of any large capacity ammunition feeding device by a licensed manufacturer or licensed importer for the purposes of testing or experimentation authorized by the Secretary.".

Subtitle B—Youth Handgun Safety

Sec. 110201. Prohibition of the Possession of a Handgun or Ammunition By, or the Private Transfer of a Handgun or Ammunition To, a Juvenile.

(a) Offense.—Section 922 of title 18, United States Code, as amended by section 110103(a), is amended by adding at the end the following new subsection:

"(x)(1) It shall be unlawful for a person to sell, deliver, or otherwise transfer to a person who the transferor knows or has reasonable cause to believe is a juvenile—

"(A) a handgun; or

"(B) ammunition that is suitable for use only in a handgun.

"(2) It shall be unlawful for any person who is a juvenile to knowingly possess—

"(A) a handgun; or

"(B) ammunition that is suitable for use only in a handgun.

Subtitle C—Licensure

Sec. 110301. Firearms Licensure and Registration To Require a Photograph and Fingerprints.

(a) Firearms Licensure.—Section 923(a) of title 18, United States Code, is amended in the second sentence by inserting "and shall include a photograph and fingerprints of the applicant" before the period.

(b) Registration.—Section 5802 of the Internal Revenue Code of 1986 is amended by inserting after the first sentence the following: "An individual required to register under this section shall include a photograph and fingerprints of the individual with the initial application.".

Sec. 110307. Notification of Names and Addresses of Firearms Licensees.

Section 923 of title 18, United States Code, is amended by adding at the end the following new subsection:

"(1) The Secretary of the Treasury shall notify the chief law enforcement officer in the appropriate State and local jurisdictions of the names and addresses of all persons in the State to whom a firearms license is issued.".

Subtitle E—Gun Crime Penalties

Sec. 110501. Enhanced Penalty for Use of a Semiautomatic Firearm during a Crime of Violence or a Drug Trafficking Crime.

(a) Amendment to Sentencing Guidelines.—Pursuant to its authority under section 994 of title 28, United States Code, the United States Sentencing Commission shall amend its sentencing guidelines to provide an appropriate enhancement of the punishment for a crime of violence (as defined in section 924(c)(3) of title 18, United States Code) or a drug trafficking crime (as defined in section 924(c)(2) of title 18, United States Code) if a semiautomatic firearm is involved.

Sec. 110502. Enhanced Penalty for Second Offense of Using an Explosive to Commit a Felony.

Pursuant to its authority under section 994 of title 28, United States Code, the United States Sentencing Commission shall promulgate amendments to the sentencing guidelines to appropriately enhance penalties in a case in which a defendant convicted under section 844(h) of title 18, United States Code, has previously been convicted under that section.

TITLE XII—Terrorism

Sec. 120004. Sentencing Guidelines Increase for Terrorist Crimes.

The United States Sentencing Commission is directed to amend its sentencing guidelines to provide an appropriate enhancement for any felony, whether committed within or outside the United States, that involves or is intended to promote international terrorism, unless such involvement or intent is itself an element of the crime.

Sec. 120005. Providing Material Support To Terrorists.

(a) Offense.—Chapter 113A of title 18, United States Code, is amended by adding the following new section:

"Sec. 2339A. Providing material support to terrorists

"(b) Offense.—A person who, within the United States, provides material support or resources or conceals or disguises the nature, location, source, or ownership of material support or resources, knowing or intending that they are to be used in preparation for, or in carrying out, a violation of section 32, 36, 351, 844 (f) or (i), 1114, 1116, 1203, 1361, 1363, 1751, 2280, 2281, 2331, or 2339 of this title or section 46502 of title 49, or in preparation for or carrying out the concealment of an escape from the commission of any such violation, shall be fined under this title, imprisoned not more than 10 years, or both.

TITLE XIV—Youth Violence

Sec. 140001. Prosecution as Adults of Certain Juveniles for Crimes of Violence.

The 4th undesignated paragraph of section 5032 of title 18, United States Code, is amended by striking "; however" and inserting ". In the application of the preceding sentence, if the crime of violence is an offense under section 113(a), 113(b),

113(c), 1111, 1113, or, if the juvenile possessed a firearm during the offense, section 2111, 2113, 2241(a), or 2241(c), 'thirteen' shall be substituted for 'fifteen' and 'thirteenth' shall be substituted for 'fifteenth'. Notwithstanding sections 1152 and 1153, no person subject to the criminal jurisdiction of an Indian tribal government shall be subject to the preceding sentence for any offense the Federal jurisdiction for which is predicated solely on Indian country (as defined in section 1151), and which has occurred within the boundaries of such Indian country, unless the governing body of the tribe has elected that the preceding sentence have effect over land and persons subject to its criminal jurisdiction. However".

Sec. 140006. Increased Penalties for Employing Children To Distribute Drugs Near Schools and Playgrounds.

Section 419 of the Controlled Substances Act (21 U.S.C. 860) is amended—

(2) by inserting after subsection (b) the following new subsection:

"(c) Notwithstanding any other law, any person at least 21 years of age who knowingly and intentionally—

"(1) employs, hires, uses, persuades, induces, entices, or coerces a person under 18 years of age to violate this section; or

"(2) employs, hires, uses, persuades, induces, entices, or coerces a person under 18 years of age to assist in avoiding detection or apprehension for any offense under this section by any Federal, State, or local law enforcement official, is punishable by a term of imprisonment, a fine, or both, up to triple those authorized by section 401.".

Sec. 140008. Solicitation of Minor To Commit Crime.

(a) Directive to Sentencing Commission.—(1) The United States Sentencing Commission shall promulgate guidelines or amend existing guidelines to provide that a defendant 21 years of age or older who has been convicted of an offense shall receive an appropriate sentence enhancement if the defendant involved a minor in the commission of the offense.

TITLE XV—Criminal Street Gangs

Sec. 150001. Criminal Street Gangs.

(a) In General.—Part I of title 18, United States Code, is amended by inserting after chapter 25 the following new chapter:

"Chapter 26—Criminal Street Gangs
"Sec. 521. Criminal street gangs
"(b) Penalty.—The sentence of a person convicted of an offense described in subsection (c) shall be increased by up to 10 years if the offense is committed under the circumstances described in subsection (d).

"(c) Offenses.—The offenses described in this section are—

"(1) a Federal felony involving a controlled substance (as defined in section 102 of the Controlled Substances Act (21 U.S.C. 802)) for which the maximum penalty is not less than 5 years;

"(2) a Federal felony crime of violence that has as an element the use or attempted use of physical force against the person of another; and

"(3) a conspiracy to commit an offense described in paragraph (1) or (2).

"(d) Circumstances.—The circumstances described in this section are that the offense described in subsection (c) was committed by a person who—

"(1) participates in a criminal street gang with knowledge that its members engage in or have engaged in a continuing series of offenses described in subsection (c);

"(2) intends to promote or further the felonious activities of the criminal street gang or maintain or increase his or her position in the gang; and

"(3) has been convicted within the past 5 years for—

"(A) an offense described in subsection (c);

"(B) a State offense—

"(i) involving a controlled substance (as defined in section 102 of the Controlled Substances Act (21 U.S.C. 802)) for which the maximum penalty is not less than 5 years' imprisonment; or

"(ii) that is a felony crime of violence that has as an element the use or attempted use of physical force against the person of another;

"(C) any Federal or State felony offense that by its nature involves a substantial risk that physical force against the person of another may be used in the course of committing the offense; or

"(D) a conspiracy to commit an offense described in subparagraph (A), (B), or (C).".

Sec. 150002. Adult Prosecution of Serious Juvenile Offenders.
Section 5032 of title 18, United States Code, is amended—
(3) in the fifth undesignated paragraph by adding at the end the following: "In considering the nature of the offense, as required by this paragraph, the court shall consider the extent to which the juvenile played a leadership role in an organization, or otherwise influenced other persons to take part in criminal activities, involving the use or distribution of controlled substances or firearms. Such a factor, if found to exist, shall weigh in favor of a transfer to adult status, but the absence of this factor shall not preclude such a transfer.".

Sec. 150007. Juvenile Anti-Drug and Anti-Gang Grants in Federally Assisted Low-Income Housing.
Grants authorized in this Act to reduce or prevent juvenile drug and gang-related activity in "public housing" may be used for such purposes in federally assisted, low-income housing.

Sec. 150008. Gang Investigation Coordination and Information Collection.
(a) Coordination.—The Attorney General (or the Attorney General's designee), in consultation with the Secretary of the Treasury (or the Secretary's designee), shall develop a national strategy to coordinate gang-related investigations by Federal law enforcement agencies.

TITLE XVI—Child Pornography

Sec. 160001. Penalties for International Trafficking in Child Pornography.
(a) Import Related Offense.—Chapter 110 of title 18, United States Code, is amended by adding at the end the following new section:

"Sec. 2258. Production of sexually explicit depictions of a minor for importation into the United States
"(a) Use of Minor.—A person who, outside the United States, employs, uses, persuades, induces, entices, or coerces any minor to engage in, or who has a minor assist any other person to engage in, or who transports any minor with the intent that the minor engage in any sexually explicit conduct for the purpose of producing any visual depiction of such conduct, intending

that the visual depiction will be imported into the United States or into waters within 12 miles of the coast of the United States, shall be punished as provided in subsection (c).

"(b) Use of Visual Depiction.—A person who, outside the United States, knowingly receives, transports, ships, distributes, sells, or possesses with intent to transport, ship, sell, or distribute any visual depiction of a minor engaging in sexually explicit conduct (if the production of the visual depiction involved the use of a minor engaging in sexually explicit conduct), intending that the visual depiction will be imported into the United States or into waters within a distance of 12 miles of the coast of the United States, shall be punished as provided in subsection (c).

"(c) Penalties.—A person who violates subsection (a) or (b), or conspires or attempts to do so—

"(1) shall be fined under this title, imprisoned not more than 10 years, or both; and

"(2) if the person has a prior conviction under this chapter or chapter 109A, shall be fined under this title, imprisoned not more than 20 years, or both."

Sec. 160002. Sense of Congress Concerning State Legislation Regarding Child Pornography.

It is the sense of the Congress that each State that has not yet done so should enact legislation prohibiting the production, distribution, receipt, or simple possession of materials depicting a person under 18 years of age engaging in sexually explicit conduct (as defined in section 2256 of title 18, United States Code) and providing for a maximum imprisonment of at least 1 year and for the forfeiture of assets used in the commission or support of, or gained from, such offenses.

TITLE XVII—Crimes against Children
Subtitle A—Jacob Wetterling Crimes against Children and Sexually Violent Offender Registration Act

Sec. 170101. Establishment of Program.

(a) In General.—

(1) State guidelines.—The Attorney General shall establish guidelines for State programs that require—

(A) a person who is convicted of a criminal offense against a victim who is a minor or who is convicted of a sexually violent offense to register a current address with a designated

State law enforcement agency for the time period specified in subparagraph (A) of subsection (b)(6); and

(B) a person who is a sexually violent predator to register a current address with a designated State law enforcement agency unless such requirement is terminated under subparagraph (B) of subsection (b)(6).

(b)(6) Length of registration.—

(A) A person required to register under subparagraph (A) of subsection (a)(1) shall continue to comply with this section until 10 years have elapsed since the person was released from prison, placed on parole, supervised release, or probation.

(B) The requirement of a person to register under subparagraph (B) of subsection (a)(1) shall terminate upon a determination, made in accordance with paragraph (2) of subsection (a), that the person no longer suffers from a mental abnormality or personality disorder that would make the person likely to engage in a predatory sexually violent offense.

Subtitle C—Missing and Exploited Children

Sec. 170301. Short Title.

This subtitle may be cited as the "Morgan P. Hardiman Task Force on Missing and Exploited Children Act".

Sec. 170302. Purpose.

The purpose of this subtitle is to establish a task force comprised of law enforcement officers from pertinent Federal agencies to work with the National Center for Missing and Exploited Children (referred to as the "Center") and coordinate the provision of Federal law enforcement resources to assist State and local authorities in investigating the most difficult cases of missing and exploited children.

TITLE XVIII—Rural Crime
Subtitle A—Drug Trafficking in Rural Areas

Sec. 180102. Rural Crime and Drug Enforcement Task Forces.

(a) Establishment.—The Attorney General, in consultation with the Governors, mayors, and chief executive officers of State and local law enforcement agencies, may establish a Rural Crime and Drug Enforcement Task Force in judicial districts that encompass significant rural lands. Assets seized as a result of investigations initiated by a Rural Crime and Drug Enforcement Task Force and forfeited under Federal law shall be used, consistent with the guidelines on equitable sharing established by the Attorney General and of the Secretary of the Treasury, primarily to enhance the operations of the task force and its participating State and local law enforcement agencies.

Sec. 180103. Rural Drug Enforcement Training.

(a) Specialized Training for Rural Officers.—The Director of the Federal Law Enforcement Training Center shall develop a specialized course of instruction devoted to training law enforcement officers from rural agencies in the investigation of drug trafficking and related crimes.

Sec. 180104. More Agents for the Drug Enforcement Administration.

There are authorized to be appropriated for the hiring of additional Drug Enforcement Administration agents—

(1) $12,000,000 for fiscal year 1996;
(2) $20,000,000 for fiscal year 1997;
(3) $30,000,000 for fiscal year 1998;
(4) $40,000,000 for fiscal year 1999; and
(5) $48,000,000 for fiscal year 2000.

Subtitle B—Drug Free Truck Stops and Safety Rest Areas

Sec. 180201. Drug Free Truck Stops and Safety Rest Areas.

(a) Short Title.—This section may be cited as the "Drug Free Truck Stop Act".

(b) Amendment to Controlled Substances Act.—

(1) In general.—Part D of the Controlled Substances Act (21 U.S.C. 801 et seq.) is amended by inserting after section 408 the following new section:

"(b) First Offense.—A person who violates section 401(a)(1) or section 416 by distributing or possessing with intent to distribute a controlled substance in or on, or within 1,000 feet of, a truck stop or safety rest area is (except as provided in subsection (b)) subject to—

"(1) twice the maximum punishment authorized by section 401(b); and

"(2) twice any term of supervised release authorized by section 401(b) for a first offense.

"(c) Subsequent Offense.—A person who violates section 401(a)(1) or section 416 by distributing or possessing with intent to distribute a controlled substance in or on, or within 1,000 feet of, a truck stop or a safety rest area after a prior conviction or convictions under subsection (a) have become final is subject to—

"(1) 3 times the maximum punishment authorized by section 401(b); and

"(2) 3 times any term of supervised release authorized by section 401(b) for a first offense.".

(c) Sentencing Guidelines.—Pursuant to its authority under section 994 of title 28, United States Code, and section 21 of the Sentencing Act of 1987 (28 U.S.C. 994 note), the United States Sentencing Commission shall promulgate guidelines, or shall amend existing guidelines, to provide an appropriate enhancement of punishment for a defendant convicted of violating section 409 of the Controlled Substances Act, as added by subsection (b).

TITLE XIX—Federal Law Enforcement

Sec. 190001. Federal Judiciary and Federal Law Enforcement.

(a) Authorization of Additional Appropriations for the Federal Judiciary.—

Federal judiciary.—There are authorized to be appropriated for the activities of the Federal Judiciary to help meet the increased demands for judicial activities, including supervised release, pre-trial, and probation services, that will result from enactment into law of this Act—

(A) $30,000,000 for fiscal year 1996;
(B) $35,000,000 for fiscal year 1997;
(C) $40,000,000 for fiscal year 1998;
(D) $40,000,000 for fiscal year 1999; and
(E) $55,000,000 for fiscal year 2000.

(b) Authorization of Additional Appropriations for the Department of Justice.—There is authorized to be appropriated for the activities and agencies of the Department of Justice, in addition to sums authorized elsewhere in this section, to help meet the increased demands for Department of Justice activities that will result from enactment into law of this Act—

(A) $40,000,000 for fiscal year 1996;
(B) $40,000,000 for fiscal year 1997;
(C) $40,000,000 for fiscal year 1998;
(D) $40,000,000 for fiscal year 1999; and
(E) $39,000,000 for fiscal year 2000.

(c) Authorization of Additional Appropriations for the Federal Bureau of Investigation.—There is authorized to be appropriated for the activities of the Federal Bureau of Investigation, to help meet the increased demands for Federal Bureau of Investigation activities that will result from enactment into law of this Act—

    (A) $35,000,000 for fiscal year 1996;

    (B) $40,000,000 for fiscal year 1997;

    (C) $50,000,000 for fiscal year 1998;

    (D) $60,000,000 for fiscal year 1999; and

    (E) $60,000,000 for fiscal year 2000.

    (d) Authorization of Additional Appropriations for United States Attorneys.—There is authorized to be appropriated for the account Department of Justice, Legal Activities, "Salaries and expenses, United States Attorneys", to help meet the increased demands for litigation and related activities which will result from enactment into law of this Act—

    (A) $5,000,000 for fiscal year 1996;

    (B) $8,000,000 for fiscal year 1997;

    (C) $10,000,000 for fiscal year 1998;

    (D) $12,000,000 for fiscal year 1999; and

    (E) $15,000,000 for fiscal year 2000.

    (e) Authorization of Additional Appropriations for the Department of the Treasury.—There is authorized to be appropriated for the activities of the Bureau of Alcohol, Tobacco, and Firearms, the United States Customs Service, the Financial Crimes Enforcement Network, the Federal Law Enforcement Training Center, the Criminal Investigation Division of the Internal Revenue Service, and the United States Secret Service to help meet the increased demands for Department of the Treasury activities that will result from enactment into law of this Act—

    (A) $30,000,000 for fiscal year 1995;

    (B) $70,000,000 for fiscal year 1996;

    (C) $90,000,000 for fiscal year 1997;

    (D) $110,000,000 for fiscal year 1998;

    (E) $125,000,000 for fiscal year 1999; and

    (F) $125,000,000 for fiscal year 2000.

TITLE XX—Police Corps and Law Enforcement Officers Training and Education
Subtitle A—Police Corps

Sec. 200101. Short Title.

This subtitle may be cited as the "Police Corps Act".

Sec. 200102. Purposes.

The purposes of this subtitle are to—

(1) address violent crime by increasing the number of police with advanced education and training on community patrol; and

(2) provide educational assistance to law enforcement personnel and to students who possess a sincere interest in public service in the form of law enforcement.

Sec. 200104. Establishment of Office of the Police Corps and Law Enforcement Education.

There is established in the Department of Justice, under the general authority of the Attorney General, an Office of the Police Corps and Law Enforcement Education.

Sec. 200108. Police Corps Training.

(a) In General.—(1) The Director shall establish programs of training for Police Corps participants. Such programs may be carried out at up to 3 training centers established for this purpose and administered by the Director, or by contracting with existing State training facilities. The Director shall contract with a State training facility upon request of such facility if the Director determines that such facility offers a course of training substantially equivalent to the Police Corps training program described in this subtitle.

(b) Training Sessions.—A participant in a State Police Corps program shall attend two 8-week training sessions at a training center, one during the summer following completion of sophomore year and one during the summer following completion of junior year. If a participant enters the program after sophomore year, the participant shall complete 16 weeks of training at times determined by the Director.

(c) Further Training.—The 16 weeks of Police Corps training authorized in this section is intended to serve as basic law enforcement training but not to exclude further training of participants by the State and local authorities to which they will be assigned. Each State plan approved by the Director under section 10 shall include assurances that following completion of a participant's course of education each participant shall receive appropriate additional training by the State or local authority to which the participant is assigned. The time spent by a participant in such additional training, but not the time spent in Police Corps training, shall be counted toward fulfillment of the participant's 4-year service obligation.

(d) Course of Training.—The training sessions at training centers established under this section shall be designed to provide basic law enforcement training, including vigorous physical and mental training to teach participants self-discipline and organizational loyalty and to impart knowledge and understanding of legal processes and law enforcement.

TITLE XXI—State and Local Law Enforcement
Subtitle C—DNA Identification

Sec. 210301. Short Title.

This subtitle may be cited as the "DNA Identification Act of 1994".

(c) DNA Identification Grants.

(1) In General.—Title I of the Omnibus Crime Control and Safe Streets Act of 1968 (42 U.S.C. 3711 et seq.), as amended by section 210201(a) is amended—

(C) by inserting after part W the following new part:

"Part X—DNA Identification Grants

"Sec. 2401. Grant Authorization.

"The Attorney General may make funds available under this part to States and units of local government, or combinations thereof, to carry out all or a substantial part of a program or project intended to develop or improve the capability to analyze deoxyribonucleic acid (referred to in this part as 'DNA') in a forensic laboratory.

Sec. 210304. Index To Facilitate Law Enforcement Exchange of DNA Identification Information.

(a) Establishment of Index.—The Director of the Federal Bureau of Investigation may establish an index of—

(1) DNA identification records of persons convicted of crimes;

(2) analyses of DNA samples recovered from crime scenes; and

(3) analyses of DNA samples recovered from unidentified human remains.

Subtitle D—Police Pattern or Practice

Sec. 210401. Cause of Action.

(a) Unlawful Conduct.—It shall be unlawful for any governmental authority, or any agent thereof, or any person acting on behalf of a governmental authority, to engage in a pattern or practice of conduct by law enforcement officers or by officials or employees of any governmental agency with responsibility for the administration of juvenile justice or the incarceration of juveniles that deprives persons of rights, privileges, or immunities secured or protected by the Constitution or laws of the United States.

(b) Civil Action by Attorney General.—Whenever the Attorney General has reasonable cause to believe that a violation of paragraph (1) has occurred, the Attorney General, for or in the name of the United States, may in a civil action obtain appropriate equitable and declaratory relief to eliminate the pattern or practice.

Sec. 210402. Data on Use of Excessive Force.

(a) Attorney General To Collect.—The Attorney General shall, through appropriate means, acquire data about the use of excessive force by law enforcement officers.

(b) Limitation on Use of Data.—Data acquired under this section shall be used only for research or statistical purposes and may not contain any information that may reveal the identity of the victim or any law enforcement officer.

(c) Annual Summary.—The Attorney General shall publish an annual summary of the data acquired under this section.

Subtitle E—Improved Training and Technical Automation

Sec. 210501. Improved Training and Technical Automation.

(a) Grants.—

(1) In general.—The Attorney General shall, subject to the availability of appropriations, make grants to State, Indian tribal, and local criminal justice agencies and to nonprofit organizations for the purposes of improving criminal justice agency efficiency through computerized automation and technological improvements.

TITLE XXII—Motor Vehicle Theft Prevention

Sec. 220001. Short Title.

This title may be cited as the "Motor Vehicle Theft Prevention Act".

Sec. 220002. Motor Vehicle Theft Prevention Program.

(a) In General.—Not later than 180 days after the date of enactment of this section, the Attorney General shall develop, in cooperation with the States, a national voluntary motor vehicle theft prevention program (in this section referred to as the "program") under which—

(1) the owner of a motor vehicle may voluntarily sign a consent form with a participating State or locality in which the motor vehicle owner—

(A) states that the vehicle is not normally operated under certain specified conditions; and

(B) agrees to—

(i) display program decals or devices on the owner's vehicle; and

(ii) permit law enforcement officials in any State to stop the motor vehicle and take reasonable steps to determine whether the vehicle is being operated by or with the permission of the owner, if the vehicle is being operated under the specified conditions; and

(2) participating States and localities authorize law enforcement officials in the State or locality to stop motor vehicles displaying program decals or devices under specified conditions and take reasonable steps to determine whether the vehicle is being operated by or with the permission of the owner.

TITLE XXIII—Victims of Crime
Subtitle A—Victims of Crime

Sec. 230102. Sense of the Senate Concerning the Right of a Victim of a Violent Crime or Sexual Abuse To Speak at an Offender's Sentencing Hearing and Any Parole Hearing.

It is the sense of the Senate that—

(1) the law of a State should provide for a victim's right of allocution at a sentencing hearing and at any parole hearing if the offender has been convicted of a crime of violence or sexual abuse;

(2) such a victim should have an opportunity equivalent to the opportunity accorded to the offender to address the sentencing court or parole board and to present information in relation to the sentence imposed or to the early release of the offender; and

(3) if the victim is not able to or chooses not to testify at a sentencing hearing or parole hearing, the victim's parents, legal

guardian, or family members should have the right to address the court or board.

TITLE XXIV—Protections for the Elderly

Sec. 240001. Missing Alzheimer's Disease Patient Alert Program.
(a) Grant.—The Attorney General shall, subject to the availability of appropriations, award a grant to an eligible organization to assist the organization in paying for the costs of planning, designing, establishing, and operating a Missing Alzheimer's Disease Patient Alert Program, which shall be a locally based, proactive program to protect and locate missing patients with Alzheimer's disease and related dementias.

Sec. 240002. Crimes against the Elderly.
(a) In General.—Pursuant to its authority under the Sentencing Reform Act of 1984 and section 21 of the Sentencing Act of 1987 (including its authority to amend the sentencing guidelines and policy statements) and its authority to make such amendments on an emergency basis, the United States Sentencing Commission shall ensure that the applicable guideline range for a defendant convicted of a crime of violence against an elderly victim is sufficiently stringent to deter such a crime, to protect the public from additional crimes of such a defendant, and to adequately reflect the heinous nature of such an offense.

TITLE XXV—Senior Citizens against Marketing Scams

Sec. 250001. Short Title.
This Act may be cited as the "Senior Citizens Against Marketing Scams Act of 1994".

Sec. 250002. Enhanced Penalties for Telemarketing Fraud.
(a) Offense.—Part I of title 18, United States Code, is amended—
(2) by inserting after chapter 113 the following new chapter:

"Chapter 113A—Telemarketing Fraud

"Sec. 2326. Enhanced penalties
"A person who is convicted of an offense under section 1028, 1029, 1341, 1342, 1343, or 1344 in connection with the conduct of telemarketing—

"(1) may be imprisoned for a term of up to 5 years in addition to any term of imprisonment imposed under any of those sections, respectively; and

"(2) in the case of an offense under any of those sections that—

"(A) victimized ten or more persons over the age of 55; or

"(B) targeted persons over the age of 55, may be imprisoned for a term of up to 10 years in addition to any term of imprisonment imposed under any of those sections, respectively.

"Sec. 2327. Mandatory restitution

"(a) In General.—Notwithstanding section 3663, and in addition to any other civil or criminal penalty authorized by law, the court shall order restitution for any offense under this chapter.

Sec. 250003. Increased Penalties for Fraud against Older Victims.

(a) Review.—The United States Sentencing Commission shall review and, if necessary, amend the sentencing guidelines to ensure that victim related adjustments for fraud offenses against older victims over the age of 55 are adequate.

Sec. 250004. Rewards for Information Leading To Prosecution and Conviction.

Section 3059 of title 18, United States Code, is amended by adding at the end the following new subsection:

"(c)(1) In special circumstances and in the Attorney General's sole discretion, the Attorney General may make a payment of up to $10,000 to a person who furnishes information unknown to the Government relating to a possible prosecution under section 2326 which results in a conviction.

Sec. 250008. Information Network.

(a) Hotline.—The Attorney General shall, subject to the availability of appropriations, establish a national toll-free hotline for the purpose of—

(1) providing general information on telemarketing fraud to interested persons; and

(2) gathering information related to possible violations of this Act.

(b) Action on Information Gathered.—The Attorney General shall work in cooperation with the Federal Trade Commission to ensure that information gathered through the hotline shall be acted on in an appropriate manner.

TITLE XXVII—Presidential Summit on Violence and National Commission on Crime Prevention and Control

Sec. 270001. Presidential Summit.

Congress calls on the President to convene a national summit on violence in America prior to convening the Commission established under this title.

Sec. 270002. Establishment; Committees and Task Forces; Representation.

(a) Establishment and Appointment of Members.—There is established a commission to be known as the "National Commission on Crime Control and Prevention". The Commission shall be composed of 28 members appointed as follows:

(1) 10 persons by the President, not more than 6 of whom shall be of the same major political party.

(2) 9 persons by the President pro tempore of the Senate, 5 of whom shall be appointed on the recommendation of the Majority Leader of the Senate and the chairman of the Committee on the Judiciary of the Senate, and 4 of whom shall be appointed on the recommendation of the Minority Leader of the Senate and the ranking minority member of the Committee on the Judiciary of the Senate.

(3) 9 persons appointed by the Speaker of the House of Representatives, in consultation with the chairman of the Committee on the Judiciary of the House of Representatives, and 4 of whom shall be appointed on the recommendation of the Minority Leader of the House of Representatives, in consultation with the ranking member of the Committee on the Judiciary.

(b) Committees and Task Forces.—The Commission shall establish committees or task forces from among its members for the examination of specific subject areas and the carrying out of other functions or responsibilities of the Commission, including committees or task forces for the examination of the subject areas of crime and violence generally, the causes of the demand for drugs, violence in schools, and violence against women, as described in subsections (b) through (e) of section 270004.

TITLE XXVIII—Sentencing Provisions

Sec. 280003. Direction To United States Sentencing Commission Regarding Sentencing Enhancements for Hate Crimes.

(a) Definition.—In this section, "hate crime" means a crime in which the defendant intentionally selects a victim, or in the case of a property crime, the property that is the object of the crime, because of the actual or perceived race, color, religion, national origin, ethnicity, gender, disability, or sexual orientation of any person.

(b) Sentencing Enhancement.—Pursuant to section 994 of title 28, United States Code, the United States Sentencing Commission shall promulgate guidelines or amend existing guidelines to provide sentencing enhancements of not less than 3 offense levels for offenses that the finder of fact at trial determines beyond a reasonable doubt are hate crimes. In carrying out this section, the United States Sentencing Commission shall ensure that there is reasonable consistency with other guidelines, avoid duplicative punishments for substantially the same offense, and take into account any mitigating circumstances that might justify exceptions.

TITLE XXIX—Computer Crime

Sec. 290001. Computer Abuse Amendments Act of 1994.

(a) Short Title.—This subtitle may be cited as the "Computer Abuse Amendments Act of 1994".

(b) Prohibition.—Section 1030(a)(5) of title 18, United States Code, is amended to read as follows:

"(5)(A) through means of a computer used in interstate commerce or communications, knowingly causes the transmission of a program, information, code, or command to a computer or computer system if—

"(i) the person causing the transmission intends that such transmission will—

"(I) damage, or cause damage to, a computer, computer system, network, information, data, or program; or

"(II) withhold or deny, or cause the withholding or denial, of the use of a computer, computer services, system or network, information, data, or program; and

"(ii) the transmission of the harmful component of the program, information, code, or command—

"(I) occurred without the authorization of the persons or entities who own or are responsible for the computer system receiving the program, information, code, or command; and

"(II)(aa) causes loss or damage to one or more other persons of value aggregating $1,000 or more during any 1-year period; or

"(bb) modifies or impairs, or potentially modifies or impairs, the medical examination, medical diagnosis, medical treatment, or medical care of one or more individuals; or

"(B) through means of a computer used in interstate commerce or communication, knowingly causes the transmission of a program, information, code, or command to a computer or computer system—

"(i) with reckless disregard of a substantial and unjustifiable risk that the transmission will—

"(I) damage, or cause damage to, a computer, computer system, network, information, data, or program; or

"(II) withhold or deny or cause the withholding or denial of the use of a computer, computer services, system, network, information, data, or program; and

"(ii) if the transmission of the harmful component of the program, information, code, or command—

"(I) occurred without the authorization of the persons or entities who own or are responsible for the computer system receiving the program, information, code, or command; and

"(II)(aa) causes loss or damage to one or more other persons of a value aggregating $1,000 or more during any 1-year period; or

"(bb) modifies or impairs, or potentially modifies or impairs, the medical examination, medical diagnosis, medical treatment, or medical care of one or more individuals;".

(d) Civil Action.—Section 1030 of title 18, United States Code, is amended by adding at the end thereof the following new subsection:

"(g) Any person who suffers damage or loss by reason of a violation of the section, other than a violation of subsection (a)(5)(B), may maintain a civil action against the violator to obtain compensatory damages and injunctive relief or other equitable relief. Damages for violations of any subsection other than subsection (a)(5)(A)(ii)(II)(bb) or (a)(5)(B)(ii)(II)(bb) are limited to economic damages. No action may be brought under this subsection unless such action is begun within 2 years of the date of the act complained of or the date of the discovery of the damage.".

TITLE XXXI—Violent Crime Reduction Trust Fund

Sec. 310001. Creation of Violent Crime Reduction Trust Fund.

(a) Violent Crime Reduction Trust Fund.—There is established a separate account in the Treasury, known as the "Violent Crime Reduction Trust Fund" (referred to in this section as the "Fund") into which shall be transferred, in accordance with subsection (b), savings realized from implementation of section 5 of the Federal Workforce Restructuring Act of 1994 (5 U.S.C. 3101 note; Public Law 103-226).

(c) Appropriations from the Fund.—(1) Amounts in the Fund may be appropriated exclusively for the purposes authorized in this Act and for those expenses authorized by any Act enacted before this Act that are expressly qualified for expenditure from the Fund.

TITLE XXXII—Miscellaneous
Subtitle I—Other Provisions

Sec. 320904. Gun-Free School Zones.

Section 922(q) of title 18, United States Code, is amended—

(2) by inserting after "(q)" the following new paragraph:

"(1) The Congress finds and declares that—

"(A) crime, particularly crime involving drugs and guns, is a pervasive, nationwide problem;

"(B) crime at the local level is exacerbated by the interstate movement of drugs, guns, and criminal gangs;

"(C) firearms and ammunition move easily in interstate commerce and have been found in increasing numbers in and around schools, as documented in numerous hearings in both the Judiciary Committee of the House of Representatives and Judiciary Committee of the Senate;

"(D) in fact, even before the sale of a firearm, the gun, its component parts, ammunition, and the raw materials from which they are made have considerably moved in interstate commerce;

"(E) while criminals freely move from State to State, ordinary citizens and foreign visitors may fear to travel to or through certain parts of the country due to concern about violent crime and gun violence, and parents may decline to send their children to school for the same reason;

"(F) the occurrence of violent crime in school zones has resulted in a decline in the quality of education in our country;

"(G) this decline in the quality of education has an adverse impact on interstate commerce and the foreign commerce of the United States;

"(H) States, localities, and school systems find it almost impossible to handle gun-related crime by themselves; even States, localities, and school systems that have made strong efforts to prevent, detect, and punish gun-related crime find their efforts unavailing due in part to the failure or inability of other States or localities to take strong measures; and

"(I) Congress has power, under the interstate commerce clause and other provisions of the Constitution, to enact measures to ensure the integrity and safety of the Nation's schools by enactment of this subsection.".

Sec. 320915. Law Enforcement Personnel.

It is the sense of the Senate that law enforcement personnel should not be reduced and calls upon the President of the United States to exempt Federal law enforcement positions from Executive Order 12839 and other Executive memoranda mandating reductions in the Federal workforce.

Sec. 320917. Extension of Statute of Limitations for Arson.

(a) In General.—Section 844(i) of title 18, United States Code, is amended by adding at the end the following: "No person shall be prosecuted, tried, or punished for any noncapital offense under this subsection unless the indictment is found or the information is instituted within 7 years after the date on which the offense was committed.".

Sec. 320921. First Time Domestic Violence Offender Rehabilitation Program.

(a) Sentence of Probation.—Section 3561 of title 18, United States Code, is amended—

(2) by inserting the following new subsection after subsection (a):

"(b) Domestic Violence Offenders.—A defendant who has been convicted for the first time of a domestic violence crime shall be sentenced to a term of probation if not sentenced to a term of imprisonment. The term 'domestic violence crime' means a crime of violence for which the defendant may be prosecuted in a court of the United States in which the victim or intended victim is the spouse, former spouse, intimate partner, former intimate partner, child, or former child of the defendant, or any relative defendant, child, or former child of the defendant, or any other relative of the defendant.".

Brady Handgun Violence Prevention Act, 1993 (excerpt)

AN ACT
To provide for a waiting period before the purchase of a handgun, and for the establishment of a national instant criminal background check system to be contacted by firearms dealers before the transfer of any firearm.

Be it enacted by the Senate and House of Representatives of the United States of America in Congress assembled,

Title I—Brady Handgun Control

Sec. 101. Short Title.

This title may be cited as the "Brady Handgun Violence Prevention Act."

Sec. 102. Federal Firearms License Required To Conduct Criminal Background Check before Transfer of Firearm To Non-Licensee.

(a) Interim Provision.—

(1) In General.—Section 922 of title 18, United States Code, is amended by adding at the end the following:

"(s)(1) Beginning on the date that is 90 days after the date of enactment of this subsection and ending on the day before the date that is 60 months after such date of enactment, it shall be unlawful for any licensed importer, licensed manufacturer, or licensed dealer to sell, deliver, or transfer a handgun to an individual who is not licensed under section 923, unless—

"(A) after the most recent proposal of such transfer by the transferee—

"(i) the transferor has—

"(I) received from the transferee a statement of the transferee containing the information described in paragraph (3);

"(II) verified the identity of the transferee by examining the identification document presented;

"(III) within 1 day after the transferee furnishes the statement, provided notice of the contents of the statement to the chief law enforcement officer of the place of residence of the transferee; and

"(IV) within 1 day after the transferee furnishes the statement, transmitted a copy of the statement to the chief law enforcement officer of the place of residence of the transferee; and

"(ii) (I) 5 business days (meaning days on which State offices are open) have elapsed from the date the transferor furnished notice of the contents of the statement to the chief law enforcement officer, during which period the transferor has not received information from the chief law enforcement officer that receipt or possession of the handgun by the transferee would be in violation of Federal, State, or local law; or

"(II) the transferor has received notice from the chief law enforcement officer that the officer has no information indicating that receipt or possession of the handgun by the transferee would violate Federal, State, or local law;

"(B) the transferee has presented to the transferor a written statement, issued by the chief law enforcement officer of the place of residence of the transferee during the 10-day period ending on the date of the most recent proposal of such transfer by the transferee, stating that the transferee requires access to a handgun because of a threat to the life of the transferee or of any member of the household of the transferee;

"(C)(i) the transferee has presented to the transferor a permit that—

"(I) allows the transferee to possess or acquire a handgun; and

"(II) was issued not more than 5 years earlier by the State in which the transfer is to take place; and

"(ii) the law of the State provides that such a permit is to be issued only after an authorized government official has verified that the information available to such official does not indicate that possession of a handgun by the transferee would be in violation of the law;

"(D) the law of the State requires that, before any licensed importer, licensed manufacturer, or licensed dealer completes the transfer of a handgun to an individual who is not licensed under section 923, an authorized government official verify that the information available to such official does not indicate that possession of a handgun by the transferee would be in violation of law;

"(E) the Secretary has approved the transfer under section 5812 of the Internal Revenue Code of 1986; or

"(F) on application of the transferor, the Secretary has certified that compliance with subparagraph (A)(i)(III) is impracticable because—

"(i) the ratio of the number of law enforcement officers of the State in which the transfer is to occur to the number of square miles of land area of the State does not exceed 0.0025;

"(ii) the business premises of the transferor at which the transfer is to occur are extremely remote in relation to the chief law enforcement officer; and

"(iii) there is an absence of telecommunications facilities in the geographical area in which the business premises are located.

"(2) A chief law enforcement officer to whom a transferor has provided notice pursuant to paragraph (1)(A)(i)(III) shall make a reasonable effort to ascertain within 5 business days whether receipt or possession would be in violation of the law, including research in whatever State and local recordkeeping systems are available and in a national system designated by the Attorney General.

"(3) The statement referred to in paragraph (1)(A)(i)(I) shall contain only—

"(A) the name, address, and date of birth appearing on a valid identification document (as defined in section 1028(d)(1)) of the transferee containing a photograph of the transferee and a description of the identification used;

"(B) a statement that the transferee—

"(i) is not under indictment for, and has not been convicted in any court of, a crime punishable by imprisonment for a term exceeding 1 year;

"(ii) is not a fugitive from justice;

"(iii) is not an unlawful user of or addicted to any controlled substance (as defined in section 102 of the Controlled Substances Act);

"(iv) has not been adjudicated as a mental defective or been committed to a mental institution;

"(v) is not an alien who is illegally or unlawfully in the United States;

"(vi) has not been discharged from the Armed Forces under dishonorable conditions; and

"(vii) is not a person who, having been a citizen of the United States, has renounced such citizenship;

"(C) date the statement is made; and

"(D) notice that the transferee intends to obtain a handgun from the transferor.

"(4) Any transferor of a handgun who, after such transfer, receives a report from a chief law enforcement officer containing information that receipt or possession of the handgun by the transferee violates Federal, State, or local law shall, within 1 business day after receipt of such request, communicate any information related to the transfer that the transferor has about the transfer and the transferee to—

"(A) the chief law enforcement officer of the place of business of the transferor; and

"(B) the chief law enforcement officer of the place of residence of the transferee.

"(5) Any transferor who receives information, not otherwise available to the public, in a report under this subsection shall not disclose such information except to the transferee, to law enforcement authorities, or pursuant to the direction of a court of law.

"(6)(A) Any transferor who sells, delivers, or otherwise transfers a handgun to a transferee shall retain the copy of the statement of the transferee with respect to the handgun transaction, and shall retain evidence that the transferor has complied with subclauses (III) and (IV) of paragraph (1)(A)(i) with respect to the statement.

"(B) Unless the chief law enforcement officer to whom a statement is transmitted under paragraph (1)(A)(i)(IV) determines that a transaction would violate Federal, State, or local law—

"(i) the officer shall, within 20 business days after the date the transferee made the statement on the basis of which the notice was provided, destroy the statement, any record containing information derived from the statement, and any record created as a result of the notice required by paragraph (1)(A)(i)(III);

"(ii) the information contained in the statement shall not be conveyed to any person except a person who has a need to know in order to carry out this subsection; and

"(iii) the information contained in the statement shall not be used for any purpose other than to carry out this subsection.

"(C) If a chief law enforcement officer determines that an individual is ineligible to receive a handgun and the individual requests the officer to provide the reason for such determination, the officer shall provide such reasons to the individual in writing within 20 business days after receipt of the request.

"(7) A chief law enforcement officer or other person responsible for providing criminal history background information pursuant to this subsection shall not be liable in an action at law for damages—

"(A) for failure to prevent the sale or transfer of a handgun to a person whose receipt or possession of the handgun is unlawful under this section; or

"(B) for preventing such a sale or transfer to a person who may lawfully receive or possess a handgun.

"(8) For purposes of this subsection, the term 'chief law enforcement officer' means the chief of police, the sheriff, or an equivalent officer or the designee of any such individual.

"(9) The Secretary shall take necessary actions to ensure that the provisions of this subsection are published and disseminated to licensed dealers, law enforcement officials, and the public."

(2) Handgun Defined: Section 921(a) of title 18, United States Code, is amended by adding at the end the following:

"(29) The term 'handgun' means—

"(A) a firearm which has a short stock and is designed to be held and fired by the use of a single hand; and

"(B) any combination of parts from which a firearm described in subparagraph (A) can be assembled.

(b) Permanent Provision: Section 922 of title 18, United States Code, as amended by subsection (a)(1), is amended by adding at the end the following:

"(t)(1) Beginning on the date that is 30 days after the Attorney General notifies licensees under section 103(d) of the Brady Handgun Violence Prevention Act that the national instant criminal background check system is established, a licensed importer, licensed manufacturer, or licensed dealer shall not transfer a firearm to any other person who is not licensed under this chapter, unless—

"(A) before the completion of the transfer, the licensee contacts the national instant criminal background check system established under section 103 of that Act;

"(B)(i) the system provides the licensee with a unique identification number; or

"(ii) 3 business days (meaning a day on which State offices are open) have elapsed since the licensee contacted the system, and the system has not notified the licensee that the receipt of a firearm by such other person would violate subsection (g) or (n) of this section; and

"(C) the transferor has verified the identity of the transferee by examining a valid identification document (as defined in section 1028(d)(1) of this title) of the transferee containing a photograph of the transferee.

"(2) If receipt of a firearm would not violate section 922 (g) or (n) or State law, the system shall—

"(A) assign a unique identification number to the transfer;

"(B) provide the licensee with the number; and

"(C) destroy all records of the system with respect to the call (other than the identifying number and the date the number was assigned) and all records of the system relating to the person or the transfer.

"(3) Paragraph (1) shall not apply to a firearm transfer between a licensee and another person if—

"(A)(i) such other person has presented to the licensee a permit that—

"(I) allows such other person to possess or acquire a firearm; and

"(II) was issued not more than 5 years earlier by the State in which the transfer is to take place; and

"(ii) the law of the State provides that such a permit is to be issued only after an authorized government official has verified that the information available to such official does not indicate that possession of a firearm by such other person would be in violation of law;

"(B) the Secretary has approved the transfer under section 5812 of the Internal Revenue Code of 1986; or

"(C) on application of the transferor, the Secretary has certified that compliance with paragraph (1)(A) is impracticable because—

"(i) the ratio of the number of law enforcement officers of the State in which the transfer is to occur to the number of square miles of land area of the State does not exceed 0.0025;

"(ii) the business premises of the licensee at which the transfer is to occur are extremely remote in relation to the chief law enforcement officer (as defined in subsection (s)(8)); and

"(iii) there is an absence of telecommunications facilities in the geographical area in which the business premises are located.

"(4) If the national instant criminal background check system notifies the licensee that the information available to the system does not demonstrate that the receipt of a firearm by such other person would violate subsection (g) or (n) or State law, and the licensee transfers a firearm to such other person, the licensee shall include in the record of the transfer the unique identification number provided by the system with respect to the transfer.

"(5) If the licensee knowingly transfers a firearm to such other person and knowingly fails to comply with paragraph (1) of this subsection with respect to the transfer and, at the time such other person most recently proposed the transfer, the national instant criminal background check system was operating and information was available to the system demonstrating that receipt of a firearm by such other person would violate subsection (g) or (n) of this section or State law, the Secretary may, after notice and opportunity for a hearing, suspend for not more than 6 months or revoke any license issued to the licensee under section 923, and may impose on the licensee a civil fine of not more than $5,000.

"(6) Neither a local government nor an employee of the Federal Government or of any State or local government, responsible for providing information to the national instant criminal background check system shall be liable in an action at law for damages—

"(A) for failure to prevent the sale or transfer of a firearm to a person whose receipt or possession of the firearm is unlawful under this section; or

"(B) for preventing such a sale or transfer to a person who may lawfully receive or possess a firearm."

(c) Penalty: Section 924(a) of title 18, United States Code, is amended—

(1) in paragraph (1), by striking "paragraph (2) or (3) of"; and

(2) by adding at the end the following:

"(5) Whoever knowingly violates subsection (s) or (t) of section 922 shall be fined not more than $1,000, imprisoned for not more than 1 year, or both."

Sec. 103. National Instant Criminal Background Check System.

(a) Determination of Timetables.—Not later than 6 months after the date of enactment of this Act, the Attorney General shall—

(1) determine the type of computer hardware and software that will be used to operate the national instant criminal background check system and the means by which State criminal records systems and the telephone or electronic device of licensees will communicate with the national system;

(2) investigate the criminal records system of each State and determine for each State a timetable by which the State

should be able to provide criminal records on an on-line capacity basis to the national system; and

(3) notify each State of the determinations made pursuant to paragraphs (1) and (2).

(b) Establishment of System: Not later than 60 months after the date of the enactment of this Act, the Attorney General shall establish a national instant criminal background check system that any licensee may contact, by telephone or by other electronic means in addition to the telephone, for information, to be supplied immediately, on whether receipt of a firearm by a prospective transferee would violate section 922 of title 18, United States Code, or State law.

(c) Expedited Action by the Attorney General.—The Attorney General shall expedite—

(1) the upgrading and indexing of State criminal history records in the Federal criminal records system maintained by the Federal Bureau of Investigation;

(2) the development of hardware and software systems to link State criminal history check systems into the national instant criminal background check system established by the Attorney General pursuant to this section; and

(3) the current revitalization initiatives by the Federal Bureau of Investigation for technologically advanced fingerprint and criminal records identification.

(d) Notification of Licensees.—On establishment of the system under this section, the Attorney General shall notify each licensee and the chief law enforcement officer of each State of the existence and purpose of the system and the means to be used to contact the system.

(e) Administrative Provisions.—

(1) Authority To Obtain Official Information.— Notwithstanding any other law, the Attorney General may secure directly from any department or agency of the United States such information on persons for whom receipt of a firearm would violate subsection (g) or (n) of section 922 of title 18, United States Code or State law, as is necessary to enable the system to operate in accordance with this section. On request of the Attorney General, the head of such department or agency shall furnish such information to the system.

(2) Other authority: The Attorney General shall develop such computer software, design and obtain such telecommunications and computer hardware, and employ such personnel, as are necessary to establish and operate the system in accordance with this section.

(f) Written Reasons Provided on Request.—If the national instant criminal background check system determines that an individual is ineligible to receive a firearm and the individual requests the system to provide the reasons for the determination, the system shall provide such reasons to the individual, in writing, within 5 business days after the date of the request.

(g) Correction of Erroneous System Information.—If the system established under this section informs an individual contacting the system that receipt of a firearm by a prospective transferee would violate subsection (g) or (n) of section 922 of title 18, United States Code or State law, the prospective transferee may request the Attorney General to provide the prospective transferee with the reasons therefor. Upon receipt of such a request, the Attorney General shall immediately comply with the request. The prospective transferee may submit to the Attorney General information to correct, clarify, or supplement records of the system with respect to the prospective transferee. After receipt of such information, the Attorney General shall immediately consider the information, investigate the matter further, and correct all erroneous Federal records relating to the prospective transferee and give notice of the error to any Federal department or agency or any State that was the source of such erroneous records.

(h) Regulations.—After 90 days' notice to the public and an opportunity for hearing by interested parties, the Attorney General shall prescribe regulations to ensure the privacy and security of the information of the system established under this section.

(i) Prohibition Relating To Establishment of Registration Systems with Respect To Firearms.—No department, agency, officer, or employee of the United States may—

(1) require that any record or portion thereof generated by the system established under this section be recorded at or transferred to a facility owned, managed, or controlled by the United States or any State or political subdivision thereof; or

(2) use the system established under this section to establish any system for the registration of firearms, firearm owners, or firearm transactions or dispositions, except with respect to persons prohibited by section 922 (g) or (n) of title 18, United States Code or State law, from receiving a firearm.

(j) Definitions.—As used in this section:

(1) Licensee.—The term "licensee" means a licensed importer (as defined in section 921(a)(9) of title 18, United States Code), a

licensed manufacturer (as defined in section 921(a)(10) of that title), or a licensed dealer (as defined in section 921(a)(11) of that title).

(2) Other Terms: The terms "firearm", "handgun", "licensed importer", "licensed manufacturer", and "licensed dealer" have the meanings stated in section 921(a) of title 18, United States Code, as amended by subsection (a)(2).

(k) Authorization of Appropriations.—There are authorized to be appropriated, which may be appropriated from the Violent Crime Reduction Trust Fund established by section 1115 of title 31, United States Code, such sums as are necessary to enable the Attorney General to carry out this section.

Sec. 104. Remedy for Erroneous Denial of Firearm.

(a) In General: Chapter 44 of title 18, United States Code, is amended by inserting after section 925 the following new section:

"Sec. 925A. Remedy for erroneous denial of firearm: "Any person denied a firearm pursuant to subsection (s) or (t) of section 922—

"(1) due to the provision of erroneous information relating to the person by any State or political subdivision thereof, or by the national instant criminal background check system established under section 103 of the Brady Handgun Violence Prevention Act; or

"(2) who was not prohibited from receipt of a firearm pursuant to subsection (g) or (n) of section 922, may bring an action against the State or political subdivision responsible for providing the erroneous information, or responsible for denying the transfer, or against the United States, as the case may be, for an order directing that the erroneous information be corrected or that the transfer be approved, as the case may be. In any action under this section, the court, in its discretion, may allow the prevailing party a reasonable attorney's fee as part of the costs."

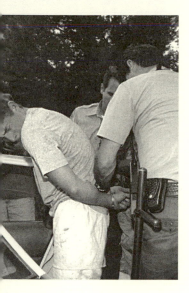

Directory of Organizations

Private and State Organizations

The following agencies and organizations have been formed to combat some aspect of crime. Publications lists may not be complete in some cases because of the large number the organization distributes. A full list can be obtained by contacting the organization. In a few cases, the agency does not produce or distribute publications.

Aid to Incarcerated Mothers (AIM)
32 Rutland Street, 4th Floor
Boston, MA 02118
(617) 536-0058

AIM is a small agency local to the Boston area that helps imprisoned mothers with family duties, visits, counseling, legal rights, and reintegration into the community when they are released from prison.

Publications: Staying Together, published three times per year.

Alternative Schools Network (ASN)
1807 West Sunnyside, Suite 1-D
Chicago, IL 60640
(312) 728-4030
e-mail: altschools@aol.com

This is a network of more than 40 nonpublic schools in the Chicago area that is funded by both public and private money. In the area of crime, its main focus is the prevention of delinquency.

Publications: ASN News (monthly); *Alternative Curriculum* (biannual); *Directory of Schools* (annual); books; reprints.

American Correctional Association (ACA)
4380 Forbes Boulevard
Lanham, MD 20706-4322
(301) 918-1800
(800) ACA-JOIN
(301) 918-1900 (FAX)

This group directs its efforts toward improving correctional institutions and their employees. It also works with prisoners after they have served their time and accredits corrections programs and institutions.

Publications: Corrections Today, published seven times per year; *On the Line* (bimonthly); *Directory of Correctional Institutions and Agencies* (annual); *Proceedings of the Annual Congress of Correction; Correction Officers Resource Guide; Careers in Corrections.* A list of publications is available.

American Society of Criminology (ASC)
1314 Kinnear Road, Suite 212
Columbus, OH 43212
(614) 292-9207
(614) 292-6767 (FAX)
e-mail: internet76551.201@compuserve.com

This organization is made up of academics and students interested in advancing the study and development of criminology.

Publications: American Society of Criminology—Member Directory (annual); *The Criminologist* (bimonthly); *Criminology: An Interdisciplinary Journal* (quarterly); proceedings from annual meetings.

Bureau of National Affairs, Inc. (BNA)
1231 25th Street, N.W.
Washington, DC 20037
(202) 452-4323
(202) 452-4200
(202) 822-8092 (FAX)
e-mail: bna_+@bna.com

The BNA is a privately owned publishing company that is not devoted exclusively to crime. Areas of crime it deals with include criminal law and industrial and government security.

A publications list is available.

Center for Governmental Research, Inc.
37 South Washington Street
Rochester, NY 14608
(716) 325-6360
(716) 325-2612 (FAX)

The center is a nonprofit consulting group that concentrates on the Rochester, New York, area. It maintains social and economic data, distributes publications, and conducts research in a variety of government-related areas, including criminal justice.

Publications: Research notes (irregular), reports.

Center for Studies in Criminal Justice (CSCJ)
University of Chicago Law School
1111 East 60th Street
Chicago, IL 60637
(312) 702-9493
(312) 702-0730 (FAX)

The center conducts research projects relating to all aspects of criminal justice—punishment, offenders, and sentencing.

Publications: Books, papers, articles.

Center for the Study of Crime, Delinquency, and Corrections
Southern Illinois University at Carbondale
Mail Code 4504
Carbondale, IL 62901
(618) 453-5701
(618) 453-6377 (FAX)

This is a research center that provides information on crime control, criminal justice education and training, criminal justice history, and crime prevention.

Publications: Journal articles, training manuals, and books.

Constitutional Rights Foundation (CRF)
601 South Kingsley Drive
Los Angeles, CA 90005

(213) 487-5590
(213) 386-0459 (FAX)

Funded with public and private money from a wide variety of sources, this foundation produces educational programs and materials aimed at educating young people about the legal system.

Publications: Bill of Rights in Action (quarterly); *Letters of Liberty; Criminal Justice in America; International Law in a Global Age; Law in Social Studies Series;* games; lesson plans; program guides; filmstrips.

Correctional Education Association (CEA)
4380 Forbes Boulevard
Lanham, MD 20706
(800) 783-1232

This organization has a diverse membership composed of educators, administrators, corrections officials, counselors, librarians, and others who want to improve the quality of programs and staff in the area of correctional education.

Publications: CEA News and Notes; Directory of Correctional Educators (annual); *Yearbook of Correctional Educators; Journal of Correctional Education* (quarterly); *Learning behind Bars; Selected Educational Programs in Prisons, Jails, and Juvenile Facilities; Standards for Adult and Juvenile Correctional Educational Programs.*

Correctional Service Federation—U.S.A. (CSF/USA)
436 West Wisconsin Avenue, Room 500
Milwaukee, WI 53203
(414) 271-2512
(414) 271-4605 (FAX)

This agency focuses on the rehabilitation of offenders and disseminates information on the subject.

Publications: Directory, newsletter.

Crime and Justice Foundation (CJF)
95 Berkeley Street, Suite 202
Boston, MA 02116
(617) 426-9800
(617) 338-1054 (FAX)
e-mail: candjf@aol.com

This is a nonprofit, private group that aims to encourage understanding of the workings of the criminal justice system.

Publications: Perspective (newsletter); data; technical reports; *Comparative Analysis of Standards for the Adult Correctional Agencies; Comparative Analysis of Standards for Juvenile Probation and Aftercare Services;* training and policy manuals.

Crime Prevention and Criminal Justice Branch
Centre for Social Development and Humanitarian Affairs
Department of Economic and Social Affairs
United Nations, Room E1233
P.O. Box 500
A-1400
Vienna, Austria
26 31 42 72
26 31 42 69

As part of the United Nations, this branch collects and disseminates international crime information and aims to develop international criminal justice and crime prevention guidelines.

Publications: Crime Prevention and Criminal Justice Newsletter; International Review of Criminal Policy (annual); proceedings of UN crime congresses.

Crime Stoppers International (CSI)
P.O. Box 30413
Albuquerque, NM 87190-0413
(800) 245-0009

Regional crime stoppers programs exist in the United States and Canada. They provide information on, and rewards for information that leads to solving, significant crimes in their areas.

Criminal Justice Center
Sam Houston State University
Huntsville, TX 77341
(409) 294-1635
(409) 294-1653 (FAX)

The center is funded in part with federal and state money. It oversees an academic program and provides continuing education for judges, attorneys, and law enforcement personnel.

Criminal Justice Research and Training Center
Criminal Justice Division
Box 19595
University of Texas at Arlington
Arlington, TX 76019
(817) 273-3320
(817) 272-5673 (FAX)

The center conducts research, surveys, and training programs and provides assistance to agencies involved in criminal justice.

Publications: Surveys, training manuals, a crime lab operations manual.

Delaware Center for Justice
501 Shipley Street
Wilmington, DE 19801
(302) 658-7174
(302) 658-7170 (FAX)

The center has a broad interest in the criminal justice system of the state of Delaware and provides public education on a variety of criminal justice issues.

Publications: Criminal Justice Bibliography for Delaware; Study of Women's Correctional Institutions (Delaware); Delaware Correctional Standards and Goals; Delaware Basics Study; data; bibliographies; standards; reprints.

Delaware Humanities Forum
1812 Newport Gap Pike
Wilmington, DE 19808
(302) 633-2400
(302) 633-1888 (FAX)
e-mail: hhofmann@strauss.udel.edu

This organization, funded by the National Endowment for the Humanities, supports programs in a broad spectrum of the humanities, including criminal justice.

Publications: Newsletter (quarterly).

Families Against Mandatory Minimums Foundation (FAMM)
1001 Pennsylvania Avenue, N.W., Suite 200-S
Washington, DC 20004
(202) 457-5790
(202) 457-8564 (FAX)

e-mail: FAMM@ix.netcom.com
homepage: http://www.famm.org

This organization, founded in 1991, aims to overturn mandatory minimum sentencing laws for convicted criminals.

Publications: FAMM-gram (biennial).

Friends Outside (FO)
3031 Tischway, Suite 507
San Jose, CA 95128
(408) 985-8807
(408) 985-8839 (FAX)

Helping former convicts successfully reintegrate into society, fighting crime, and fighting poverty are this group's primary objectives. It sponsors programs, support groups, and emergency services.

Publications: Newsletter (monthly).

Houston-Galveston Area Council
3555 Timmons Lane, Suite 500
Houston, TX 77027
(713) 627-3200
(713) 621-8129 (FAX)

This association of 145 local governments directs regional planning and technical services involving area problems, including criminal justice, in a 13-county region of Texas.

Publications: Spectrum (monthly), technical reports, bibliographies, data compilations, annual report, annual work plans.

Illinois Criminal Justice Information Authority
Statistical Analysis Center
120 South Riverside Plaza, Suite 1016
Chicago, IL 60606-3997
(312) 793-8550
(312) 793-8422 (FAX)

This organization concentrates on crime, corrections, and courts in the state of Illinois. It answers inquiries, conducts seminars, and maintains statistical information that is available to the public.

Publications: Compiler (bimonthly), data compilations, books, software.

International Association of Addictions and Offender Counseling (IAAOC)
c/o American Counseling Association
5999 Stevenson Avenue
Alexandria, VA 22304-3300
(800) 364-2262
(800) 473-2329 (FAX)

This group aims to improve rehabilitation programs for offenders and to better the working conditions of public offender counseling staffs.

Publications: IAAOC Report (quarterly); *Journal of Addictions and Offender Counseling* (semiannual).

International Association of Correctional Officers (IACO)
1333 South Wabash
Box 53
Chicago, IL 60605
(312) 996-5401
(312) 413-0458 (FAX)

This organization is made up of many members interested in improving all aspects of corrections, developing new services, and encouraging cooperation among corrections personnel.

Publications: Keeper's Voice Magazine, pamphlets, brochures.

International Society of Crime Prevention Practitioners (ISCPP)
1696 Connor Drive
Pittsburgh, PA 15129-9035
(412) 655-1600
(412) 655-1665 (FAX)

The ISCPP is made up of professionals from around the world who are interested in advancing crime prevention practices through dialogue and training.

Publications: Practitioner (bimonthly); *Basic Crime Prevention Curriculum* (annual).

Inter-University Consortium for Political and Social Research (ICPSR)
426 Thompson
Room 4080, Institute for Social Research
Ann Arbor, MI 48109
(313) 764-2570

(313) 764-8041 (FAX)
e-mail: netmail@icpsr.umich.edu
homepage: http://www.icpsr.umich.edu

This organization—housed within the Institute for Social Research (ISR) at the University of Michigan—gathers, disseminates, and analyzes data on social sciences. More than 300 universities are members.

Justice Research and Statistics Association (JRSA)
444 North Capitol Street, N.W., Suite 445
Washington, DC 20001
(202) 624-8560
(202) 624-5269 (FAX)
e-mail: cjinfo@jrsa.org

This association of professionals in the area of criminal justice aims to improve the collection, analysis, and distribution of criminal justice statistics.

Publications: Directory of Criminal Justice Issues in the States (annual); *JRSA Forum* (quarterly).

Kansas Bureau of Investigation
Statistical Analysis Center
1620 Tyler
Topeka, KS 66612
(913) 232-6000

The center maintains criminal justice data on the state of Kansas and has a missing persons database, probation database, and other information systems.

Publications: Criminal Justice Directory for Kansas; Annual Juvenile Report; Employment and Expenditures in Criminal Justice; Traffic Safety; Annual Crime in Kansas; Missing Children Bulletin.

Kansas City Crime Commission
106 West 11th Street, Suite 1430
Kansas City, MO 64105
(816) 421-8102
(816) 421-5055 (FAX)

The commission aims to encourage public interest in crime prevention, distribute crime data and information, aid law enforcement agencies, and conduct research in criminology in the Kansas City area.

Kentucky Department of Corrections
State Office Building
Frankfort, KY 40601
(502) 564-4360
(502) 564-5642 (FAX)

Criminal psychology, crime prevention, and correctional programs in Kentucky form the focus of this agency.

Publications: Periodic reports.

**Louisiana Commission on Law Enforcement
and the Administration of Criminal Justice**
1885 Wooddale Boulevard, Room 708
Baton Rouge, LA 70806
(504) 925-4418
(504) 925-1998 (FAX)

This commission administers federal money from the Office of Juvenile Justice and Delinquency Prevention, crime victim funds, and other sources. Money goes to research, information systems, juvenile crime prevention, victims, and state prisons.

Publications: Juvenile Justice Data Book (annual); *Louisiana Statute Digest; Louisiana Jail Standards;* technical studies.

Missouri Department of Public Safety
P.O. Box 749
Jefferson City, MO 65102
(573) 751-4905
(573) 751-5399 (FAX)
homepage: http://www.dps.state.mo.us

This agency receives funding through several pieces of federal legislation and focuses primarily on criminal justice in the state of Missouri.

Publications: Crime prevention brochures.

Monroe County Public Safety Laboratory
Public Safety Building, Room 524
150 Plymouth Avenue South
Rochester, NY 14614
(716) 428-5678
(716) 428-5834 (FAX)

This crime laboratory serves the western New York area and conducts training for law enforcement officials, scientific research, and testing associated with forensic science.

Narcotic Educational Foundation of America
24509 Walnut Street, Suite 201
Santa Clarita, CA 91321
(805) 287-0198
(805) 287-9825 (FAX)

The foundation is a nonprofit organization that encourages the prevention of drug abuse and crime through education.

Publications: Motion pictures, brochures, booklets, pamphlets, posters, and reference sheets.

National Center for Juvenile Justice (NCJJ)
710 5th Avenue, Suite 3000
Pittsburgh, PA 15219
(412) 227-6950
(412) 227-6955 (FAX)

This organization collects juvenile justice statistics, encourages research in juvenile justice, assists juvenile courts, and develops juvenile justice–related programs.

Publications: Juvenile Court Statistics (annual); *KINDEX: An Index to Periodical Literature Concerning Children* (annual); studies; reports.

National Center for Neighborhood Enterprise
1367 Connecticut Avenue, N.W.
Washington, DC 20036
(202) 331-1103
(202) 296-1541 (FAX)

Although this organization does not deal exclusively with crime, the group stresses community development as a weapon against crime.

Publications: Policy Dispatch (monthly), research summaries, articles, reprints, papers.

National Center on Institutions and Alternatives (NCIA)
635 Slaters Lane, Suite G-100
Alexandria, VA 22314

(703) 684-0373
(703) 684-6037 (FAX)
e-mail: ncia@itc.apc.org

The center aims to improve conditions of incarceration and to look into alternatives to mental hospitals and current prison structures.

Publications: Darkness Closes In: National Study of Jail Suicides; Specialized Foster Care for Hard-to-Place Juveniles; Scared Straight: Second Look.

National Coalition for Jail Reform
c/o Rutgers University
School of Criminal Justice
15 Washington Street
Newark, NJ 07102
(201) 648-5204

This coalition is made up of approximately 40 organizations with an interest in jail reform.

Publications: How To Look at Your Jail; Pretrial Detention; Waiting for Justice; The Public Inebriate; Juveniles and Jail; Jail: The New Mental Institution; Jail Is Not the Answer; reports; reviews; journal articles; brochures; data; reprints.

National Criminal Justice Reference Service (NCJRS)
Box 6000
Rockville, MD 20850
(301) 251-5500 (all functions)
(800) 851-3420 (National Institute of Justice)
(800) 638-8736 (Juvenile Justice Clearinghouse)
(800) 732-3277 (Justice Statistics Clearinghouse)

A major, federally funded national clearinghouse for crime information of all kinds.

Publications: NIJ Reports (bimonthly); *Document Retrieval Index (DRI); Selected Libraries in Microfiche; Topical Bibliographies; Publications of the National Institute of Justice; International Summaries; Directory of Criminal Justice Information Sources; Books in Brief;* topical booklets.

National Juvenile Detention Association (NJDA)
c/o Eastern Kentucky University
301 Perkins Building

Richmond, KY 40475
(606) 622-6259
(606) 622-2333 (FAX)
e-mail: njdadeh@aol.com

This organization encourages training, education, and communication among juvenile detention facilities.

Publications: Journal for Juvenile Justice and Detention Services (semiannual); *NJDA News* (quarterly); *NJDA Publications* (quarterly); videotapes.

National Office for Social Responsibility
in the Private Sector, Inc.
222 South Washington Street
Alexandria, VA 22314
(703) 549-5305
(703) 836-7269 (FAX)

Funded by the Office of Juvenile Justice and Delinquency Prevention, this office tries to link public and private resources for criminal justice, juvenile justice, and corrections.

National Prison Project (NPP)
1875 Connecticut Avenue, N.W., Suite 410
Washington, DC 20009
(202) 234-4830
(202) 234-4890 (FAX)

This organization lobbies for, and provides educational programs to promote, improved prison conditions and alternative sentencing methods.

Publications: National Prison Project Journal (quarterly); *Inmates and Officers, AIDS and Prisons: The Facts; Prisoner's Assistance Directory; TB and Prisons: The Facts; Status Report.*

New Jersey Association on Correction (NJAC)
986 South Broad Street
Trenton, NJ 08611
(609) 396-8900
(609) 396-8999 (FAX)

This is a voluntary and nonprofit group dedicated to directly assisting both victims and offenders of sexual assault and domestic violence. Through its Public Education and Policy division, NJAC aims to improve the criminal justice system.

Publications: NJAC News and Views (quarterly); Alternative Sentencing for Corrections: A Manual; position papers; research reports.

New York State Division of Criminal Justice Services (DCJS)
Executive Park Tower
Stuyvesant Plaza, Tower Building
Albany, NY 12203
(518) 457-6113
(518) 485-7593 (FAX)

This division provides assistance and information on criminal justice in the state of New York to agencies and officials for the purpose of formulating policy. It also serves as a central location for a large amount of criminal justice data and distributes federal money.

Publications: Criminal Law Review (monthly); *Crime and Justice Annual Report; County Criminal Justice Profiles* (annual); *Felony Processing: Indictment through Disposition* (quarterly); *Comprehensive Juvenile Justice Plan* (annual); periodic reports. A complete publications list is available.

Ohio Statistical Analysis Center
Governor's Office of Criminal Justice Services
Ohio Department of Development
400 East Town Street, Suite 120
Columbus, OH 43215-4242
(614) 466-7782
(614) 466-0308 (FAX)

The center is funded in part by the Bureau of Justice Statistics and distributes data and research on criminal justice.

Publications: Research summaries, data, bibliographies, directories. A full publications list is available.

Ohio Violence Prevention Center
Governor's Office of Criminal Justice Services
Ohio Department of Development
400 East Town Street, Suite 120
Columbus, OH 43215-4242
(614) 466-7782
(614) 466-0308 (FAX)

This is a new agency dedicated to the prevention of violence in the state of Ohio. It is housed under the same office as the Ohio Statistical Analysis Center.

Osborne Association (OA)
135 East 15th Street
New York, NY 10003
(212) 673-6633
(212) 979-7652 (FAX)

This association advises interested criminal justice agencies and aims to cut the population in correctional institutions. It also provides support services to ex-convicts, people on probation, and parolees.

Police Executive Research Forum
1120 Connecticut Avenue, N.W., Suite 930
Washington, DC 20036
(202) 466-7820
(202) 466-7826 (FAX)

This group aims to improve police service through professionalism, research, experimentation, and debate on criminal justice issues.

Publications: Problem-Solving Quarterly; Subject to Debate (bimonthly newsletter); *Asset Forfeiture Bulletin.*

Prison Fellowship Ministries (PFM)
P.O. Box 17500
Washington, DC 20041
(703) 478-0100

This organization seeks to motivate Christians to minister to inmates, ex-inmates, and victims of crimes and sponsors a variety of seminars and other programs inside prisons.

Publications: Convicted: New Hope for Ending America's Crime Crisis; Jubilee (monthly); *Kingdoms in Conflict; Justice Report; Life Sentence; Loving God.*

Prison Ministry of Yokefellow's International
P.O. Box 482
Rising Sun, MD 21911
(410) 658-2661

A religious group that tries to develop small groups among inmates, to encourage improved corrections methods, and to support the establishment of local halfway houses.

Publications: Yokefellow News (quarterly), brochures, pamphlets.

Safer Society Program and Press (SSPP)
P.O. Box 340
Brandon, VT 05733-0340
(802) 247-3132
(802) 247-4233 (FAX)

This agency's sole purpose is to address sexual abuse problems and provide aid to both offenders and victims. It is sponsored by the New York State Council of Churches.

Publications: Adults as Molested Children: A Survival Manual for Women and Men; Treating the Male Victim of Sexual Assault: Issues and Intervention Strategies; The Youthful Sex Offender: The Rationale and Goals of Early Intervention and Treatment; self-help and other books; audiocassettes; videocassettes.

Search Group, Inc. (SEARCH)
7311 Greenhaven Drive, Suite 145
Sacramento, CA 95831
(916) 392-2550
(916) 392-8440 (FAX)
BBS: telnet search.org

This nonprofit organization receives money from the Bureau of Justice Statistics. It operates a publicly accessible electronic bulletin board that contains a variety of criminal justice information and addresses of other World Wide Web sites of interest.

Publications: Interface (semiannual), reports, reprints, journal articles, bibliographies.

**Sellin Center for Studies in Criminology
and Criminal Law (SCSCCL)**
University of Pennsylvania
3733 Spruce Street, Room 437
Philadelphia, PA 19104
(215) 898-7411
(215) 898-3098 (Library)
(215) 898-6590 (FAX)

The center is mainly a research-oriented criminology group and is supported largely through funding from the National Institute of Justice.

Publications: Criminal Violence; Criminal Violence and Race: A Selected Bibliography; Criminal Violence: Biological Correlates and Determinants: A Selected Bibliography; Criminal Violence: Psychological Correlates and Determinants: A Selected Bibliography; Domestic Criminal Violence: A Selected Bibliography; The Violent Offender in the Criminal Justice System: A Selected Bibliography; Evaluating Criminology; Criminology Index; Delinquency in a Birth Cohort.

The Sentencing Project (TSP)
918 F Street, N.W., Suite 501
Washington, DC 20004
(202) 628-0871
(202) 628-1091 (FAX)

This organization is interested in educating people about the sentencing procedures of the criminal justice system and in encouraging officials to consider alternative sentencing programs.

Publications: Americans behind Bars: A Comparison of International Rates of Incarceration; Americans behind Bars: One Year Later; Young Black Men and the Criminal Justice System: A Growing National Problem; reports.

Shoplifters Anonymous (SA)
380 North Broadway, Suite 206
Jericho, NY 11753
(516) 932-0165
(800) 848-9595
(516) 932-9393 (FAX)

This group hopes to reform adults and juveniles who have shoplifting problems through education programs, counseling, and support groups.

Publications: Newsletter (quarterly).

TIPS Program
Educational Resource and Information Center
606 Delsea Drive
Sewell, NJ 08080

(609) 582-7000
(609) 582-4206 (FAX)

This program is designed to teach students in grades K-8 how to resolve conflicts and avoid becoming crime victims. Staff members train instructors how to implement individual programs in classrooms.

University of Wisconsin–Madison
Law Library, Reference Desk
975 Bascom Mall
Madison, WI 53706
(608) 262-3394
(608) 262-2775 (FAX)

The library provides reference information to residents of Wisconsin on the improvement of that state's criminal justice system. The library has absorbed the former Criminal Justice Reference and Information Center and all of its holdings.

University of Wisconsin–Platteville
Elton S. Karmann Library
1 University Plaza
Platteville, WI 53818-3099
(608) 342-1688
(608) 342-1645 (FAX)
e-mail: reference@uwplatt.edu

This library holds criminal justice materials, government publications, and many other materials, and it accepts reference inquiries via e-mail.

Publications: List of periodicals; *University of Wisconsin System Index to Master's Theses and Seminar Papers—University Cluster Institutions;* SWAMI (Southwest Wisconsin Audiovisual Media Index); SWULP (Southwest Wisconsin Union List of Periodicals).

**USCCCN National Clearinghouse
on Satanic Crime in America**
P.O. Box 1092
South Orange, NJ 07079
(908) 549-2599
e-mail: uscccn@haven.ios.com

This group provides information to the public and law enforcement agencies on occult-influenced crimes against animals and humans.

Publications: The American Focus on Satanic Crime; The USCCCN Focus; The American Focus on Rape Series; The New Youth Pastor's Handbook; White Collar Crime 101 Prevention Handbook; The Occult Awareness Training Manual on Satanism.

Volunteers in Prevention, Probation, Prisons (VIP)
163 Madison Avenue, Suite 120
Detroit, MI 48226
(313) 964-1110
(313) 964-1145 (FAX)

This group encourages volunteer programs in criminal justice that address prevention, parole, prosecution, prison, and probation.

Publications: Reprints, motion pictures, books, reports, brochures, tapes, leaflets.

Wisconsin Department of Justice
Division of Law Enforcement Services
Crime Information Bureau
P.O. Box 2718
Madison, WI 53701
(608) 266-7314

This state agency is primarily concerned with missing persons information and adult criminal records. It operates a computerized system for the state's criminal justice agencies.

Publications: Law Enforcement Bulletin (monthly).

Wisconsin Office of Justice Assistance
30 West Mifflin Street, Suite 330
Madison, WI 53702
(608) 266-3323

This agency is funded in part by the Bureau of Justice Statistics (BJS) and through several federal acts. It stresses technical aid and service. Areas it addresses include the entire criminal justice system and statistics.

Publications: Wisconsin Juvenile Justice Improvement Plan (annual); *Sexual Assaults in Wisconsin* (annual); *Uniform Crime Reports* (annual/semiannual); *Jail Reports* (annual).

Federal Agencies

The United States Department of Justice

The United States Department of Justice (see Figure 5.1) employs thousands of people and encompasses a number of federal crime agencies. It is responsible for a wide variety of activities in the fight against crime—investigations, enforcing immigration and drug laws, crime prevention, and law enforcement, to name a few. Its attorneys represent the United States in Supreme Court cases and provide legal counsel to members of the executive branch. The president of the United States selects an attorney general to head the department. Following is a partial list of offices and agencies, specifically related to crime, contained inside the Department of Justice.

Office of the Attorney General
Department of Justice
Tenth Street and Constitution Avenue, N.W.
Washington, DC 20530
(202) 514-2000

Appointed by the president, the Attorney General heads the Department of Justice, represents the United States in legal matters, and gives legal advice to the executive branch of the federal government.

Drug Enforcement Administration (DEA)
Public Affairs Section
Department of Justice
Washington, DC 20537
(202) 307-7977

Four drug enforcement agencies merged in 1973 to form the DEA. The DEA conducts operations around the country involving the enforcement of federal drug laws. Interstate and international trafficking, manufacture and distribution of controlled substances, and seizing assets linked to drug trafficking constitute its major duties. It sometimes works with other law

U.S. DEPARTMENT OF JUSTICE

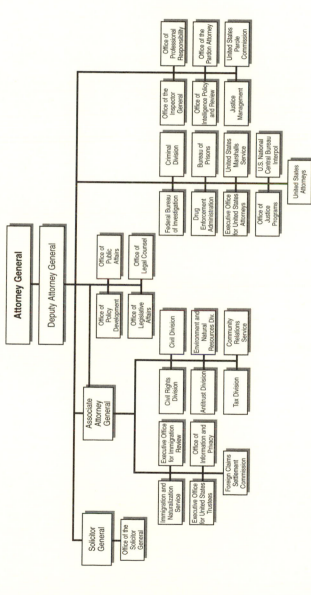

Figure 5.1   U.S. Department of Justice

enforcement agencies around the world and supplies them with training and information. The El Paso Intelligence Center (EPIC), a drug intelligence center, is managed by the DEA.

Federal Bureau of Investigation (FBI)
Office of Public Affairs
J. Edgar Hoover Building
Ninth Street and Pennsylvania Avenue, N.W.
Washington, DC 20535
(202) 324-3000

Established in 1908, the FBI consists of 10 divisions and has 56 field offices. Its duties include collecting evidence and tracking down witnesses connected with cases involving violations of federal law. The FBI frequently assists state and local law enforcement agencies in investigations, forensics, and fingerprint identification. The following areas constitute its main focus: drugs, violent crime, white-collar crime, foreign counterintelligence, and counterterrorism.

Federal Bureau of Prisons
Office of the General Counsel
320 First Street, N.W.
Washington, DC 20534
(202) 307-3198

This agency establishes and oversees federal prisons around the country. Connected with the bureau, the National Institute of Corrections provides support to state and local corrections agencies.

U.S. Marshals Service
Office of Policy and Communications
Department of Justice
600 Army Navy Drive, Suite 1260
Arlington, VA 22202
(202) 307-9065

Established in 1789, the U.S. Marshals Service employs more than 3,500 people and operates more than 400 offices in the United States and its territories. The service is in part a security agency, providing protection for courts and judges. Marshals also guard federal prisoners in custody and in transport, confiscate and sell property of drug traffickers, operate the Federal Witness Security Program, and arrest federal fugitives.

United States Parole Commission
Office of the Chairman
Department of Justice
5550 Friendship Boulevard
Chevy Chase, MD 20815
(301) 492-5990

The nine members of the United States Parole Commission, appointed by the president, grant and supervise parole for federal prisoners. The commission may also change or revoke parole. The Comprehensive Crime Control Act of 1984 abolished the commission and, as of November 1, 1997, it will cease to exist.

Community Relations Service (CRS)
Department of Justice
5550 Friendship Boulevard, Suite 330
Chevy Chase, MD 20815
(301) 492-5929

Created under the Civil Rights Act of 1964, the Community Relations Service aims to resolve racial conflicts arising in communities around the country. Members of the service, based in ten regional and three field offices throughout the United States, often intervene directly in local disputes. Mediators become involved on the service's initiative or at the request of state and local officials. When appropriate, the CRS seeks to cooperate with other state, local, and private organizations.

Office of Justice Programs (OJP)
633 Indiana Avenue, N.W.
Washington, DC 20531
(202) 307-0781

The Office of Justice Programs encompasses five program bureaus, whose duties include collecting and analyzing statistics and developing programs to prevent and fight crime. An assistant attorney general oversees the office. State agencies receive grants from the OJP for drug control, juvenile justice programs, and other anticrime programs. In February 1995, the OJP established the Victim Compensation Grant Program, which provides crime victims with money and assistance.

• **Bureau of Justice Assistance (BJA).** As part of the Office of Justice Programs, the BJA aids state and local law enforcement by providing money and other assistance. In addition, it operates national crime prevention programs such as the Regional Information Sharing System and the National Crime Prevention Campaign.

• **Bureau of Justice Statistics (BJS)** [(800) 732-3277]. The BJS collects and publishes statistics on crime across the nation. The National Crime Victimization Survey, conducted by the BJS, is one of two main sources of national crime data (along with the FBI's *Uniform Crime Reports*). Through interviews with U.S. households, the bureau compiles its crime victimization rates.

The bureau also publishes bulletins and special reports, updates other branches of government on pertinent crime data, and helps state governments develop crime statistics programs. People interested in reference information about crime statistics should contact the Justice Statistics Clearinghouse at (800) 732-3277. The Drugs and Crime Data Center and Clearinghouse, managed by the BJS, provides information and data on drugs and crime. It can be reached at (800) 666-3332 or Box 6000, Rockville, MD 20850.

• **National Institute of Justice (NIJ).** The NIJ, contained within the Office of Justice Programs, is a research and development agency. Its employees research effective crime policy and sponsor programs to support others involved in criminal justice. The institute also evaluates new and existing anticrime programs and publishes parts of its research.

• **Office of Juvenile Justice and Delinquency Prevention (OJJDP).** Juvenile crime and missing and exploited children are the two main focuses of this agency. Created as a result of the Juvenile Justice and Delinquency Prevention Act of 1974, the office is divided into five divisions. Each division takes responsibility for different aspects of the office's mission, which include a grant program for states, prevention, funding innovative nonprofit organizations, providing training programs for those involved in criminal justice, and distributing information.

The Juvenile Justice Clearinghouse, which maintains information on juvenile delinquency and justice, can be contacted at (800) 638-8736.

In 1984, the Missing Children's Assistance Act created the Missing Children's Program, run by the OJJDP, which involves researching and collecting information on missing and exploited children.

• **Office for Victims of Crime (OVC).** A large part of this agency's focus is carrying out the Victims of Crime Act of 1984. One of the act's major provisions is the creation of the Crime Victims Fund, which receives money collected from convicted federal criminals. States receive this money in grants to assist crime victims with medical costs and other expenses resulting from victimization. Fund money also goes to states for the support of programs that assist crime victims.

The OVC works with other agencies in administering programs for victims of drug-related crimes and tries to coordinate crime victims assistance services nationwide. It funds the National Victims Resources Center, which can be reached at (800) 627-6872.

Immigration and Naturalization Service (INS)
Office of Information
Department of Justice
425 I Street, N.W.
Washington, DC 20536
(202) 514-4316

In addition to processing legal visitors and immigrants to the United States, the INS enforces immigration laws. The agency oversees 21 border patrol sectors, 4 regional administrative offices, 33 districts, and 3 offices abroad. INS officials apprehend and deport illegal aliens and prevent them from receiving illegal employment and benefits.

Office of the Assistant Attorney General,
Criminal Division
Department of Justice
Tenth Street and Pennsylvania Avenue, N.W.
Washington, DC 20530
(202) 514-2601

The Department of Justice's Criminal Division supervises and applies federal criminal laws. More than 90 attorneys work with the division and are involved in litigating, formulating policy, and giving advice.

Office of the Assistant Attorney General, Environment
and Natural Resources Division
Department of Justice
Tenth Street and Pennsylvania Avenue, N.W.

Washington, DC 20530
(202) 514-2701

This division's main activity in the area of criminal law is the enforcement of civil and criminal environmental law.

Tax Division
Office of the Attorney General
Department of Justice
Tenth Street and Pennsylvania Avenue, N.W.
Washington, DC 20530
(202) 514-2901

Attorneys with the tax division prosecute cases of tax evasion, fraud, delinquency, and other offenses involving revenue laws. In general, the division assists the Internal Revenue Service in legal matters. Organized crime, drug trafficking, and financial corruption are frequent targets.

U.S. Attorneys

One U.S. attorney serves in each federal judicial district in the country. Additional attorneys work in U.S. territories. Appointed by the president, these attorneys prosecute federal criminal cases, represent the United States in civil cases, and assist the government in collecting debts.

Department of the Treasury

The Department of the Treasury also contains several offices that are active in crime control. The Bureau of Alcohol, Tobacco, and Firearms tries to control illegal trafficking in explosives, firearms, cigarettes, alcohol, and pornography. It also aims to ensure that those legally involved in these industries receive adequate protection at both the consumer and retail levels.

U.S. Customs agents monitor imported goods and seize illegal drugs and other contraband when necessary. In addition, they enforce export control laws and try to prevent exports of high-tech illegal weapons.

The main training facility of the Federal Law Enforcement Center is located in Glynco, Georgia. The agency works with more than 70 law enforcement organizations and trains police officers and investigators in basic skills. It also provides a number of specialized training programs, such as programs in law enforcement photography and white-collar crime.

U.S. Secret Service agents protect the president and vice president, as well as their families. The president-elect and vice president-elect, as well as former presidents and their families, also receive Secret Service protection, as do visiting foreign officials and some representatives of the United States traveling abroad. The agents' duties also include investigating monetary fraud of many sorts, including fraudulent use of government benefits and credit card fraud.

Uniform Crime Reporting Programs

The following agencies collect uniform crime reporting data in their respective states.

Alabama Criminal Justice
Information Center
770 Washington Avenue, Suite 350
Montgomery, AL 36130
(205) 242-4900, ext. 225

Arkansas Crime Information Center
One Capitol Mall, 4D-200
Little Rock, AR 72201
(501) 682-2222

Bureau of Criminal Statistics
Department of Justice
P.O. Box 903427
Sacramento, CA 94203
(916) 227-3554

Bureau of Identification
Illinois State Police
726 South College Street
Springfield, IL 62704
(217) 782-8263

Bureau of Research and Development
Pennsylvania State Police
1800 Elmerton Avenue
Harrisburg, PA 17110
(717) 783-5536

Central Records Division
Maryland State Police Department
1711 Belmont Avenue
Baltimore, MD 21244
(410) 298-3883

Crime Reporting and Field Services
State Bureau of Investigation
Division of Criminal Information
407 North Blount Street
Raleigh, NC 27601
(919) 733-3171

Criminal Identification Bureau
Department of Law Enforcement
700 South Stratford Drive
Meridian, ID 83680
(208) 327-7130

Criminal Information Services
Nevada Highway Patrol
555 Wright Way
Carson City, NV 89711
(702) 687-5713

Data Processing Division
Metropolitan Police Department
300 Indiana Avenue, N.W.
Washington, DC 20001
(202) 727-4301

Georgia Crime Information Center
Georgia Bureau of Investigation
P.O. Box 370748
Decatur, GA 30037
(404) 244-2614

Information Services Section
Bureau of Criminal Investigation
Attorney General's Office
P.O. Box 1054
Bismarck, ND 58502
(701) 221-5500

Iowa Department of Public Safety
Wallace State Office Building
Des Moines, IA 50319
(515) 281-8422

Kansas Bureau of Investigation
1620 Southwest Tyler Street
Topeka, KS 66612
(913) 232-6000

Kentucky State Police
Information Services Branch
1250 Louisville Road
Frankfort, KY 40601
(502) 227-8783

Law Enforcement Data Systems Division
Oregon Department of State Police
400 Public Service Building
Salem, OR 97310
(503) 378-3057

Louisiana Commission on Law Enforcement
1885 Wooddale Boulevard, 12th Floor
Baton Rouge, LA 70806
(504) 925-4440

Montana Board of Crime Control
303 North Roberts
Helena, MT 59620
(406) 444-3604

Office of Information Systems Management
Minnesota Department of Public Safety
444 Cedar Street
Suite 100-H, Town Square
Saint Paul, MN 55101
(612) 296-7589

Office of Justice Assistance
222 State Street, 2nd Floor
Madison, WI 53703
(608) 266-3323

Records Management Division
Department of State Police
P.O. Box 27472
Richmond, VA 23261-7472
(804) 674-2023

Rhode Island State Police
P.O. Box 185
North Scituate, RI 02857
(401) 647-3311

South Carolina Law Enforcement Division
P.O. Box 21398
Columbia, SC 29221-1398
(803) 896-7162

South Dakota Statistical Analysis Center
c/o 500 East Capitol Avenue
Pierre, SD 57501
(605) 773-6310

State Bureau of Identification
P.O. Box 430
Dover, DE 19903
(302) 739-5875

Statistical Services
New York State Division of
  Criminal Justice Services
8th Floor, Mail Room
Executive Park Tower Building, Stuyvesant Plaza
Albany, NY 12203
(518) 457-8381

Uniform Crime Report
Division of State Police
10 Hazen Drive
Concord, NH 03305
(603) 271-2509

Uniform Crime Reporting
Arizona Department of Public Safety
P.O. Box 6638
Phoenix, AZ 85005
(602) 223-2263

Uniform Crime Reporting
Colorado Bureau of Investigation
690 Kipling Street
Denver, CO 80215
(303) 239-4300

Uniform Crime Reporting
Criminal Records Section
Division of Criminal Investigation
316 West 22nd Street
Cheyenne, WY 82002
(307) 777-7625

Uniform Crime Reporting
Division of State Police
P.O. Box 7068
West Trenton, NJ 08628-0068
(609) 882-2000, ext. 2392

Uniform Crime Reporting
Utah Department of Public Safety
4501 South 2700 West
Salt Lake City, UT 84119
(801) 965-4445

Uniform Crime Reporting Bureau
Crime Records Division
Texas Department of Public Safety
P.O. Box 4143
Austin, TX 78765-4143
(512) 465-2091

Uniform Crime Reporting Division
Maine State Police
36 Hospital Street, Station #42
Augusta, ME 04333
(207) 624-7004

Uniform Crime Reporting Program
294 Colony Street
Meriden, CT 06450
(203) 238-6653

Uniform Crime Reporting Program
Crime Prevention Program
Department of the Attorney General
810 Richards Street, Suite 701
Honolulu, HI 96813
(808) 586-1416

Uniform Crime Reporting Program
Washington Association of Sheriffs and Police Chiefs
P.O. Box 826
Olympia, WA 98507
(206) 586-3221

Uniform Crime Reporting Program
725 Jefferson Road
South Charleston, WV 25309
(304) 746-2159

Uniform Crime Reporting Section
Department of Public Safety Information System
5700 East Tudor Road
Anchorage, AK 99507
(907) 269-5659

Uniform Crime Reporting Section
Michigan State Police
7150 Harris Drive
Lansing, MI 48913
(517) 322-5542

Uniform Crime Reporting Section
Nebraska Commission on Law Enforcement
  and Criminal Justice
P.O. Box 94946
Lincoln, NE 68509
(402) 471-3982

Uniform Crime Reporting Section
Oklahoma State Bureau of Investigation
6600 North Harvey, Suite 300
Oklahoma City, OK 73116
(405) 848-6724

Uniform Crime Reports
Crime Reporting Unit
CIS, 5th Floor
Massachusetts State Police
1010 Commonwealth Avenue
Boston, MA 02215
(617) 566-4500

Uniform Crime Reports Section
Special Services Bureau
Florida Department of Law Enforcement
P.O. Box 1489
Tallahassee, FL 32302
(904) 487-1179

Vermont Department of Public Safety
P.O. Box 189
Waterbury, VT 05676
(802) 244-8786

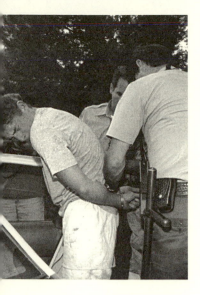

Print Resources

The many books, reference books, government documents, and periodicals in this section constitute a wide spectrum of resources on many aspects of crime, written from a variety of perspectives and intended for different audiences. Books and government documents published before 1980 are not included unless they played a significant role in history.

Books

Albanese, Jay S. *Myths and Realities of Crime and Justice,* 2d ed. Niagara Falls, NY: Apocalypse Publishing Co., 1986.

This book offers analysis of crime and criminal justice practices in the United States.

Allen, Bud, and Diana Bosta. *Games Criminals Play: How You Can Profit by Knowing Them.* Susanville, CA: Rae John Publishers, 1981.

An examination of common criminal swindles and how people can protect themselves from them.

Allen, Harry E., et al. *Crime and Punishment: An Introduction to Criminology.* New York and London: Free Press and Collier Macmillan, 1981.

Subjects addressed in this book include corrections, criminals, and the criminal justice system.

215

Alloway, David Nelson. *A Survey of the Crime Problem in America,* rev. ed. Lexington, MA: Ginn Custom Publishers, 1981.
This book serves as an overview of crime problems in the United States.

American Society of Newspaper Editors, American Newspaper Publishers Association Foundation (ANPA). *Free Press and Fair Trial.* Washington, DC: ANPA Foundation, 1982.
The conflicts and balance between the constitutional rights of the press's freedom to report and a defendant's right to a fair trial form the focus of this book.

Athens, Lonnie H. *The Creation of Dangerous Violent Criminals.* New York: Routledge, 1989.
This book focuses on psychological factors that contribute to violent crime and criminals and would be of use to those who are interested in criminal psychology.

Bartol, Curt R. *Criminal Behavior: A Psychosocial Approach.* Englewood Cliffs, NJ: Prentice Hall, 1980.
An academic analysis of criminal behavior and psychology.

Bazelon, David L. *Questioning Authority: Justice and Criminal Law.* New York: Knopf, 1987.
Criminal liability, insanity, and criminal justice are among the topics discussed in this book.

Bean, Philip, and David Whynes. *Barbara Wootton—Social Science and Public Policy: Essays in Her Honour.* New York: Tavistock Publications, 1986.
The essays in this book address a variety of subjects, including criminal justice, but not all are devoted to crime.

Bennett, Georgette. *Crimewarps: The Future of Crime in America.* New York: Anchor Books, 1989.
A book of interest to crime forecasters that examines possible future trends in crime in the United States.

Bennett, Vivo, and Cricket Clagett. *1,001 Ways To Avoid Getting Mugged, Murdered, Robbed, Raped, or Ripped Off.* New York: Mason/Charter, 1977.
A thorough investigation of swindles and deceptions commonly used by con artists, with advice on how to prevent oneself from falling victim to them.

Block, Alan A., and William Chambliss. *Organizing Crime.* New York: Elsevier, 1981.
A book that describes various aspects of organized criminal activity.

Blumstein, Alfred, et al. *Criminal Careers and "Career Criminals."* Washington, DC: National Academy Press, 1986.

The crime and criminal behavior analyses in this volume are taken from the Panel on Research on Criminal Careers, the Committee on Research on Law Enforcement and the Administration of Justice, the Commission on Behavioral and Social Sciences Education, and the National Research Council.

Bopp, William J., and James J. Vardalis. *Crimes against Women.* Springfield, IL: Thomas, 1987.
     This book describes crimes committed against women and how to prevent them.

Bouza, Anthony V. *How To Stop Crime.* New York: Plenum Press, 1993.
     A general book concerned with prevention and criminal justice in the fight against crime.

Braithwaite, John. *Corporate Crime in the Pharmaceutical Industry.* London: Routledge and Kegan Paul, 1984.
     Case studies of commercial crimes and corrupt practices in the pharmaceutical industry.

————. *Crime, Shame, and Reintegration.* New York: Cambridge University Press, 1989.
     A book that addresses problems associated with criminals, their crimes, and their rehabilitation into society after the fact.

Brantingham, Paul J., and Patricia Brantingham. *Patterns in Crime.* New York and London: Macmillan and Collier Macmillan, 1984.
     This work describes historical crime patterns.

Bright, Jon. *Crime Prevention in America: A British Perspective.* Chicago: Office of International Criminal Justice, University of Illinois at Chicago, 1992.
     Crime prevention and problems in U.S. inner cities form the focus of this book.

Bursik, Robert J., Jr., and Harold G. Grasmick. *Neighborhoods and Crime: The Dimensions of Effective Community Control.* New York and Toronto: Lexington Books and Maxwell Macmillan Canada, 1993.
     This book addresses problems with and solutions to crime in neighborhoods.

Castleman, Michael. *Crime Free—Stop Your Chances of Being Robbed, Raped, Mugged or Burglarized by 90 Percent: Foolproof Techniques to Protect You, Your Family or Your Business.* New York: Simon and Schuster, 1984.
     This book contains a great deal of information on safety and precautionary measures people can take to reduce their chances of being victimized by crime.

Chambliss, William J. *Exploring Criminology.* New York: Macmillan, 1988.

As part of Macmillan's Criminal Justice series, this book serves as an inquiry into various aspects of criminology.

Chermak, Steven. *Victims in the News: Crime and the American News Media.* Boulder, CO: Westview Press, 1995.
An examination of problems and issues surrounding crime victims in the media.

Citizens Crime Commission of New York City, Regional Plan Association. *Downtown Safety, Security and Economic Development: A Joint Report.* New York: Downtown Research and Development Center, 1985.
A New York report on urban renewal and development, as well as on safety and prevention measures to accompany that renewal and development.

Cohen, Stanley. *Against Criminology.* New Brunswick, NJ: Transaction Books, 1988.
An analytical look at criminology.

————. *Visions of Social Control: Crime, Punishment, and Classification.* New York: Polity Press, 1985.
An analysis of crime and corrections from a social perspective with a focus on prevention and criminal behavior.

Collins, James J., Jr., ed. *Drinking and Crime: Perspectives on the Relationships between Alcohol Consumption and Criminal Behavior.* New York: Guilford Press, 1981.
A compilation of essays that address problems associated with alcohol and criminal behavior. The book is part of the Guilford Alchohol Studies Series.

Conklin, John E. *Criminology.* New York: Macmillan, 1986.
A general look at criminology.

Cooper, H. H. A. *The Hostage-Takers.* Boulder, CO: Paladin Press, 1981.
General subjects addressed in this book include hostages, hostage negotiations, terrorists, police training, and crisis management.

Curtis, Lynn A., ed. *Policies To Prevent Crime: Neighborhood, Family, and Employment Strategies.* Newbury Park, CA: Sage Publications, 1987.
As part of the Annals of the American Academy of Political and Social Science series, this book addresses violent crime and crime prevention.

Davidson, R. N. *Crime and Environment.* New York: St. Martin's Press, 1981.
This book examines the influence of environment on criminal behavior.

Davis, James R. *Street Gangs: Youth, Biker, and Prison Groups.* Dubuque, IA: Kendall/Hunt Publishing Company, 1982.

Gangs, terrorism, violence, and juvenile delinquency are addressed in this book.

Davis, Robert C., Arthur J. Lurigio, and Dennis P. Rosenbaum, eds. *Drugs and the Community: Involving Community Residents in Combatting the Sale of Illegal Drugs.* Springfield, IL: C. C. Thomas, 1993.

A compilation of essays on community anticrime programs, drug enforcement in public housing, drug activity, urban gangs, and other related topics.

Debner, Claudia, and Terry O'Neill, eds. *Crime and Criminals: Opposing Viewpoints.* St. Paul, MN: Greenhaven Press, 1984.

This book presents opposing viewpoints on gun control, white-collar crime, criminal justice, crime prevention, and other subjects.

Dintino, Justin J., and Frederick T. Martens. *Police Intelligence Systems in Crime Control: Maintaining a Delicate Balance in a Liberal Democracy.* Springfield, IL: C. C. Thomas, 1983.

This book examines the role of police, intelligence, and law enforcement in society.

Dobson, Terry, with Judith Shepherd-Chow. *Safe and Alive: How To Protect Yourself, Your Family, and Your Property against Violence.* Los Angeles: J. P. Tarcher, 1981.

This book contains advice on how to secure oneself and one's possessions to avoid becoming a crime victim.

Doleschal, Eugene. *Prevention of Crime and Delinquency.* Davis, CA: International Dialogue Press, 1984.

This work is part of the Dialogue Books series, and its main focus is on crime prevention.

Dudley, William, ed. *Crime and Criminals: Opposing Viewpoints.* San Diego, CA: Greenhaven Press, 1989.

In this work, opposing arguments are presented on the causes of crime, gun control, treatment of criminals, and other crime-related issues.

Eitzen, D. Stanley, and Doug A. Timmer. *Criminology: Crime and Criminal Justice.* New York: Wiley, 1985.

This book takes a general look at crime and criminal justice.

Ekerstrvm, Malin. *Crooks and Squares: Lifestyles of Thieves and Addicts in Comparison to Conventional People.* New Brunswick, NJ: Transaction Books, 1985.

Examines psychological aspects of deviant and criminal behavior in comparison with behavior that is considered normal.

Evans, David J., and David Herbert, eds. *The Geography of Crime.* New York: Routledge, 1989.

Environmental and psychological factors in connection with crime prevention are discussed.

Eysenck, Hans J., and Gisli H. Gudjonsson. *The Causes and Cures of Criminality.* New York: Plenum Press, 1989.
 This book addresses psychological factors connected to preventing crime and rehabilitating criminals.

Fairchild, Erika S., and Vincent J. Webb, eds. *The Politics of Crime and Criminal Justice.* Beverly Hills, CA: Sage Publications, 1985.
 Political aspects of criminal justice are discussed. The book is part of the Perspectives in Criminal Justice series.

Farrington, David P., Lloyd E. Ohlin, and James Q. Wilson. *Understanding and Controlling Crime: Toward a New Research Strategy.* New York: Springer-Verlag, 1986.
 A report commissioned by the John D. and Catherine T. MacArthur Foundation for the Research in Criminology series. General subjects addressed include crime and its prevention.

Figlio, Robert M., Simon Hakim, and George F. Rengert, eds. *Metropolitan Crime Patterns.* Monsey, NY: Criminal Justice Press, 1986.
 An analysis of metropolitan and suburban trends in criminal activity.

Flowers, Ronald B. *Minorities and Criminality.* New York: Greenwood Press, 1988.
 This book looks into discrimination and crimes against minorities. It is part of the Contributions in Criminology and Penology series.

Fox, Vernon Brittain. *Introduction to Criminology.* Englewood Cliffs, NJ: Prentice Hall, 1985.
 A general book on criminology that touches on criminal psychology and criminal justice areas.

Frazier, Mansfield B. *From behind the Wall: Commentary on Crime, Punishment, Race, and the Underclass by a Prison Inmate,* 1st ed. New York: Paragon House, 1995.
 A prisoner's analysis of the criminal justice system. The book addresses sociological aspects of crime, prevention, and racism.

Friedberg, Ardy, and Research Forecasts, Inc. *America Afraid: How Fear of Crime Changes the Way We Live.* New York: Research Forecasts, Inc., 1983.
 Public opinion, fear, and perception of crime are examined.

Gibbons, Don C. *Society, Crime, and Criminal Behavior,* 5th ed. Englewood Cliffs, NJ: Prentice Hall, 1987.
 This book was published in a previous edition as *Society, Crime and Criminal Careers.* It examines various aspects of crime and criminal behavior in the United States.

Goldstein, Herman. *Problem-Oriented Policing.* Philadelphia: Temple University Press, 1990.

A look at preventing crime through law enforcement methods that target factors that lead to criminal activity.

Gonzalez, Alfredo, and Shirley Better, with Ralph Dawson. *Gang Violence Prevention: Perspectives and Strategies,* 1st ed. Los Angeles: Edmund G. "Pat" Brown Institute of Public Affairs, California State University, 1990.

This book presents viewpoints on preventing violent crime associated with gang activity.

Gordon, Diana R. *The Justice Juggernaut: Fighting Street Crime, Controlling Citizens.* New Brunswick, NJ: Rutgers University Press, 1990.

As part of the Crime, Law, and Deviance Series, this book looks at ways to prevent and punish street crime.

Graham, John. *Crime Prevention Strategies in Europe and North America.* Helsinki, Finland: Helsinki Institute for Crime Prevention and Control, 1990.

This outline of crime prevention measures is published by an institute affiliated with the United Nations.

Greenberg, Martin S., and R. Barry Ruback. *After the Crime: Victim Decision Making.* New York: Plenum Press, 1992.

This work probes psychological problems associated with crime victimization. It is part of a series called Perspectives in Law and Psychology.

Hagan, John. *Crime and Disrepute.* Thousand Oaks, CA: Pine Forge Press, 1994.

Written from a sociological perspective, this book examines crime and deviant behavior.

Haskell, Martin R., and Lewis Yablonsky. *Criminology: Crime and Criminality.* Boston: Houghton Mifflin, 1983.

A general look into criminology, corrections, crime, and criminals.

Hazlehurst, Kayleen M., ed. *Popular Justice and Community Regeneration: Pathways of Indigenous Reform.* Westport, CT: Praeger, 1995.

This book contains perspectives on social problems, development, crime prevention, and justice.

Heinz, Ann, Herbert Jacob, and Robert L. Lineberry. *Crime in City Politics.* New York: Longman, 1983.

An examination of crimes associated with city political activity. The book is part of the Longman Professional Studies in Law and Public Policy series.

Hippchen, Leonard Joseph, and Yong S. Yim. *Terrorism, International Crime, and Arms Control.* Springfield, IL: Thomas, 1982.

This book examines international crime problems and issues, particularly terrorism and arms traffic.

Hobbs, Dick, ed. *Professional Criminals.* Brookfield, VT: Dartmouth, 1995.

Analyses of professional criminals, their behavior, and recidivism. The book is part of the International Library of Criminology, Criminal Justice, and Penology series.

Hodgins, Sheilagh, ed. *Mental Disorder and Crime.* Newbury Park, CA: Sage Publications, 1993.

A work that looks into psychological problems associated with crime and criminal behavior—especially violent crime.

Holt, Angela Luby. *Medicare/Medicaid Fraud and Abuse: Two Issues and Two Responsibilities.* New York: National League for Nursing, 1980.

This book details problems with the abuse of federal Medicare and Medicaid health care assistance programs.

Hyde, Margaret O. *The Rights of the Victim.* New York: F. Watts, 1983.

The author examines in simple terms the rights of people who have been victimized by crimes.

Jacob, Herbert. *The Frustration of Policy: Responses to Crime by American Cities.* Boston: Little, Brown, 1984.

A look into municipal law enforcement and other action against crime in the United States.

Jenkins, Philip. *Crime and Justice: Issues and Ideas.* Monterey, CA: Brooks/Cole Publishing Company, 1984.

This book examines prominent issues in crime and criminal justice. It is part of the Contemporary Issues in Crime and Justice Series.

Johnson, Elmer H., ed. *Handbook on Crime and Delinquency Prevention.* New York: Greenwood Press, 1987.

This book serves as a general manual for crime prevention and includes ideas for combating juvenile delinquency.

Johnson, Ray, with Carroll Stoianoff. *Ray Johnson's Total Security: How You Can Protect Yourself from Crime.* New York: New American Library, 1984.

A general book on steps people can take to keep themselves from becoming crime victims.

Jones, David Arthur. *History of Criminology: A Philosophical Perspective.* Westport, CT: Greenwood Press, 1986.

This book examines criminology from a historical and theoretical perspective. It is part of the Contributions in Criminology and Penology series.

Kohn, Alexander. *False Prophets.* New York: Basil Blackwell, 1986.

A work that describes problems with fraud in science and with medical ethics.

Kooistra, Paul. *Criminals as Heroes: Structure, Power and Identity.* Bowling Green, OH: Bowling Green State University Popular Press, 1989.

An academic perspective on outlaws and famous criminals and their activity.

Krebs, Dennis R., Kenneth C. Henry, and Mark B. Gabriele. *When Violence Erupts: A Survival Guide for Emergency Responders.* St. Louis: Mosby, 1990.

This book talks about crimes and violence against emergency medical personnel. It also describes prevention and safety precautions.

Lab, Steven P. *Crime Prevention: Approaches, Practices, and Evaluations,* 2d ed. Cincinnati, OH: Anderson Publishing Co., 1992.

The author analyzes the effectiveness of crime prevention strategies in the United States.

Larson, Calvin J. *Crime—Justice and Society.* Bayside, NY: General Hall, 1984.

A general look into crime and justice issues in our society.

LeShan, Eda J. *The Roots of Crime: What You Need To Know about Crime and What You Can Do about It.* New York: Four Winds Press, 1981.

Subjects addressed in this book include the roots of crime in children and poor treatment of criminals in prison. It also includes interviews with convicted criminals.

Lindquist, John H. *Misdemeanor Crime: Trivial Criminal Pursuit.* Newbury Park, CA: Sage Publications, 1988.

This book examines the hunt for people who commit minor criminal offenses. It is part of the Studies in Crime, Law, and Justice series.

Lombroso, Cesare. *Crime, Its Causes and Remedies.* Boston: Little, Brown, 1911.

Written by an Italian scientist, this book provides historical perspective on hypothesized relationships between crime and physical makeup.

Long, Robert Emmet, ed. *Criminal Sentencing.* New York: H. W. Wilson, 1995.

Michael J. Mandel, Jill Smolowe, Hanna Rosin, Richard Lacayo, and Glenn Pierce are among the contributors to this book. Subjects addressed include sentencing, capital punishment, and criminal justice.

Lotz, Roy Edward. *Crime and the American Press.* New York: Praeger, 1991.

This book looks at the relationship among crime, journalism, reporting, and the press. It is part of the Praeger Series in Political Communication.

Lspez-Rey y Arrojo, Manuel. *A Guide to United Nations Criminal Policy.* Brookfield, VT: Gower, 1985.
This book outlines UN policy on crime prevention and criminal justice. It is part of the Cambridge Studies in Criminology series.

Lynch, Michael J., and W. Byron Groves. *A Primer in Radical Criminology.* New York: Harrow and Heston, 1986.
The authors describe Marxist and radical approaches to criminology.

Malinchak, Alan A. *Crime and Gerontology.* Englewood Cliffs, NJ: Prentice Hall, 1980.
Crimes against elderly people, prevention, and elderly offenders are addressed.

Mann, Stephanie, with M. C. Blakeman. *Safe Homes, Safe Neighborhoods: Stopping Crime Where You Live.* Berkeley, CA: Nolo Press, 1993.
A manual for curbing and preventing crime through neighborhood organizational efforts and personal safety precautions.

Mannle, Henry W., and J. David Hirschel. *Fundamentals of Criminology.* Englewood Cliffs, NJ: Prentice Hall, 1988.
A basic book that examines criminology.

MacNamara, Donal E. J., and Lloyd McCorkle. *Crime, Criminals, and Corrections.* New York: John Jay Press, 1982.
The authors conduct a general examination of crime, victims, and the criminal justice system.

MacNamara, Donal E. J., and Philip John Stead, eds. *New Dimensions in Transnational Crime.* New York: John Jay Press, 1982.
The subject of this book is offenses in modern international crime.

McCaghy, Charles H. *Deviant Behavior: Crime, Conflict, and Interest Groups,* 2d ed. New York and London: Macmillan and Collier Macmillan, 1985.
The author examines relationships between deviant behavior and criminal activity, with an academic perspective.

McDonald, Hugh C. *Survival.* New York: Ballantine Books, 1982.
Avoiding and preventing crime are addressed.

McGuigan, Patrick B., and Jon S. Pascale, eds. *Crime and Punishment in Modern America.* Washington, DC: Institute for Government and Politics of the Free Congress Research and Education Foundation, 1986.
The contributors address prominent current issues in U.S. criminal justice.

McGurn, Thomas P., with Christine N. Kelly. *The Woman's Bible for Survival in a Violent Society.* New York: Stein and Day, 1984.
Safety measures women can take to increase their security and prevent crimes against them are the foci of this book.

Meier, Robert F. *Crime and Society.* Boston: Allyn and Bacon, 1989.
A general look at crime and criminal justice in our society.

————, ed. *Major Forms of Crime.* Beverly Hills, CA: Sage Publications, 1984.
Part of the Sage Criminal Justice Annuals series, this work describes prominent types of crime in society.

Milton S. Eisenhower Foundation. *Youth Investment and Community Reconstruction: Street Lessons on Drugs and Crime for the Nineties.* Washington, DC: Milton S. Eisenhower Foundation, 1990.
A modern look at urban youth crime problems, drug abuse, crime prevention, and community development.

Moore, Mark H., et al. *Dangerous Offenders: The Elusive Target of Justice.* Cambridge, MA: Harvard University Press, 1984.
This book discusses violent criminals and the criminal justice system in the United States.

National Crime Prevention Institute. *Understanding Crime Prevention.* Boston: Butterworths, 1986.
A work that investigates crime prevention measures in buildings and elsewhere.

National Institute for Citizen Education in the Law, National Crime Prevention Council. *Teens, Crime, and the Community: Education and Action for Safer Schools and Neighborhoods.* St. Paul, MN: West, 1992.
This book describes crimes committed by and against young people in schools and communities.

Neely, Richard. *Take Back Your Neighborhood: Organizing a Citizen's Patrol Force To Fight Crime in Your Community.* New York: Donald I. Fine, 1990.
The author describes how people can organize groups to prevent crime in their neighborhoods.

Nettler, Gwynn. *Explaining Crime,* 3rd ed. New York: McGraw-Hill, 1984.
Part of the McGraw-Hill Series on Crime and Criminal Justice, this book is a general work on crime.

————. *Explaining Criminals.* Cincinnati, OH: Anderson Publishing Company, 1982.
This general analysis of criminals is part of the series Criminal Careers

Novak, Michael. *Character and Crime: An Inquiry into the Causes of the Virtue of Nations.* Notre Dame, IN: Brownson Institute, 1986.
The author analyzes crime in the context of nations' moral conditions. The book is part of the Modern Catholic series, and the text comes from an Aquinas Fund Lecture on Responsible Citizenship sponsored by the International Society of Criminology.

O'Block, Robert L. *Security and Crime Prevention.* St. Louis: Mosby, 1981.

    This book examines security measures in buildings and industry.

Ochberg, Frank M., ed. *Post-Traumatic Therapy and Victims of Violence.* New York: Brunner/Mazel, 1988.

    This book examines psychological issues, including stress disorders, associated with crime victimization.

Pepinsky, Harold E., and Paul Jesilow. *Myths That Cause Crime.* Cabin John, MD: Seven Locks Press, 1984.

    The authors analyze possible causes of crime.

Podolefsky, Aaron, and Frederic Dubow. *Strategies for Community Crime Prevention: Collective Responses to Crime in Urban America.* Springfield, IL: C. C. Thomas, 1981.

    This work is based on reactions to a crime project conducted at the Center for Urban Affairs. Subjects addressed include communities, prevention, and social control.

Prins, Herschel A. *Bizarre Behaviours: Boundaries of Psychiatric Disorder.* New York: Tavistock/Routledge, 1990.

    Written from a psychological persepective, this book looks into behaviors that may point to criminal activity.

Public Agenda Foundation. *Crime: What We Fear, What Can Be Done.* Dayton, OH: National Issues Forum, 1986.

    Part of the National Issues Forum series, this book offers analysis of the crime problem and potential solutions. Subjects addressed include the administration of criminal justice and prevention.

Reid, Sue Titus. *Crime and Criminology,* 3rd ed. New York: Holt, Rinehart, and Winston, 1982.

    A general book on criminology.

Rohr, Janelle, ed. *Violence in America: Opposing Viewpoints.* San Diego, CA: Greenhaven Press, 1990.

    The contributors debate causes of violence, family and teen violence, serial killers, violence prevention, and other aspects of crime. The book is part of the Opposing Viewpoints series.

Rosenbaum, Dennis P., ed. *Community Crime Prevention: Does It Work?* Beverly Hills, CA: Sage Publications, 1986.

    This book offers a critical and analytical look at community and neighborhood crime prevention. It is part of the Sage Criminal Justice System Annuals series.

Salasin, Susan E., ed. *Evaluating Victim Services.* Beverly Hills, CA: Sage Publications, 1981.

    A compilation of writings on services available to aid crime victims, written in conjunction with the Evaluation Research Society.

Saney, Parviz. *Crime and Culture in America: A Comparative Perspective.* New York: Greenwood Press, 1986.

This book is part of the Contributions in Criminology and Penology series and examines criminal behavior, justice, and U.S. culture.

Scheingold, Stuart A. *The Politics of Law and Order: Street Crime and Public Policy.* New York: Longman, 1984.

Part of the Longman Professional Studies in Law and Public Policy, this book probes the relationship between politics and public crime control policy.

Scott, Joseph E., and Travis Hirschi, eds. *Controversial Issues in Crime and Justice.* Newbury Park, CA: Sage Publications, 1987.

The contributors examine various aspects of crime and criminal justice. The book is part of the Studies in Crime, Law, and Justice series.

Sedgwick, Jeffrey Leigh. *Law Enforcement Planning: The Limits of an Economic Analysis.* Westport, CT: Greenwood Press, 1984.

Part of the Contributions in Criminology and Penology series, this book provides a critical look at law enforcement planning.

Sheley, Joseph F. *America's "Crime Problem": An Introduction to Criminology.* Belmont, CA: Wadsworth Publishing Company, 1985.

A general look at crime and criminology in the United States.

———, ed. *Exploring Crime: Readings in Criminology and Criminal Justice.* Belmont, CA: Wadsworth, 1987.

A collection of writings on crime, criminal justice, prevention, and criminal psychology.

Shelley, Louise I. *Crime and Modernization: The Impact of Industrialization and Urbanization on Crime.* Carbondale, IL: Southern Illinois University Press, 1981.

This book is part of the Science and International Affairs Series and explores relationships among crime, urbanization, and technology.

Shook, Lyle L. *Cry, Cities! Crime, Cost of Living and Quality of Life in American Cities!* Mankato, MN: Gabriel Books, 1982.

This book examines the factors, including crime, that influence the quality of life in U.S. cities.

Siegel, Larry J. *Criminology.* St. Paul, MN: West Publishing Company, 1983.

A general book on criminology.

Skogan, Wesley G., ed. *Reactions to Crime and Violence.* Thousand Oaks, CA: Sage Periodicals Press, 1995.

This book is a compilation of essays on crime in communities, fear in urban life, women and crime, community organization, firearms, crime prevention, fear on campuses, and other issues related to crime. Contributors include Bonnie S. Fisher, David McDowell, Vincent F. Sacco, Paul Ekblom, Ralph B. Taylor, and Susan F. Bennett.

Skogan, Wesley G., and Michael G. Maxfield. *Coping with Crime: Individual and Neighborhood Reactions.* Beverly Hills, CA: Sage Publications, 1981.

The authors examine crime victimization and prevention at the individual and community levels. The book is part of the Sage Library of Social Research.

Stop the Violence, Start Something. Raleigh: North Carolina Crime Prevention Division, 1995.

A book on crime prevention issued by the North Carolina Department of Public Safety.

Territo, Leonard, James Halstead, and Max Bromley. *Crime and Justice in America: A Human Perspective,* 2d ed. St. Paul, MN: West Publishing Company, 1989.

An analysis of criminal behavior, crime, and criminal justice in the United States.

Thomas, Andrew Peyton. *Crime and the Sacking of America: The Roots of Chaos.* Washington, DC: Brassey's, 1994.

A look into causes of the crime problem in the United States.

Thomas, Charles Wellington, and John R. Hepburn. *Crime, Criminal Law, and Criminology.* Dubuque, IA: W. C. Brown, 1983.

This book is a general analysis of criminal justice, criminal law, and criminology.

Timmer, Doug A., and D. Stanley Eitzen. *Crime in the Streets and Crime in the Suites: Perspectives on Crime and Criminal Justice.* Boston: Allyn and Bacon, 1989.

The authors present differing viewpoints on crime and criminal justice issues.

Tonry, Michael, and David P. Farrington, eds. *Building a Safer Society: Strategic Approaches to Crime Prevention.* Chicago: University of Chicago Press, 1995.

This book is composed of essays on community, situational, and other types of crime prevention.

Trojanowicz, Robert C., and Bonnie Bucqueroux. *Community Policing: A Contemporary Perspective.* Cincinnati, OH: Anderson Publishing Company, 1990.

An analysis of the increasingly popular method of law enforcement known as community policing. The book also contains updates from communities that have established community policing programs.

Tucker, William. *Vigilante, the Backlash against Crime in America.* New York: Stein and Day, 1985.

The author analyzes citizen vigilante reactions to crime problems in the United States.

Van Ness, Daniel W. *Crime and Its Victims: What We Can Do.* Downer's Grove, IL: InterVarsity Press, 1986.

Written from a religious perspective, this book examines crime, victims, and punishment. It contains a forward by Charles Colson and is part of the Impact Books series.

Vetter, Harold J., and Ira J. Silverman. *Criminology and Crime: An Introduction.* New York: Harper and Row, 1986.
A general introductory book on criminology.

Von Brook, Patricia, Mark A. Siegel, and Carol D. Foster, eds. *Gambling: Crime or Recreation?* Wylie, TX: Information Plus, 1988.
A short booklet that explains common gambling practices, both legal and illegal.

Wadman, Robert C., and Sir Stanley E. Bailey. *Community Policing and Crime Prevention in America and England.* Chicago: Office of International Criminal Justice, University of Illinois at Chicago, 1993.
An analysis of community policing programs in the United States and Great Britain.

Walker, Samuel. *Sense and Nonsense about Crime: A Policy Guide,* 2d ed. Pacific Grove, CA: Brooks/Cole Publishing Company, 1989.
A general book on crime and criminal justice policy.

Weiss, Karel, ed. *The Prison Experience: An Anthology.* New York: Delacorte Press, 1976.
This book is a compilation of writings by prisoners and their families and friends that address the prison experience.

White, Bertha Rothe. *The Crimes and Punishment Primer.* Dobbs Ferry, NY: Oceana Publications, 1986.
This work is primarily concerned with criminal law and is part of the Legal Almanac series.

Wickman, Peter M., and Phillip Whitten, with Robert Levey. *Criminology, Perspectives on Crime and Criminality.* Lexington, MA: D. C. Heath, 1980.
Viewpoints on aspects of criminal behavior, crime, and criminology are presented.

Wilkins, Leslie T. *Consumerist Criminology.* Totowa, NJ: Barnes and Noble, 1984.
The book offers a critical look at criminology and is part of the Cambridge Studies in Criminology series.

Williams, Franklin P., III, and Marilyn D. McShane. *Criminological Theory.* Englewood Cliffs, NJ: Prentice Hall, 1988.
A general look into theoretical aspects of criminology.

Wilson, James Q. *Thinking about Crime,* 2d ed., rev. Beverly Hills, CA: Basic Books, 1983.
An examination of crime, criminal justice, and punishment from an academic and sociological perspective.

Wilson, James Q., and Richard J. Herrnstein. *Crime and Human Nature.* New York: Simon and Schuster, 1985.

The authors examine crime and criminal behavior in the theoretical context of human nature.

Wilson, James Q., and Joan Petersilia, eds. *Crime.* San Francisco: Institute for Contemporary Studies Press, 1995.

A collection of essays on medical factors in crime, criminal justice research, juvenile crime, the family, and other related subjects.

Wilson, James Q., and Michael Tonry, eds. *Drugs and Crime.* Chicago: University of Chicago Press, 1990.

A compilation of writings on narcotics and crime. The book is part of the Crime and Justice series.

Wright, James D., and Peter H. Rossi. *Armed and Considered Dangerous: A Survey of Felons and Their Firearms.* Hawthorne, NY: Aldine de Gruyter, 1986.

This book presents information on guns and on felons who own them.

Wright, Kevin N. *The Great American Crime Myth.* Westport, CT: Greenwood Press, 1985.

An analytical examination of crime in the United States that is part of the Contributions in Criminology and Penology series.

Reference Books

American Correctional Association. *International Directory of Correctional Administrations.* College Park, MD: American Correctional Association, 1987. 232 pages.

For each of the many countries included, the reference contains demographics, a history of its legal system, and a list of its correctional institutions.

———. *National Jail and Adult Detention Directory.* College Park, MD: American Correctional Association, 1979–. 456 pages.

A comprehensive directory of names, addresses, and other information on detention facilities in the United States.

———. *National Juvenile Detention Directory.* Laurel, MD: American Correctional Association, 1992. 295 pages.

Describes juvenile detention facilities in the United States and lists their names and addresses.

———. *Probation and Parole Directory.* College Park, MD: American Correctional Association, 1981–. 530 pages.

A directory of names and addresses of probation departments in the United States and Canada. Both adult and juvenile departments are included.

Bailey, William G., ed. *Police Science.* New York: Garland Publishing, 1989. 718 pages.

A fairly detailed and excellent reference for information on crimes, investigation, history, and police action.

Becker, Harold K., and Donna Lee Becker. *Handbook of the World's Police.* Metuchen, NJ: Scarecrow Press, 1986. 340 pages.

This handbook gives a brief summary of the demography, history, government, and police forces of the world's nations. It is a useful resource for gathering basic information about law enforcement around the world.

Crimes and Punishment. Reference ed., 8 vols. New York: Marshall Cavendish, 1985.

This eight-volume reference series chronicles the activities of famous criminals. It is written in narrative form and contains a large number of historical photographs.

De Sola, Ralph. *Crime Dictionary.* New York: Facts on File, 1982. 219 pages.

This crime dictionary defines nearly every term/acronym related to crime, police, prisons, courts, and other aspects of criminal justice.

Fay, John J. *The Police Dictionary and Encyclopedia.* Springfield, IL: Charles T. Thomas, 1988. 370 pages.

A detailed dictionary of terms associated with crime and police investigation. Five useful appendixes are entitled "Felony Definitions by State," "Minimum and Maximum Felony Sentences by State," "Capital Offenses by State," "Method of Execution by State," and "Social Security Number Index."

Grau, Joseph J., ed. *Criminal and Civil Investigation Handbook.* New York: McGraw-Hill, 1981. 1094 pages.

A collection of essays by multiple authors covering a wide variety of criminal investigation techniques for white-collar crime, terrorism, computer crime, narcotics, and more. The essays are written at a fairly academic level, and the book is not as readable as some of the others listed here.

Hallett, Michael A., and Dennis J. Palumbo. *United States Criminal Justice Interest Groups: Institutional Profiles.* Westport, CT: Greenwood Press, 1993. 130 pages.

A directory of criminal justice organizations, with their functions, publications, and purposes.

International City/County Mangagement (ICMA). *Police Salaries.* Washington, DC: ICMA, 1993. 55 pages.

This small booklet lists data on police and their salaries, by rank, in the United States.

Jaffe, Jerome H., M.D., editor-in-chief. *Encyclopedia of Drugs and Alcohol.* 4 vols. New York: Simon and Schuster Macmillan, 1995.

A well-written and thorough guide to drugs and alcohol, their abuse, treatment, and relation to crime. The series also contains an extensive directory of drug and alcohol treatment programs.

Kadish, Sanford H., editor-in-chief. *Encyclopedia of Crime and Justice.* 5 vols. New York: Free Press, 1983.

This reference series is very thorough and is a good overall reference on crime and the justice system. Articles on each subject are written by professionals in an academic style.

Kurian, George Thomas. *World Encyclopedia of Police Forces and Penal Systems.* New York: Facts on File, 1989. 582 pages.

This lengthy reference gives fairly detailed descriptions of police forces and penal systems around the world. It includes information on how the systems are structured; how each country recruits, trains, and educates its police; and, in many cases, the country's crime statistics.

McCaghy, Charles H. *Crime in American Society,* 2d ed. New York: Macmillan, 1987. 401 pages.

A textbook that describes various aspects of crime in the United States. The book is very general and takes both a theoretical and a historical approach to understanding crime.

Nash, Jay Robert. *Encyclopedia of World Crime.* 5 vols. Wilmette, IL: Crimebooks, 1990.

A very comprehensive reference series that highlights famous criminals, crimes, and crime fighters. The set also contains a large dictionary, appendixes on important crime-related court decisions and landmark crime legislation, and a large index.

————. *World Encyclopedia of Organized Crime.* New York: Paragon House, 1989. 624 pages.

A reference book devoted to all aspects of international organized crime, including major figures and historical roots.

National Police Chiefs and Sheriffs Information Bureau. *National Directory of Law Enforcement Administrators.* Milwaukee, WI: National Police Chiefs and Sheriffs Information Bureau, 1986. 505 pages.

A directory of state correctional agencies, prosecutors, municipal law enforcement agencies, campus law enforcement, federal and international agencies, state police, and highway patrols, with names and addresses.

Nemeth, Charles P. *Anderson's Directory of Criminal Justice Education, 1986–87.* Cincinnati, OH: Anderson Publishing Company, 1986. 692 pages.

A comprehensive guide to criminal justice education programs in the United States, with descriptions and addresses. The directory includes criminology-, law-, and justice-related programs.

Rowland, Desmond, and James Bailey. *The Law Enforcement Handbook.* New York: Facts on File, 1983. 294 pages.

A handbook on police methods of patrol and investigation. This manual is a concise, readable resource for understanding common offenses and how police investigate them.

Sifakis, Carl. *Encyclopedia of American Crime.* Smithmark, NY: Facts on File, 1982. 802 pages.

This reference book is devoted primarily to famous criminals and their activities, but it also contains biographical information on noted crime fighters.

Torres, Donald. *Handbook of Federal Police and Investigative Agencies.* Westport, CT: Greenwood Press, 1985. 411 pages.

Contains detailed descriptions of the functions and duties of federal agencies, with diagrams that show agencies' internal structures.

Williams, Vergil L. *Dictionary of American Penology.* Westport, CT: Greenwood Press, 1979. 530 pages.

A large dictionary of terms associated with penology.

Government Documents

Most government documents can be found in federal depositories, by contacting the United States Government Printing Office, or by contacting the agency that produces the document.

Bibliography on Crime Forecasting and Related Topics. Washington, DC: U.S. Department of Justice, Bureau of Justice Statistics [prepared by the research team Knowlton Johnson et al., in collaboration with the Project Advisory Group, James Fox, Robert Willstadter, Clinton Goff], 1983.

A bibliographical reference for information on crime forecasting.

Bickman, Leonard, et al. *Citizen Crime Reporting Projects.* Washington, DC: U.S. Department of Justice, National Institute of Justice, 1982.

This document provides analysis of citizen-based crime prevention programs.

Buchanan, Robert A., and Karen L. Whitlow. *Guidelines for Developing, Implementing and Revising an Objective Prison Classification System.* Washington, DC: U.S. Department of Justice, National Institute of Justice, 1987.

Part of the National Institute of Justice's Research Report series, this document contains a framework for reforms in the prison system.

Buracker, Carroll D., and William K. Stover. *Automated Fingerprint Identification: Regional Application of Technology.* Washington, DC: Federal Bureau of Investigation, U.S. Department of Justice, 1984.

This document is reprinted from the *FBI Law Enforcement Bulletin* and describes potential regional uses for modern fingerprinting technology.

Bureau of Justice Assistance (BJA). *Understanding Community Policing: A Framework for Action.* Washington, DC: BJA, 1994.

This BJA report describes community policing and advocates the implementation of more programs.

Bureau of Justice Statistics. *Drugs, Crime and the Justice System: A National Report.* Washington, DC: U.S. Government Printing Office, 1992.

Drug abuse, relationships between drugs and crime, and drug use in the justice system are addressed in this report.

Chelimsky, Eleanor, et al. *Security and the Small Business Retailer.* Washington, DC: U.S. Department of Justice, Law Enforcement Assistance Administration, National Institute of Law Enforcement and Criminal Justice, 1978.

Preventing crime against small businesses is the subject of this report.

Cisneros, Henry G. *Defensible Space: Deterring Crime and Building Community.* Washington, DC: U.S. Department of Housing and Urban Development, 1995.

Crime prevention through building design and security measures in public housing projects form the foci of this report.

Cohen, Jacqueline. *Incapacitating Criminals: Recent Research Findings by Jacqueline Cohen.* Washington, DC: U.S. Department of Justice, National Institute of Justice, 1983.

A Department of Justice report on research on crime, criminals, and punishment.

Comptroller General of the United States, General Accounting Office. *Stronger Federal Effort Needed in Fight against Organized Crime: Report.* Washington, DC: U.S. General Accounting Office, 1981.

A report that advocates a stepped-up federal law enforcement presence in the battle against organized crime.

Computer Crime: Criminal Justice Resource Manual. Washington, DC: Bureau of Justice Statistics, U.S. Department of Justice, 1980.

A 392-page manual on computer crime. As computer technology has advanced rapidly since this publication was written, the information is not fully up-to-date.

Crime and the Elderly. Bethesda, MD: U.S. Department of Health and Human Services, Public Health Service, National Institutes of Health, 1985.

Part of the series Age Page, this document addresses crime against the elderly and prevention.

Crime Control and Criminal Records. Washington, DC: U.S. Department of Justice, Bureau of Justice Statistics, 1985.

A Bureau of Justice Statistics special report on criminal records.

Crime Prevention Awareness Manual. Washington, DC: General Services Administration, Federal Protection and Safety Division, 1985.

This document serves as a general handbook on crime prevention.

Criminal Aliens: INS' Detention and Deportation Activities in the New York City Area: Briefing Report to the Honorable Alfonse M. D'Amato. Washington, DC: U.S. Senate, U.S. General Accounting Office, 1986.

This document reports on Immigration and Naturalization Service deportations and other actions taken against aliens around New York City.

Criminal Cases in Five States, 1983–86. Washington, DC: U.S. Department of Justice, Office of Justice Programs, Bureau of Justice Statistics (BJS), 1989.

This special BJS report summarizes and analyzes criminal cases in five U.S. states during a four-year period.

Criminal Justice: New Technologies and the Constitution, Special Report. Washington, DC: Congress of the United States, Office of Technology Assessment, 1988.

A report on new technology as it relates to constitutional rights, criminal justice, and law enforcement.

Cronin, Roberta C. *Innovative Community Partnerships: Working Together for Change: Program Summary.* Washington, DC: U.S. Department of Justice, Office of Justice Programs, Office of Juvenile Justice and Delinquency Prevention, 1994.

Subjects considered in this report include community policing, crime prevention, and neighborhood watch programs.

Delinquency Prevention Works: Program Summary. Washington, DC: U.S. Department of Justice, Office of Justice Programs, Office of Juvenile Justice and Delinquency Prevention, 1995.

The focus of this program summary is the prevention of both crime and delinquency.

Dodge, Lowell. *Criminal Aliens: INS Enforcement: Statement of Lowell Dodge, Director, Administration of Justice Issues, General Government Division, Before the Subcommittee on Immigration, Refugees, and International Law, Committee on the Judiciary, House of Representatives.* Washington, DC: U.S. General Accounting Office, 1989.

This document is concerned with aliens and immigrants who commit crimes in the United States.

Dodge, Richard W. *Response to Screening Questions in the National Crime Survey.* Washington, DC: U.S. Department of Justice, Bureau of Justice Statistics, 1985.

Analysis of the National Crime Survey, one of the most prominent sources of national crime statistics.

DuBow, Fred, Edward McCabe, and Gail Kaplan. *Reactions to Crime: A Critical Review of the Literature.* Washington, DC: U.S. Department of Justice, Law Enforcement Assistance Administration, National Institute of Law Enforcement and Criminal Justice. 1980.

The authors analyze information available about public opinion on criminal activity.

Duncan, J. T. Skip. Edited by John Slone. *Citizen Crime Prevention Tactics: A Literature Review and Selected Bibliography.* Washington, DC: U.S. Department of Justice, National Institute of Justice, 1980.

This publication lists and analyzes literature available on community and citizen crime prevention activities.

Earls, Felton, and Albert J. Reiss Jr. *Breaking the Cycle: Predicting and Preventing Crime.* Washington, DC: U.S. Department of Justice, Office of Justice Programs, National Institute of Justice, 1994.

This document is a National Institute of Justice research report containing suggestions for preventing crime and juvenile delinquency.

Finn, Peter. *Victims.* Washington, DC: U.S. Department of Justice, National Institute of Justice, 1988.

This document addresses victims of crime and is part of the Crime File series.

————. *Victims: A Study Guide.* Rockville, MD: U.S. Department of Justice, National Institute of Justice, 1986.

A study guide for the previous document.

Gang and Drug Policy. Washington, DC: U.S. Department of Justice, Office of Justice Programs, Office of Juvenile Justice and Delinquency Prevention, 1991.

Subjects addressed in this document include juvenile delinquency, gang violence, drug abuse, and crime, as well as government policy to combat these problems.

Garofalo, James, and Maureen McLeod. *Improving the Use and Effectiveness of Neighborhood Watch Programs.* Washington, DC: U.S. Department of Justice, National Institute of Justice, 1988.

This document is part of the Research in Action series and outlines suggestions for improving neighborhood watch crime prevention programs.

Gladis, Stephen D. *The Hostage/Terrorist Situation and the Media.* Washington, DC: U.S. Department of Justice, Federal Bureau of Investigation, 1984.

The author of this report analyzes conflicts and relationships between the press and law enforcement in dealing with dangerous situations involving terrorists and hostages.

"Got a Minute? You Could Stop a Crime: Take a Bite out of Crime." Washington, DC: U.S. Department of Justice, Office of Justice Assistance, Research, and Statistics, 1984.

This document contains information on what individuals can do to help prevent crime.

Graham, Mary G. *Controlling Drug Abuse and Crime: A Research Update.* Washington, DC: U.S. Department of Justice, National Institute of Justice, 1987.

This is a short update on research about drug abuse. It is part of the Research in Action series.

Greenberg, Stephanie W., William M. Rohe, and Jay R. Williams. *Informal Citizen Action and Crime Prevention at the Neighborhood Level: Synthesis and Assessment of the Research.* Washington, DC: U.S. Department of Justice, National Institute of Justice, 1985.

A National Institute of Justice research report that analyzes citizen and community participation in crime prevention efforts.

———. *Informal Citizen Action and Crime Prevention at the Neighborhood Level: Executive Summary.* Washington, DC: U.S. Department of Justice, National Institute of Justice, 1985.

A summary of the previous document.

Halleck, Seymour L. *The Mentally Disordered Offender.* Rockville, MD: U.S. Department of Health and Human Services, Public Health Service, Alcohol, Drug Abuse, and Mental Health Administration, National Institute of Mental Health, 1987.

The author examines relationships between psychological problems and criminal behavior, as well as issues in forensic psychiatry.

Handbook on the Comprehensive Crime Control Act of 1984 and Other Criminal Statutes Enacted by the 98th Congress. Washington, DC: U.S. Department of Justice, 1984.

This manual serves as a guide to federal anticrime legislation during the term of the 98th Congress, in particular the Comprehensive Crime Control Act of 1984.

Heinz, Anne M. *Governmental Responses to Crime, Legislative Responses to Crime: The Changing Content of Criminal Law.* Washington, DC: U.S. Department of Justice, National Institute of Justice, 1982.

The author elaborates on new types of and trends in criminal law.

Herrnstein, Richard J. *Biology and Crime: A Study Guide.* Rockville, MD: U.S. Department of Justice, National Institute of Justice, 1986.

Part of the Crime File series, this report probes potential relationships between biology and crime.

Hoffman, Peter B. *Predicting Criminality: A Study Guide.* Rockville, MD: U.S. Department of Justice, National Institute of Justice, 1986.

The author examines criminals, criminal behavior, and recidivism. The guide is part of the Crime File series.

Hollander, Brian, et al. *Reducing Residential Crime and Fear: The Hartford Neighborhood Crime Prevention Program: Executive Summary.* Corrected printing. Washington, DC: U.S. Department of Justice, Law Enforcement Assistance Administration, National Institute of Law Enforcement and Criminal Justice, 1980.

A summary of the Hartford Neighborhood Crime Prevention Program. Topics addressed include crime and crime prevention in the state of Connecticut.

How To Gain Access to BJS Data. Washington, DC: U.S. Department of Justice, Bureau of Justice Statistics, 1984.

This document describes information available from the Bureau of Justice Statistics.

How To Protect Children: Take a Bite out of Crime. Washington, DC: U.S. Department of Justice, Office of Justice Assistance, Research, and Statistics, 1984.

This publication gives information on preventing children from becoming crime victims.

Jacob, Herbert, and Robert L. Lineberry. *Governmental Responses to Crime: Crime on Urban Agendas.* Washington, DC: U.S. Department of Justice, National Institute of Justice, 1982.

Subjects addressed in this report include crime in urban areas, law enforcement, and criminal justice.

Jacob, Herbert, and Robert L. Lineberry, with Ann M. Heinz, Michael J. Rich, and Duane H. Swank. *Governmental Responses to Crime: Crime and Governmental Responses in American Cities.* Washington, DC: U.S. Department of Justice, Center for Urban Affairs and Policy, 1982.

The authors of this 135-page document describe and analyze law enforcement and other methods city governments use to combat crime in their areas.

Kalish, Carol B. *International Crime Rates.* Washington, DC: U.S. Department of Justice, Bureau of Justice Statistics, 1988.

A Bureau of Justice Statistics Special Report, this document describes and analyzes the crime rates of various countries.

Kaplan, John. *Heroin.* Washington, DC: U.S. Department of Justice, National Institute of Justice, 1988.

This document probes problems with heroin, drug abuse, and crime. It is part of the Crime File series.

————. *Heroin: A Study Guide.* Rockville, MD: U.S. Department of Justice, National Institute of Justice, 1986.

A study guide for the previous document.

Kelling, George L., and James K. Stewart. *Neighborhoods and Police: The Maintenance of Civil Authority.* Washington, DC: U.S. Department of Justice, Office of Justice Programs, National Institute of Justice, 1989.

Part of the Perspectives in Policing series, this document addresses police, neighborhoods, crime prevention, and neighborhood watch programs.

Klaus, Patsy A. *The Costs of Crime to Victims.* Washington, DC: U.S. Department of Justice, Office of Justice Programs, Bureau of Justice Statistics, 1994.

The author analyzes the economic toll crime takes on its victims. The document is part of the Crime Data Brief series and also contains statistical information.

Kravitz, Marjorie, sup. ed. *Crime Analysis: A Selected Bibliography.* Compiled by Margaret N. Emig and Robert O. Heck. Washington, DC: National Criminal Justice Reference Service [prepared for the Institute of Justice, U.S. Department of Justice, by Aspen Systems Corp.; distributed by the National Criminal Justice Reference Service], 1980.

A bibliography of literature and information on crime analysis.

Langan, Patrick A., and Lawrence A. Greenfield. *Career Patterns in Crime.* Washington, DC: U.S. Department of Justice, Bureau of Justice Statistics (BJS), 1983.

A BJS special report that analyzes recidivism, criminal behavior, and statistics.

Lehnen, Robert G., and Wesley G. Skogan, eds. *The National Crime Survey: Working Papers.* Washington, DC: U.S. Department of Justice, Bureau of Justice Statistics, 1982.

This document contains information on the National Crime Survey, a main source of national crime statistics.

Mendelsohn, Harold A., and Garrett J. O'Keefe. *Media Campaigns and Crime Prevention: An Executive Summary.* Washington, DC: U.S. Department of Justice, National Institute of Justice, 1982.

This document examines media publicity efforts to fight crime.

Milavsky, J. Ronald. *TV and Violence.* Washington, DC: U.S. Department of Justice, National Institute of Justice, 1988.

This report is part of the Crime File series, and it investigates violence on television.

———. *TV and Violence: A Study Guide.* Rockville, MD: U.S. Department of Justice, National Institute of Justice, 1986.

A study guide for the previous document.

Moore, Mark Harrison, Robert C. Trojanowicz, and George L. Kelling. *Crime and Policing.* Washington, DC: U.S. Department of Justice, National Institute of Justice, 1988.

Part of the Perspectives in Policing series, this document analyzes law enforcement and crime.

National Crime Prevention Council. *Working as Partners with Community Groups.* Washington, DC: U.S. Department of Justice, Office of Justice Programs, Bureau of Justice Assistance, 1994.

This document addresses community policing, neighborhood watch programs, and other community-based crime prevention efforts. It is a Bureau of Justice Assistance Community Partnerships Bulletin.

National Criminal Justice Reference Service. *Crime Analysis.* Washington, DC: U.S. Department of Justice, National Institute of Justice, 1980.
    The subject of this document is analysis of crime.

National Institute of Justice (U.S.). *National Institute of Justice Publications, 1984–1988.* Washington, DC: U.S. Department of Justice, National Institute of Justice, 1988.
    This document lists the publications of the National Institute of Justice between 1984 and 1988.

National Institute of Law Enforcement and Criminal Justice, Office of Technology Transfer. *Periodicals Catalog.* Published annually. Washington, DC: U.S. Department of Justice, Law Enforcement Assistance Administration, National Institute of Law Enforcement and Criminal Justice, Office of Technology Transfer, 1972–.
    This publication lists periodicals concerned with crime, law enforcement, drug abuse, criminal behavior, and justice.

Newman, Oscar, and Karen A. Franck. *Factors Influencing Crime and Instability in Urban Housing Developments.* Washington, DC: U.S. Department of Justice, National Institute of Justice, 1980.
    A 302-page report on security and crime in public housing developments.

————. *Factors Influencing Crime and Instability in Urban Housing Developments: Executive Summary.* Washington, DC: U.S. Department of Justice, National Institute of Justice, 1980.
    This document is a summary of the previous report.

Office of Congressional and Public Affairs. *Personal Security Handbook: How You and Your Family Can Minimize Risks to Personal Safety.* Arlington, VA: U.S. Department of Justice, U.S. Marshals Service, 1991.
    A manual containing information on how people can protect themselves from criminal activity.

Operation Weed and Seed: Implementation Manual. Washington, DC: U.S. Department of Justice, Executive Office for Weed and Seed, 1992.
    A handbook of guidelines for the Operation Weed and Seed program, which is aimed at crime prevention.

Pennell, Susan, Christine Curtis, and Joel Henderson. *Guardian Angels: An Assessment of Citizen Response to Crime.* Washington, DC: U.S. Department of Justice, National Institute of Justice, 1986.
    A National Institute of Justice analysis of the Guardian Angels, a citizen patrol group that has taken root in some U.S. cities.

Peterson, Mark A., and Harriet B. Braiker, with Suzanne M. Polich. *Doing Crime: A Survey of California Prison Inmates.* Washington, DC: U.S. Department of Justice, National Institute of Justice, 1980.

This document contains a survey and analysis of inmates in the state of California.

Pointer, W. Donald, and Marjorie Kravitz. *The Handicapped Offender: A Selected Bibliography.* Washington, DC: U.S. Department of Justice, National Institute of Corrections, National Institute of Justice, 1981.

A bibliography that lists sources of information on handicapped people who break the law.

President's Commission on Law Enforcement and Administration of Justice. *Crime in a Free Society: Selections from the President's Commission on Law Enforcement and Administration of Justice.* Belmont, CA: Dickenson Publishing Company, 1968.

A report of historical interest. It contains findings of the Johnson administration's Commission on Law Enforcement and Administration of Justice, which conducted a thorough investigation of crime and criminal justice in the United States in the late 1960s.

President's Commission on Organized Crime. *The Cash Connection: Organized Crime, Financial Institutions, and Money Laundering.* Washington, DC: President's Commission on Organized Crime, 1984.

This report contains results of an inquiry into links between organized crime and financial institutions.

————. *Organized Crime and Money Laundering. Record of Hearing II, March 14, 1984, New York, NY.* Washington, DC: President's Commission on Organized Crime, 1985.

This document contains the text of a hearing on money laundering that was part of the work of the President's Commission on Organized Crime.

————. *Organized Crime of Asian Origin. Record of Hearing III, October 23–25, 1984, New York, NY.* Washington, DC: President's Commission on Organized Crime, 1985.

This document is the text of a hearing on Asian organized crime.

Preventing Burglary and Robbery Loss. Rev. February 1977. Washington, DC: U.S. Small Business Administration, 1980.

This report contains suggestions for building security, building design, alarms, and other measures aimed at preventing burglaries.

Products and Services/National Institute of Justice/NCJRS. Rockville, MD: U.S. Department of Justice, National Institute of Justice, 1983.

This document describes publications, services, and other products available from the National Criminal Justice Reference Service.

Reaves, Brian A. *Using NIBRS Data To Analyze Violent Crime.* Washington, DC: U.S. Department of Justice, Office of Justice Programs, Bureau of Justice Statistics, 1993.

This Bureau of Justice Statistics technical report examines the use of incident-based reporting data in evaluating violent crime.

Redesign of the National Crime Survey. Washington, DC: U.S. Department of Justice, Office of Justice Programs, Bureau of Justice Statistics, 1989.

This document examines the reworking of the National Crime Survey, a prominent source of national crime statistics.

Report to the Nation on Crime and Justice: Technical Appendix. Washington, DC: U.S. Department of Justice, Bureau of Justice Statistics, 1988.

A general report on the state of crime and criminal justice in the United States.

Residential Security Manual: Burglary. Washington, DC: General Services Administration, Federal Protection and Safety Division, 1985.

A guide to protecting residential areas from burglary.

Rosenbaum, Dennis P. *Update on NIJ-Sponsored Research: Six New Reports.* Washington, DC: U.S. Department of Justice, Office of Justice Programs, National Institute of Justice, 1994.

Narcotics control, drug abuse, crime, and crime prevention are among the topics addressed in these National Institute of Justice research reports.

Rosenbaum, Dennis P., Arthur J. Lurigio, and Paul J. Lavrakas. *Crime Stoppers: A National Evaluation of Program Operations and Effects.* Washington, DC: U.S. Department of Justice, National Institute of Justice, 1987.

Part of the Research in Brief series, this document analyzes crime stoppers programs in the United States.

Safe Haven Program. Washington, DC: Bureau of Justice Statistics, 1994.

A description of the Safe Haven Program. Issues addressed include juvenile delinquency, drug abuse, and crime prevention.

San Diego: Public Attitudes about Crime. Washington, DC: U.S. Department of Justice, Law Enforcement Assistance Administration, National Criminal Justice Information and Statistics Service [prepared for the Law Enforcement Assistance Administration by the Bureau of the Census], 1980.

This report measures public opinion on crime and justice issues in San Diego.

Shenk, J. Frederick, and Patsy A. Klaus. *The Economic Cost of Crime to Victims.* Washington, DC: U.S. Department of Justice, Bureau of Justice Statistics, 1984.

A Bureau of Justice Statistics report that evaluates the economic burden crime places on its victims.

Sherman, Lawrence W. *Neighborhood Safety.* Washington, DC: U.S. Department of Justice, National Institute of Justice, 1988.
A report, part of the Crime File series, on security in neighborhoods in the United States.

———. *Neighborhood Safety: A Study Guide.* Rockville, MD: U.S. Department of Justice, National Institute of Justice, 1986.
A study guide for the previous document.

———. *Repeat Offenders.* Washington, DC: U.S. Department of Justice, National Institute of Justice, 1988.
This document presents analysis of repeat criminal lawbreakers and is part of the Crime File series.

———. *Repeat Offenders: A Study Guide.* Rockville, MD: U.S. Department of Justice, National Institute of Justice, 1986.
A study guide for the previous document.

Skogan, Wesley G., et al. *The Reactions to Crime Project: Executive Summary.* Washington, DC: U.S. Department of Justice, National Institute of Justice, 1982.
The focus of this project report is public opinion on crime, justice, and victimization.

Smith, Barbara E. *Non-Stranger Violence: The Criminal Court's Response.* Washington, DC: U.S. Department of Justice, National Institute of Justice, 1983.
This report describes the effectiveness and actions of criminal courts in cases involving violence toward victims who know their attackers.

Smith, Wendy Serbin. *Victimless Crime: A Selected Bibliography.* Washington, DC: U.S. Department of Justice, Law Enforcement Assistance Administration, National Institute of Law Enforcement and Criminal Justice, 1977.
A bibliography of resources on crime without victims.

Solicited Research Programs, Fiscal Year 1985. Washington, DC: U.S. Department of Justice, National Institute of Justice (NIJ), 1985.
This document describes NIJ research programs planned for 1985.

Spergel, Irving, et al. *Gang Suppression and Intervention: Community Models: Research Summary.* Washington, DC: U.S. Department of Justice, Office of Justice Programs, Office of Juvenile Justice and Delinquency Prevention, 1994.
A synopsis of research information on curbing gang activity through community intervention.

Sykes, Gresham M. *The Future of Crime.* Rockville, MD: U.S. Department of Health and Human Services, Public Health Service, Alcohol, Drug Abuse, and Mental Health Administration, National Institute of Mental Health, Center for Studies of Crime and Delinquency, 1980.

Part of the Crime and Delinquency Issues series, this report outlines potential issues in the future of crime.

Together We Can—Meet the Challenge: Winning the Fight against Drugs. Washington, DC: U.S. Department of Housing and Urban Development, Office of Policy Development and Research, Office of Public and Indian Housing, 1991.

Drug abuse, crime, and public housing are addressed in this document.

Understanding Community Policing: A Framework for Action. Washington, DC: Bureau of Justice Statistics, 1994.

This document describes community policing and advocates the implementation of community policing programs.

United States. *Joint Resolution to Designate October 1994 as "Crime Prevention Month."* Washington, DC: U.S. Government Printing Office, 1994.

This document is the text of a resolution naming October 1994 "Crime Prevention Month."

Urban Crime Prevention Program: Guideline Manual. Washington, DC: Department of Justice, Law Enforcement Assistance Administration, 1980.

A handbook for implementing an urban crime prevention program published by the now-defunct Law Enforcement Assistance Administration.

U.S. Bureau of the Census. *Miami: Public Attitudes about Crime.* Washington, DC: U.S. Department of Justice, Law Enforcement Assistance Administration, National Criminal Justice Information and Statistics Service [prepared for the Law Enforcement Assistance Administration by the Bureau of the Census], 1980.

A National Crime Survey report describing public opinion on crime and criminal justice issues in Miami.

———. *New Orleans: Public Attitudes about Crime.* Washington, DC: U.S. Department of Justice, Law Enforcement Assistance Administration, National Criminal Justice Information and Statistics Service [prepared for the Law Enforcement Assistance Administration by the Bureau of the Census], 1980.

A National Crime Survey report of public opinion on crime and criminal justice issues in New Orleans.

U.S. Bureau of Justice Statistics. *Privacy and Security of Criminal History Information: A Guide to Research and Statistical Use.* Washington, DC: U.S. Department of Justice, Bureau of Justice Statistics, 1981.

This document serves as a guide for legally using information on offenders' past criminal activity for research and other purposes.

U.S. Congress, House of Representatives, Committee on Government Operations. *The Federal Role in Investigation of Serial Violent Crime: Forty-fifth Report.* Washington, DC: U.S. Government Printing Office, 1986.

A House report on federal government investigation of violent crime.

————, Committee on the Judiciary. *Comprehensive Drug Penalty Act of 1982: Report to Accompany H.R. 7140.* Washington, DC: U.S. Government Printing Office, 1982.

A House report on antidrug legislation that addresses narcotics, crime, and forfeiture of assets.

————. *Designer Drug Enforcement Act of 1986: Report to Accompany H.R. 5246.* Washington, DC: U.S. Government Printing Office, 1986.

This document is a House report connected with federal anti–designer drug legislation.

————, Subcommittee on Civil and Constitutional Rights. *Interstate Identification Index Pilot Program: Hearing before the Subcommittee on Civil and Constitutional Rights of the Committee on the Judiciary, House of Representatives, Ninety-seventh Congress, first session, October 22, 1981.* Washington, DC: U.S. Government Printing Office, 1983.

This report contains the text of a House hearing on the Interstate Identification Index Pilot Program. Topics addressed include public records, privacy rights, and crime.

————, Subcommittee on Courts, Civil Liberties, and the Administration of Justice. *Witness Protection Act: Hearing before the Subcommittee on Courts, Civil Liberties, and the Administration of Justice of the Committee on the Judiciary, House of Representatives, Ninety-eighth Congress, first session, on H.R. 3086, June 22, 1983.* Washington, DC: U.S. Government Printing Office, 1985.

This document is the text of a congressional hearing on the Witness Protection Act.

————, Subcommittee on Crime. *America's Crime Problem: Oversight Hearings before the Subcommittee on Crime of the Committee on the Judiciary, House of Representatives, Ninety-seventh Congress, first session, June 10, 11, and 18, 1981.* Washington, DC: U.S. Government Printing Office, 1983.

A committee hearing on violent crime, criminal justice, and other players in U.S. crime problems.

————. *Armed Career Criminal Legislation: Hearing before the Subcommittee on Crime of the Committee on the Judiciary, House of Representatives, Ninety-ninth Congress, second session, May 21, 1986.* Washington, DC: U.S. Government Printing Office, 1987.

Subjects addressed in this hearing include firearms, narcotics, sentencing, and crime.

————. *Crime and Violence in the Media: Hearing before the Subcommittee on Crime of the Committee on the Judiciary, House of Representatives, Ninety-eighth Congress, first session, 1983.* Washington, DC: U.S. Government Printing Office, 1984.

This document contains the text of a House subcommittee hearing on violence on television and in other media forms.

————. *Federal Initiatives on Crime Control: Hearings before the Subcommittee on Crime of the Committee on the Judiciary, House of Representatives, Ninety-seventh Congress, first session, May 5, 11, and 26 and June 29 and 30, 1981.* Washington, DC: U.S. Government Printing Office, 1983.

A 386-page report containing the text of House committee hearings on federal government crime control efforts.

————. *Report of the Attorney General's Task Force on Violent Crime: Hearings before the Subcommittee on Crime of the Committee on the Judiciary, House of Representatives, Ninety-seventh Congress, first session, November 4 and 18, 1981.* Washington, DC: U.S. Government Printing Office, 1983.

This document contains the text of a report by the Attorney General's Task Force on Violent Crime to a House subcommittee.

————, Subcommittee on Criminal Justice. *Revision of the Federal Criminal Code: Hearings before the Subcommittee on Criminal Justice of the Committee on the Judiciary, House of Representatives, Ninety-sixth Congress, first session, February 14, 15, 22, 27; September 6, 7, 10, 11, 12, 13, 14, 17; October 9, 11, and 25, 1979.* Washington, DC: U.S. Government Printing Office, 1981–1982.

The text of hearings before a House subcommittee on reforming the federal criminal law code.

————. *RICO Reform: Hearings before the Subcommittee on Criminal Justice of the Committee on the Judiciary, House of Representatives, Ninety-ninth Congress, first and second sessions.* Washington, DC: U.S. Government Printing Office, 1987.

Subjects addressed in this hearing include the reform of antiracketeering legislation, organized crime, and criminal procedure.

————, Select Committee on Aging. *Crime and the Elderly: New Jersey: Hearing before the Select Committee on Aging, House of Representatives, Ninety-seventh Congress, second session, August 27, 1982.* Washington, DC: U.S. Government Printing Office, 1982.

A House hearing on elderly crime victims.

————, Select Committee on Children, Youth, and Families. *Down These Mean Streets: Violence by and against America's Children: Hearing before the Select Committee on Children, Youth, and Families, House of Representatives, One Hundred First Congress, first session, May 16, 1989.* Washington, DC: U.S. Government Printing Office, 1989.

A House subcommittee hearing on the increasing problem of juvenile criminals and crime victims.

————, Senate. Committee on Commerce, Science, and Transportation. *Aviation Drug-Trafficking Control Act: Report to Accompany S. 1146.* Washington, DC: U.S. Government Printing Office, 1983.

Subjects addressed in this Senate report include drug smuggling and narcotics control.

————. *Motor Vehicle Theft Law Enforcement Act of 1984: Report to Accompany S. 1400.* Washington, DC: U.S. Government Printing Office, 1984.

The subjects of this report are auto theft and the Motor Vehicle Theft Law Enforcement Act of 1984.

————, Subcommittee on Aviation. *Aviation Drug-Trafficking Control Act: Hearing before the Subcommittee on Aviation of the Committee on Commerce, Science, and Transportation, United States Senate, Ninety-eighth Congress, first session, July 21, 1983.* Washington, DC: U.S. Government Printing Office, 1983.

Senate hearings on the Aviation Drug-Trafficking Control Act. Topics addressed include drug smuggling and narcotics control.

————, Subcommittee on Surface Transportation. *Motor Vehicle Theft Law Enforcement Act of 1983: Hearing before the Subcommittee on Surface Transportation, Committee on Commerce, Science, and Transportation, United States Senate, Ninety-eighth Congress, first session, July 19, 1983.* Washington, DC: U.S. Government Printing Office, 1983.

Senate hearings on a proposed Motor Vehicle Theft Law Enforcement Act of 1983 that address automobile theft problems.

————, Committee on Governmental Affairs, Permanent Subcommittee on Investigations. *Emerging Criminal Groups: Hearings before the Permanent Subcommittee on Investigations of the Committee on Governmental Affairs, United States Senate, Ninety-ninth Congress, second session, September 17 and 24, 1986.* Washington, DC: U.S. Government Printing Office, 1987.

This document contains the text of Senate subcommittee hearings on the increasing number of criminal groups in the United States.

————, Committee on the Judiciary. *Justice Assistance Act of 1982: Report, Together with Additional Views, of the Committee on the Judiciary, United States Senate.* Washington, DC: U.S. Government Printing Office, 1982.

A Senate report on the Justice Assistance Act of 1982 that addresses crime prevention and other crime issues.

————. *The Omnibus Victims Protection Act of 1982: Report of the Committee on the Judiciary, United States Senate, to accompany S. 2420.* Washington, DC: U.S. Government Printing Office, 1982.

A Senate report on the Omnibus Victims Protection Act of 1982 that contains information on crime victims, prevention, and criminal law.

―――――, Subcommittee on Criminal Law. *Omnibus Victims Protection Act: Hearing before the Subcommittee on Criminal Law of the Committee on the Judiciary, United States Senate, Ninety-seventh Congress, second session, May 27, 1982.* Washington, DC: U.S. Government Printing Office, 1982.

A Senate subcommittee hearing on the Omnibus Victims Protection Act. The document addresses crime victims, criminal law, prevention, and criminal justice issues.

―――――. *Pharmacy Robbery Legislation: Hearing before the Subcommittee on Criminal Law of the Committee on the Judiciary, United States Senate, Ninety-seventh Congress, second session, June 17, 1982.* Washington, DC: U.S. Government Printing Office, 1982.

This document contains the text of a Senate hearing on legislation to prevent theft from pharmacies.

―――――, Subcommittee on Juvenile Justice. *Juveniles and Dangerous Drugs: Hearing before the Subcommittee on Juvenile Justice of the Committee on the Judiciary, United States Senate, Ninety-seventh Congress, second session, January 28, 1982.* Washington, DC: U.S. Government Printing Office, 1982.

This document contains the text of Senate hearings on drug abuse, crime, juvenile delinquency, and juvenile justice.

―――――. *Relationship between Child Abuse, Juvenile Delinquency, and Adult Criminality: Hearing before the Subcommittee on Juvenile Justice of the Committee on the Judiciary, United States Senate, Ninety-eighth Congress, first session, October 19, 1983.* Washington, DC: U.S. Government Printing Office, 1984.

A Senate hearing on connections between child abuse, juvenile crime, and delinquency and the juvenile justice system.

―――――. *Violent Juvenile Crime: Hearing before the Subcommittee on Juvenile Justice of the Committee on the Judiciary, United States Senate, Ninety-seventh Congress, first session, July 9, 1981.* Washington, DC: U.S. Government Printing Office, 1981.

This document contains the text of a hearing on violent crimes committed by juveniles in the United States.

―――――, Committee on Labor and Human Resources, Subcommittee on Aging. *Impact of Crime on the Elderly: Hearing before the Subcommittee on Aging of the Committee on Labor and Human Resources, United States Senate, Ninety-eighth Congress, first session, June 28, 1983.* Washington, DC: U.S. Government Printing Office, 1984.

A Senate subcommittee hearing on the frequency and effect of crime victimization among older Americans.

————, Committee on Small Business. *Impact of Crime on Small Business: Hearing before the Committee on Small Business, United States Senate, Ninety-eighth Congress, first session, October 12, 1983.* Washington, DC: U.S. Government Printing Office, 1983.

This report contains the text of a Senate committee hearing on small business and crime victimization.

————, Subcommittee on Urban and Rural Economic Development. *The Impact of Crime on Small Business: Hearings before the Subcommittee on Urban and Rural Economic Development of the Committee on Small Business, United States Senate, Ninety-seventh Congress, second session.* Washington, DC: U.S. Government Printing Office, 1982.

This document addresses crime problems in small businesses in the United States.

————, Select Committee on Small Business. *Crime and Its Impact on Small Business: Hearing before the Select Committee on Small Business, United States Senate, Ninety-sixth Congress, second session, May 29, 1980.* Washington, DC: U.S. Government Printing Office, 1980.

A Senate committee hearing on crime and small business in the United States.

————, Special Committee to Investigate Organized Crime in Interstate Commerce. *The Kefauver Committee Report on Organized Crime,* complete and unexpurgated ed. New York: Didier, 1951.

This report is of historical interest and contains results of the Kefauver Commission inquiry into the workings and extent of organized crime in interstate commerce.

U.S. Department of the Army. *Crime Prevention Handbook.* Washington, DC: Headquarters, Department of the Army, 1982.

A crime prevention manual compiled by the U.S. Department of the Army.

U.S. Department of Housing and Urban Development, in partnership with the U.S. Department of Labor et al. *Interagency Urban Initiatives Anti-Crime Program.* Washington, DC: U.S. Department of Housing and Urban Development, 1980.

Crime, prevention, urban renewal, urban policy, and public housing are addressed in this publication.

U.S. Department of Justice, Bureau of Justice Statistics. *Report to the Nation on Crime and Justice,* 2d ed. Washington, DC: U.S. Department of Justice, Bureau of Justice Statistics (BJS), 1988.

A general BJS statistical report on crime and criminal justice in the United States.

U.S. General Accounting Office. *The FBI Has Improved Its Fingerprint Identification Service: Report.* Washington, DC: U.S. General Accounting Office, 1983.

A report that describes improvements in the Federal Bureau of Investigation's fingerprint identification service.

―――. *Federal Prisons: Trends in Offender Characteristics: Factsheet for the Chairman, Select Committee on Narcotics Abuse and Control, House of Representatives.* Washington, DC: U.S. General Accounting Office, 1989.

A document containing facts and statistics on traits of criminals in the federal prison system.

VICAP Crime Analysis Report. Quantico, VA: U.S. Department of Justice, Federal Bureau of Investigation, National Center for the Analysis of Violent Crime, 1991.

A Violent Criminal Apprehension Program (VICAP) report on violent crime in the United States.

Wallis, Allan, and Daniel Ford. *Crime Prevention through Environmental Design: An Operational Handbook.* Washington, DC: U.S. Department of Justice, National Institute of Justice, 1981.

A manual with information on preventing crime through design of buildings and other environmental factors.

Weingart, Saul N., Francis X. Hartmann, and David Osborne. *Case Studies of Community Anti-Drug Efforts.* Washington, DC: U.S. Department of Justice, Office of Justice Programs, National Institute of Justice, 1994.

Part of the Research in Brief series, this document describes different community-based efforts to fight drug problems.

What You Should Know about Preventing Thefts in the Federal Workplace. Washington, DC: U.S. General Services Administration, Federal Protective Service, Public Buildings Service, 1987.

A handbook with information on safeguarding one's belongings and preventing theft in federal offices.

Whitaker, Catherine J. *Crime Prevention Measures.* Washington, DC: U.S. Department of Justice, Bureau of Justice Statistics, 1986.

A Bureau of Justice Statistics special report on crime prevention.

―――. *The Redesigned National Crime Survey: Selected New Data.* Washington, DC: U.S. Department of Justice, Office of Justice Programs, Bureau of Justice Statistics, 1989.

This document contains information on a reformed National Crime Survey, a prominent source of national crime statistics.

―――. *Teenage Victims: A National Crime Survey Report.* Washington, DC: U.S. Department of Justice, Bureau of Justice Statistics, 1986.

A National Crime Survey report on crime victimization among teenagers in the United States.

William Brill Associates. *Household Safety and Security Survey.* Washington, DC: Office of Policy Development and Research [prepared for the U.S. Department of Housing and Urban Development, Office of Policy Development and Research, by William Brill Associates], 1980.

This document is part of the series Planning for Housing Security. Subjects addressed include security in public housing and security and crime prevention through architectural design.

Wilson, Bradford P. *Exclusionary Rule.* Washington, DC: U.S. Department of Justice, National Institute of Justice, 1988.

This report analyzes the exclusionary rule, which places restrictions on evidence allowed in criminal trials. It is part of the Crime File series.

———. *Exclusionary Rule: A Study Guide.* Rockville, MD: U.S. Department of Justice, National Institute of Justice, 1986.

A study guide for the previous document.

Wilson, Thomas F., and Paul L. Woodard. *Automated Fingerprint Identification Systems: Technology and Policy Issues.* Washington, DC: U.S. Department of Justice, Bureau of Justice Statistics [prepared by Search Group], 1987.

The authors discuss advantages, problems, and issues associated with automated fingerprint identification.

Wish, Eric D., Mary A. Toborg, and John P. Bellassai. *Identifying Drug Users and Monitoring Them during Conditional Release.* Washington, DC: U.S. Department of Justice, National Institute of Justice, Office of Communication and Research Utilization [prepared for the National Institute of Justice, U.S. Department of Justice, by Abt Associates], 1988.

Part of the National Institute of Justice's Issues and Practices series, this publication discusses drug use among convicts during parole and probation.

Wish, Eric D., et al. *An Analysis of Drugs and Crime among Arrestees in the District of Columbia: Executive Summary.* Washington, DC: U.S. Department of Justice, National Institute of Justice, 1982.

This document examines the role of drugs in the offenses committed by arrested persons in the District of Columbia.

Wolfgang, Marvin E., and Neil Alan Weiner, with W. Donald Pointer. *Criminal Violence and Race: A Selected Bibliography.* Washington, DC: U.S. Department of Justice, National Institute of Justice, 1982.

This publication lists sources of information on crime, violence, and racial issues.

———. *The Violent Offender in the Criminal Justice System: A Selected Bibliography.* Washington, DC: U.S. Department of Justice, National Institute of Justice, 1982.

A bibliography of information on crime, violence, criminal behavior, and criminal justice.

Woodard, Paul L. *Criminal Justice Information Policy: Criminal Justice "Hot" Files.* Washington, DC: U.S. Department of Justice, Bureau of Justice Statistics, 1986.

This document is concerned with issues in criminal justice.

Wright, James D., and Peter H. Rossi. *Weapons, Crime, and Violence in America: Executive Summary.* Washington, DC: U.S. Department of Justice, National Institute of Justice, 1981.
    This document contains information on violent crime, firearms, and weapons in the United States.

Wright, James D., et al. *Weapons, Crime, and Violence in America: A Literature Review and Research Agenda.* Washington, DC: U.S. Department of Justice, National Institute of Justice, 1981.
    This document is a review of information on violent crime and weapons in the United States, as well as of proposed research.

Wright, James D., et al. *Weapons, Crime, and Violence in America: An Annotated Bibliography.* Washington, DC: U.S. Department of Justice, National Institute of Justice, 1981.
    A bibliography of information on crime, violence, firearms, and other weapons in the United States.

Zedlewski, Edwin W., and Mary G. Graham, eds. *Searching for Answers: Annual Report on Drugs and Crime.* Rockville, MD: National Institute of Justice, 1990.
    A yearly report on drugs and crime prepared for the attorney general, the president, and Congress.

Uniform Crime Reports Publications

The following publications are part of the Uniform Crime Reporting Program. For information, call (202) 324-5015.

- *Age-Specific Arrest Rates and Race-Specific Arrest Rates for Selected Offenses*
- *Crime in the United States* (annual)
- *Crime Trends* (semiannual press release)
- *Hate Crime* (annual press release)
- *Hate Crime Data Collection Guidelines*
- *Hate Crime Statistics* (annual)
- *Hate Crime Statistics, 1990: A Resource Book*
- *Killed in the Line of Duty: A Study of Selected Felonious Killings of Law Enforcement Officers* (special report)
- *Law Enforcement Officers Killed* (semiannual press release)
- *Law Enforcement Officers Killed and Assaulted* (annual)
- *Manual of Law Enforcement Records*
- *National Incident-Based Reporting System (NIBRS): Volume 1— Data Collection Guidelines*
- *NIBRS: Volume 2—Data Submission Specifications*

- *NIBRS: Volume 3—Approaches to Implementing an Incident-Based Reporting (IBR) System*
- *NIBRS: Volume 4—Error Message Manual*
- *NIBRS: Supplemental Guidelines for Federal Participation*
- *Population-at-Risk Rates and Selected Crime Indicators*
- *Training Guide for Hate Crime Data Collection*
- *UCR Preliminary Annual Report* (semiannual)
- *UCR Preliminary Release, January–June* (semiannual)
- *Uniform Crime Reporting Handbook: Summary System*
- *Uniform Crime Reporting Handbook: National Incident-Based Reporting System (NIBRS)*

Periodicals

Abstracts on Crime and Juvenile Delinquency: An Index to the Microform Collection. Glen Rock, NJ: Microfilming Corporation of America. LCCN: 79-640126. ISSN: 0164-1654.

This serial was formerly called *Index to Abstracts on Crime and Juvenile Delinquency.* It indexes information on crime, criminals, and juvenile delinquency that is available on microform.

Annual Report for the Court of Special Sessions. New York: Bar Press, Annual. LCCN: sn87-20890.

A yearly report on the activity of the New York State Court of Special Sessions.

Annual Report for the Year of . . . Baltimore, MD: Criminal Justice Commission, Annual. LCCN: 92-641015.

This yearly report began publication in 1964 and contains crime information and statistics.

Annual Report—Governor's Committee on Crime, Delinquency, and Corrections. Charleston, WV: Governor's Committee on Crime, Delinquency, and Corrections, Annual. LCCN: 74-645206 r922.

A yearly report that contains information on crime, corrections, criminal justice, and federal anticrime aid in the state of West Virginia.

Annual Report of the Attorney General of the United States. Washington, DC: U.S. Department of Justice, Office of Attorney Personnel Management, Annual.

A yearly summary of the activities of the agencies housed under the U.S. Department of Justice. The document contains a list of field offices that employ attorneys, a directory of agency employment contacts, and a list of FBI field offices.

A Bibliography of Selected Rand Publications: Criminality, Justice and Public Safety. Santa Monica, CA: Rand Corporation. LCCN: sn94-33400.

This serial lists Rand publications on crime, criminals, criminal justice, and law enforcement.

California Police Gazette. San Francisco, CA: Henri St. Clair, Weekly. LCCN: sn94-52695.
A crime newspaper that has been published since 1854.

California Police Record. San Francisco, CA: Harry N. Norse, Weekly. LCCN: sn95-62197.
A weekly newspaper on crime and law enforcement.

Comprehensive Law Enforcement Plan. Carson City, NV: Commission on Crime, Delinquency and Corrections. LCCN: 77-633226 r922. ISSN: 0092-1084.
This document outlines the state of Nevada's plan for law enforcement and crime control.

Crime. Plano, TX: Information Aids, Biennial. LCCN: sn88-21841.
Part of the Information Series on Current Topics, this publication contains crime information and statistics.

Crime and Criminal Justice. Washington, DC: U.S. Government Printing Office, Superintendent of Documents, Irregular. Ceased publication in 1992. LCCN: sn93-27772.
A bibliography of information on crime and criminal justice.

Crime and Delinquency. New York: National Council on Crime and Delinquency, Quarterly. LCCN: 56-504. ISSN: 0011-1287.
Formerly the *NPPA Journal,* this periodical has commentary on crime, juvenile delinquency, and criminology.

Crime and Delinquency Abstracts. Rockville, MD: National Clearinghouse for Mental Health Information. LCCN: 66-3911.
Abstracts on sources of information about crime, delinquency, and juvenile delinquency.

Crime and Delinquency Literature. Hackensack, NJ: National Council on Crime and Delinquency, Information Center, Quarterly. LCCN: 72-621963.
Two older publications—*Information Review on Crime and Delinquency* and *Selected Highlights of Crime and Delinquency Literature*—merged to form this publication. It contains abstracts of crime literature materials.

Crime and Justice. Chicago: University of Chicago Press, Annual. LCCN: 80-642217. ISSN: 0192-3234.
A yearly review of research on crime and criminal justice.

Crime and Justice Annual Report. Albany, NY: Office of Policy Analysis, Research, and Statistical Services, Bureau of Criminal Justice Statistical Services, Annual. LCCN: 87-654457.

An annual report from the New York State Division of Criminal Justice Services. It contains crime statistics, crime information, analysis, and criminal justice information for the state of New York.

Crime and Juvenile Delinquency: A Bibliographic Guide to the Documents Update. Sanford, NC: Microfilming Corporation of America. LCCN: 79-647378 r922.
A bibliography for information on crime, corrections, juvenile delinquency, corrections, and criminology.

Crime Beat. New York: 54 Corp., Monthly. LCCN: sn91-485. ISSN: 1058-529X.
This publication began in 1991 and contains information on crime.

Crime in Arizona: An Annual Report Compiled by the Arizona Department of Public Safety. Phoenix: Arizona Department of Public Safety, Annual. LCCN: sn94-26407.
A yearly government report on criminal activity in the state of Arizona.

Crime in Florida: Annual Report. Tallahassee: Florida Department of Law Enforcement, Annual. LCCN: 95-640181.
A yearly statistical report on crime in Florida. The publication is part of the Uniform Crime Reporting program.

Crime in Kentucky: Report. Frankfort: Kentucky State Police, Annual. LCCN: 87-645191.
Part of the Uniform Crime Reporting Program, this yearly publication contains statistics on criminal activity in the state of Kentucky.

Crime in Louisiana. Baton Rouge: Louisiana Commission on Law Enforcement, Louisiana Criminal Justice Information System Division, Annual. LCCN: 79-642736.
A yearly report on crime and justice in the state of Louisiana.

Crime in Maine. Augusta: State of Maine, Department of Public Safety. LCCN: 77-640920 r92. ISSN: 0148-6292.
A crime information and statistics report for the state of Maine.

Crime in Nebraska. Lincoln: Nebraska Commission on Law Enforcement and Criminal Justice, Annual. LCCN: 79-643889.
This report was formerly published as *Offenses Known to Police: Uniform Crime Report.* It is part of the Uniform Crime Reporting program and contains statistics on crime and criminal justice in Nebraska.

Crime in Nevada. Carson City: Nevada Department of Law Enforcement Assistance, Annual. LCCN: 78-642481.
An annual summary of criminal activity in the state of Nevada.

Criminal Justice. Washington, DC: U.S. Government Printing Office, Annual. LCCN: sn94-28101.

A bibliography on crime and criminal justice information.

Criminal Justice Abstracts. Monsey, NY: Willow Tree Press, Quarterly. LCCN: 647645. ISSN: 0146-9177.

Abstracts of articles, reports, and books that deal with crime and criminal justice.

Criminal Justice History. New York: Crime and Justice History Group, Annual. LCCN: 81-640321.

This serial contains information on crime and criminal justice history. It is distributed by John Jay Press and is published in English and French.

Criminal Justice Plan. Juneau, AK: Criminal Justice Planning Agency, Annual. LCCN: 77-636000.

A yearly comprehensive government plan for criminal justice, corrections, and law enforcement in the state of Alaska.

Criminal Justice Research Bulletin. Huntsville, TX: Sam Houston State University Criminal Justice Research Center, Six times a year. LCCN: sn90-33579.

This serial contains information on crime and criminal justice research.

Criminology. Columbus, OH: American Society of Criminology. LCCN: 76-648723. ISSN: 0011-1384.

An interdisciplinary journal on crime. This journal is the official publication of the American Society of Criminology.

Criminology, Penology, and Police Science Abstracts. Amsterdam and New York: Kugler Publications, Bimonthly. LCCN: 93-660538.

Abstracts on criminology, police, crime, corrections, justice, and juvenile delinquency information. This publication was created when two others merged, *Criminology and Penology Abstracts* and *Police Science Abstracts.*

FBI Law Enforcement Bulletin. Washington, DC: U.S. Department of Justice, Federal Bureau of Investigation, Monthly. LCCN: sn79-6149.

The bulletin of the Federal Bureau of Investigation. It contains updates on current investigations and information on crime and law enforcement.

Federal Probation. Washington, DC: Administrative Office of the United States Courts, Quarterly/irregular. LCCN: sc81-3113. ISSN: 0014-9128.

A newsletter on federal crime and probation.

Felony Laws of the 50 States and the District of Columbia. Washington, DC: U.S. Department of Justice, Bureau of Justice Statistics, Annual. LCCN: 89-644114.

A yearly update of felony laws and offenses in U.S. states.

Felony Sentences in State Courts. Washington, DC: U.S. Department of Justice, Office of Justice Programs, Bureau of Justice Statistics, Biennial. LCCN: sn89-23295.

A serial that describes sentencing for felonies in U.S. state courts.

Fugitives Wanted by the Police. Washington, DC: U.S. Bureau of Investigation, Monthly. LCCN: sn87-20747.

This serial, published only between 1932 and 1935, listed wanted fugitives from justice during J. Edgar Hoover's war on "public enemies." It is published today as the *FBI Law Enforcement Bulletin.*

Georgia Criminal Justice Data. Atlanta: State Crime Commission, Division of Criminal Justice Statistics. LCCN: 76-641437.

Formerly called *Crime in Georgia,* this publication contains statistical information on criminal activity in the state of Georgia.

Incident-Based Iowa Uniform Crime Reports. Des Moines, IA: Department of Public Safety, Annual. LCCN: 95-648053.

This yearly statistical report on criminal activity in Iowa is part of the Uniform Crime Reporting program.

International Criminal Justice Review. Atlanta: College of Public and Urban Affairs, Georgia State University, Annual. LCCN: sn91-2810. ISSN: 1057-5677.

A journal on international crime and criminal justice.

International Journal of Comparative and Applied Criminal Justice. Wichita, KS: Department of Administration of Justice, Wichita State University, Semiannual. LCCN: 80-643365. ISSN: 0192-4036.

An academic journal devoted to crime and criminal justice issues.

International Journal of the Sociology of Law. London and New York: Academic Press, Quarterly. LCCN: 80-649675.

This periodical was formerly the *International Journal of Criminology and Penology.* It covers issues in jurisprudence, sociology, criminal law, correctional law, and crime.

Journal of Criminal Law, Criminology and Police Science. Chicago: Northwestern University School of Law, Quarterly. LCCN: 12-27508.

This journal on crime, criminology, law enforcement, and criminal law was orginally called the *Journal of the American Institute of Criminal Law and Criminology* and later the *Journal of Criminal Law and Criminology* before acquiring its present title.

Journal of Research in Crime and Delinquency. Thousand Oaks, CA: Sage Publications, Quarterly. LCCN: 64-9395. ISSN: 0022-4278.

This journal publishes research in the areas of criminology and crime.

Judicial, Prevention and Enforcement Activities. Washington, DC: U.S. Bureau of Indian Affairs, Division of Judicial, Prevention and Enforcement Services. LCCN: 74-641929.

A report on federal anticrime activities involving American Indians in the United States.

Medicaid Fraud Report. Washington, DC: National Association of Attorneys General, Ten issues per year. LCCN: 87-659157.

A periodic report on fraud and abuse of Medicaid money.

Michigan Public Speaks Out on Crime. Detroit: Market Opinion Research Company. LCCN: 79-640462.

Previously called *Crime in Michigan,* this serial contains the results of public opinion polls on crime in the state of Michigan.

National Crime Information Center: A Newsletter for the Criminal Justice Community. Washington, DC: U.S. Department of Justice, Federal Bureau of Investigation, Quarterly. LCCN: sn91-23460.

A newsletter with information on crime and law enforcement issues.

National Police Gazette. New York: Camp and Wilkes, Weekly. LCCN: sn94-95956.

A weekly newspaper with information on crime, law enforcement, and criminal justice issues.

New York State Criminal Justice Processing. Albany: New York State, Division of Criminal Justice Services, Office of Policy Analysis, Research and Statistical Services, Annual. LCCN: 87-643022.

A yearly report, with crime and criminal justice information and statistics for the state of New York.

The NIJ Publications Catalog. National Institute of Justice (U.S.). Washington, DC: U.S. Department of Justice, Office of Justice Programs, National Institute of Justice, Irregular.

This serial lists the publications produced by the National Institute of Justice.

North Dakota Comprehensive Criminal Justice Plan. Bismarck: Combined Law Enforcement Council. LCCN: 72-612709 r922.

This report was formerly called the *North Dakota Law Enforcement Plan.* It is a plan for law enforcement and criminal justice activity in the state of North Dakota.

NYSIBR News. Albany: New York State, Division of Criminal Justice Services, Bureau of Statistical Services, Quarterly.

The initials stand for New York State Incident-Based Reporting, and the publication contains information and statistics on criminal activity in the state of New York.

Ohio Citizen Attitudes Concerning Crime and Criminal Justice. Columbus: Governor's Office of Criminal Justice Services, Ohio Statistical Analysis Center, Biennial. LCCN: 86-641359.

Formerly published as *Ohio Citizen Attitudes,* this serial contains public opinion information on crime and criminal justice issues in Ohio.

Oklahoma Criminal Justice Action Plan. Oklahoma City: Oklahoma Crime Commission. LCCN: 77-644150 r922. ISSN: 0149-1660.

This report outlines the state of Oklahoma's plans involving criminal justice, federal anticrime aid, law enforcement, and other anticrime measures.

Oregon Law Enforcement Agencies Report of Criminal Offenses and Arrests. Salem: Law Enforcement Data System, Annual. LCCN: 89-640075.

Statistical information for the state of Oregon on crime, criminals, and arrests.

A Public Opinion Report from the Arkansas Crime Poll. Little Rock: Arkansas Crime Information Center, Annual. LCCN: WMLC 93/5458.

This report began in 1987 and contains public opinion figures on crime in Arkansas.

Regional Criminal Justice Plan. Lubbock, TX: South Plains Association of Governments. LCCN: 75-313517. ISSN: 0149-3248.

An area plan for anticrime measures and criminal justice activity in Texas.

Report of the California Crime Commission. Sacramento: California State Printing Office. LCCN: sn89-39610.

This report contains an analysis of crime in the state of California.

Report of the Crime Commission of Michigan. Lansing: Crime Commission of Michigan, Biennial. LCCN: sn89-39611.

Analysis of crime in Michigan.

Reported Crime in New York State. Albany: New York State Division of Criminal Justice Services, Bureau of Statistical Services, Annual. LCCN: sn92-35099.

This report contains information on crime in the state of New York.

Reported Offenses and Arrests: New York State. Albany: New York State Department of Correctional Services, Division of Research. LCCN: 72-611797.

This report contains statistical information on criminal offenses and arrests in the state of New York.

Security Advisor. McLean, VA: ELL Security Consultants, Bimonthly. LCCN: sn90-2435. ISSN: 1050-6381.

This publication is specifically devoted to crimes committed by animal rights activists. Subjects addressed include security systems, offenses, and prevention.

Selected Topic Digest. Washington, DC: National Criminal Justice Reference Service. LCCN: 73-641089. ISSN: 0091-9179.

A federal government source of information on crime and criminal justice issues.

Social Justice. San Francisco: Institute for the Study of Labor and Economic Crisis, Quarterly. LCCN:74-646246. ISSN: 0094-7571.

Formerly called *Crime and Social Justice,* this is a journal on crime and social issues.

Statistics Calendar. Juneau, AK: Department of Public Safety, Records and Identification Section. LCCN: 79-621578.

Subjects addressed in this Alaska serial include crime and criminal statistics.

Texas Crime Poll. Huntsville, TX: Sam Houston State University, Criminal Justice Center, Survey Research Program, Semiannual. LCCN: 80-647965.

This report contains the results of the Texas Crime Poll, which measures public opinion on crime and criminal justice issues in that state.

Tribal and Bureau Law Enforcement Services Automated Data Report (U.S. Indian Police Training Center): Navajo Area. Washington, DC: U.S. Department of the Interior, Bureau of Indian Affairs, Division of Law Enforcement Services, U.S. Indian Police Training Center. LCCN: 80-643513.

Information contained in this report includes descriptions of crime and law enforcement in Navajo Indian territory, as well as statistics.

Uniform Crime Reporting: Index Offenses Reported Final Counts for [year]. Albany, NY: Division of Criminal Justice Services, Office of Policy Analysis, Research and Statistical Services, Bureau of Criminal Justice Statistics Services, Annual. LCCN: sf94-93846.

This report prints statistical information on crimes and arrests in the state of New York and is part of the Uniform Crime Reporting Program.

Uniform Crime Reports. Lincoln: Nebraska Commission on Law Enforcement and Criminal Justice, Annual. LCCN: 86-640431 r923.

Yearly statistical information on crime and arrests in Nebraska. The publication is part of the Uniform Crime Reporting Program.

Uniform Crime Reports, Commonwealth of Pennsylvania: Annual Report. Harrisburg: Bureau of Research and Development, Pennsylvania State Police, Annual. LCCN: 75-640313.

This serial contains statistics on crime in Pennsylvania and is part of the Uniform Crime Reporting Program.

Uniform Crime Reports: State of Rhode Island. Providence: Rhode Island State Police, Annual. LCCN: 76-641582.

A compilation of crime statistics for the state of Rhode Island. It is part of the Uniform Crime Reporting Program.

United Nations Interregional Crime and Justice Research Institute: Annual Report. Rome, Italy: United Nations Interregional Crime and Justice Research Institute, Annual. LCCN: 92-640562.

This publication contains information on institute activities, international crime, and research. It was formerly published as *United Nations Social Defence Research Institute: Annual Report.*

United States Title and Code Criminal Offense Citations. Washington, DC: Administrative Office of the United States Courts, Biennial (irregular). LCCN: 90-643843.

A periodic publication that describes criminal violations of the U.S. Code.

Microforms and Microfilms

Bea, Keith, and Harry Hogan, coordinators. *Crime, Drug, and Gun Control Comparison of Major Bills under Consideration by the House Judiciary Committee, 102nd Congress.* Washington, DC: Congressional Research Service, Library of Congress, 1991.

An examination of legislation under consideration at that time to combat crime, drugs, and firearms abuse.

Bea, Keith, David Teasley, and Charles Doyle. *Crime Control Act of 1994: Selected Highlights of H.R. 3355 as Passed* [microform]. Washington, DC: Congressional Research Service, Library of Congress, 1994.

This document describes significant parts of the Violent Crime Control and Law Enforcement Act of 1994.

Bowers, Jean. *Crime Control Criminal Theory: Selected References, 1989–1991* [microfilm]. Washington, DC: Congressional Research Service, Library of Congress, 1991.

A list of references on the subjects of crime and prevention.

———. *Crime Control: Federal Response: Selected References, 1990–1991* [microfilm]. Washington, DC: Congressional Research Service, Library of Congress, 1991.

A bibliography of information on federal efforts to combat crime in the United States.

Crime and Delinquency. New York: National Council on Crime and Delinquency, Quarterly. LCCN: Microfilm LL-0133.

A quarterly serial that addresses issues in crime and juvenile delinquency.

Crime and Justice Annual Report. Albany: New York State Division of Criminal Justice Services, Office of Policy Analysis, Research, and Statistical Services, Bureau of Criminal Justice Statistical Services, Annual. LCCN: sn94-40408.

A yearly report with statistical and other crime information for the state of New York.

Crime Control Comparison of House and Senate Legislation of the 103rd Congress, Second Session [microfilm]. Washington, DC: Congressional Research Service, Library of Congress, 1994.

This microform describes House and Senate anticrime legislation under consideration during the second session of the 103rd Congress.

Doyle, Charles. *Crime Control Act of 1994 Capital Punishment Provisions Summarized* [microfilm]. Washington, DC: Congressional Research Service, Library of Congress, 1994.

The author describes new capital punishment provisions included in the Violent Crime Control and Law Enforcement Act of 1994.

————. *When the Young Violate Federal Criminal Law: Federal Juvenile Delinquency Act and Related Matters* [microform]. Washington, DC: Congressional Research Service, Library of Congress, 1993.

This document discusses juvenile criminals who violate federal laws and legislation to combat the problem.

Hogan, Harry, coordinator. *Crime and Drug Control Comparison of Pending Senate and House Bills S. 618 and H.R. 1400/S. 635* [microfilm]. Washington, DC: Congressional Research Service, Library of Congress, 1991.

An analysis of proposed anticrime and antidrug House and Senate bills, 1991.

————, coordinator. *Crime Control Act of 1990 (P.L. 101-647): Summary* [microfilm]. Washington, DC: Congressional Research Service, Library of Congress, 1991.

This document is a synopsis of the Crime Control Act of 1990.

————, coordinator. *Crime, Drug, and Gun Control Summary of S. 1241 (102nd Congress) as Passed by the Senate* [microform]. Washington, DC: Congressional Research Service, Library of Congress, 1991.

A summary of anticrime, antidrug, and gun control measures passed in the Senate bill S. 1241.

Hogan, Harry, and Keith Bea, coordinators. *Crime, Drug, and Gun Control Highlights of Conference Agreement on H.R. 3371, 102nd Congress* [microform]. Washington, DC: Congressional Research Service, Library of Congress, 1992.

This document explains anticrime, antidrug, and gun control measures in a 1992 congressional conference agreement.

Law and Legal Systems. New Canaan, CT: NewsBank, Approximately 110–170 times a year. LCCN: 91-651518. ISSN: 0737-3775.

A serial with information on crime and criminal justice issues.

Loo, Shirley. *Crime and Criminal Justice: An Alphabetical Microthesaurus of Terms Selected from the Legislative Indexing Vocabulary* [microform]. Washington, DC: Congressional Research Service, Library of Congress, 1988.

This document is part of the Major Studies and Issue Briefs of the Congressional Research Service and defines legislative words associated with crime and criminal justice.

National Institute of Justice/NCJRS, Microfiche Program [microform]. Rockville, MD: National Criminal Justice Reference Service, 1982.

Part of the Selected Library in Microfiche series, this microform describes microfiches that are part of the National Criminal Justice Reference Service's microfiche program.

National Police Gazette. New York: Camp and Wilkes, Weekly. LCCN: sf88-91824.

A weekly crime newspaper that is part of the American Periodical Series.

Pettit, Gerald. *Crime and Victimization of the Minority Elderly: A Bibliography* [microform]. San Diego: University Center on Aging, San Diego State University, College of Health and Human Services, National Resource Center on Minority Aging Populations, 1991.

A bibliography of information on crime victims who are elderly and minorities.

Roe, Tangela G. *Anti-Crime Initiatives: Community Policing and Citizen Involvement; Selected References, 1992–1994* [microform]. Washington, DC: Congressional Research Service, Library of Congress, 1994.

A list of information on community policing from 1992 to 1994.

———. *Anti-Crime Initiatives: Drug Control; Selected References, 1992–1994* [microform]. Washington, DC: Congressional Research Service, Library of Congress, 1994.

This microform lists sources of information on anti–drug control efforts between 1992 and 1994.

———. *Anti-Crime Initiatives: Issues, Approaches, and Federal Involvement; Selected References, 1992–1994* [microform]. Washington, DC: Congressional Research Service, Library of Congress, 1994.

This microform lists information sources and references on anti-crime efforts and crime issues between 1992 and 1994.

———. *Anti-Crime Initiatives: Sentencing, Prisons, and Prisoners; Selected References, 1992–1994* [microform]. Washington, DC: Congressional Research Service, Library of Congress, 1994.

This microform is a bibliography of information on prisoners, inmates, sentencing, and corrections from 1992 to 1994.

———. *Anti-Crime Initiatives: Youth and Violence; Selected References, 1992–1994* [microform]. Washington, DC: Congressional Research Service, Library of Congress, 1994.

A list of references on juveniles, violence, and crime between 1992 and 1994.

Teasley, David. *Anti-Crime Funding in the Fiscal 1995 Commerce, Justice, State Appropriations Act (H.R. 4603): A Summary* [microform]. Washington, DC: Congressional Research Service, Library of Congress, 1994.

A summary of federal spending in fiscal year 1995 on anticrime measures authorized by the Commerce, Justice, State Appropriations Act.

————. *Crime Control Act of 1990 (P.L. 101-647): Drug-Related Reports and Other Executive Branch Actions Required* [microfilm]. Washington, DC: Congressional Research Service, Library of Congress, 1991, 1994.

Subjects addressed in this document include federal law enforcement, executive branch anticrime action, and antidrug efforts resulting from the Crime Control Act of 1990.

Thomas, Kenneth R. *Anti-Stalking Statutes Background and Constitutional Analysis* [microform]. Washington, DC: Congressional Research Service, Library of Congress, 1992.

This microform addresses potential constitutional problems and other issues related to antistalking laws.

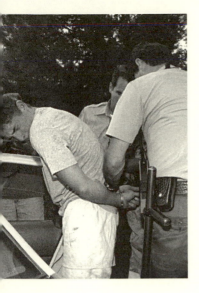

Nonprint Resources

7

M uch information that was formerly confined to libraries is becoming more readily available to anyone who has a computer, a modem, and a connection to the Internet. If you do not have access to the Internet, check with your local library. Some provide public access. Most of the Internet sites listed here contain links to other pages and electronic databases that provide additional information. The audio-visual resources given here are available at some libraries; you can also obtain them by contacting the company directly.

Audio-Visual

Bad Cops, or Cops Getting a Bad Rap?
Type: Video recording
Length: 28 minutes
Cost: $89.95
Date: 1993
Source: Films for the Humanities and Sciences
Box 2053
Princeton, NJ 08543-2053
(800) 257-5126

This video features defensive statements from police officers who have been accused of being "bad cops."

Child Sex Abusers
Type: Video recording
Length: 28 minutes
Cost: $89.95
Date: 1994
Source: Films for the Humanities and Sciences
Box 2053
Princeton, NJ 08543-2053
(800) 257-5126

Presents cases of sex abuse among children who know each other. It also contains advice on spotting a potentially abusive child.

Crime Check: Acquaintance Rape
Type: Video recording
Length: 22 minutes
Cost: $199.95
Date: 1993
Source: AIMS Media
9710 De Soto Avenue
Chatsworth, CA 91311-4409
(800) 367-2467

This video describes acquaintance rape and offers advice on how to prevent it.

Crime in the Streets
Type: Issued as a motion picture and a video recording
Length: 16 minutes
Cost: $99.95
Date: 1983
Source: AIMS Media
9710 De Soto Avenue
Chatsworth, CA 91311-4409
(800) 367-2467

A reformed mugger describes different kinds of behavior that attract or discourage theft in the city and also gives advice on protecting valuables. Intended for high school students and older.

Crime in the Suites
Type: Video recording
Length: 25 minutes

Cost: $89.95
Date: 1987
Source: Films for the Humanities and Sciences
           Box 2053
           Princeton, NJ 08543-2053
           (800) 257-5126

White-collar crime in the United States is the topic of this video. It features interviews with Professor Joseph O'Donoghue and author Georgette Bennett, as well as testimonials from people who have been involved in or victimized by white-collar crime.

Crimebusters
Type: Video recording
Length: 26 minutes
Cost: $89.95
Date: 1989
Source: Films for the Humanities and Sciences
           Box 2053
           Princeton, NJ 08543-2053
           (800) 257-5126

The subject of this video is technological advances in criminal investigation. Techniques examined include DNA fingerprinting, detecting fingerprints with lasers, and computer uses.

The Death Penalty
Type: Video recording
Length: 28 minutes
Cost: $149.00
Date: 1988
Source: Films for the Humanities and Sciences
           Box 2053
           Princeton, NJ 08543-2053
           (800) 257-5126

This video looks at the ways the death penalty is used in the United States.

Drugs in Black and White
Type: Video recording; comes with a discussion guide
Length: 41 minutes
Cost: $125.00

Date: 1990
Source: Coronet/MTI
            4350 Equity Drive
            Columbus, OH 43228
            (800) 321-3106

This video examines the extent of drug use among teenagers in the Atlanta, Georgia, vicinity.

DUI, Unlicensed To Kill
Type: Video recording
Length: 45 minutes
Cost: $149.00
Date: 1995
Source: Films for the Humanities and Sciences
            Box 2053
            Princeton, NJ 08543-2053
            (800) 257-5126

The failure of the judicial system to keep drunk drivers off the road is the topic of this video. It features an interview with an incarcerated repeat driving under the influence (DUI) offender and a discussion between families who have been victimized by drunk drivers and DUI offenders.

Kids and Drugs
Type: Video recording; comes with a discussion guide
Length: 28 minutes
Cost: $89.95
Date: 1987
Source: Films for the Humanities and Sciences
            Box 2053
            Princeton, NJ 08543-2053
            (800) 257-5126

This video presents the testimonies of five teenagers who became addicted to drugs or alcohol and recovered from their addictions.

Rape and DNA Testing
Type: Video recording
Length: 28 minutes
Cost: $89.95
Date: 1993

Source: Films for the Humanities and Sciences
Box 2053
Princeton, NJ 08543-2053
(800) 257-5126

This video presents a panel discussion about the use of DNA
testing and evidence in rape cases. The panel includes a rape
victim, attorneys, and people who have been falsely convicted
of rape.

Rape, Not Always a Stranger
Type: Video recording
Length: 25 minutes
Cost: $149.95
Date: 1988
Source: AIMS Media
9710 De Soto Avenue
Chatsworth, CA 91311-4409
(800) 367-2467

Two narrators, a rape counselor and a police officer, examine situations that can potentially lead to rape.

What Price the Drug War
Type: Video recording
Length: 58 minutes
Cost: $89.95
Date: 1994
Source: Films for the Humanities and Sciences
Box 2053
Princeton, NJ 08543-2053
(800) 257-5126

This video looks into the costs of drug use in the United States
and offers suggestions for drug control policy. Treatment for
drug addicts is also discussed.

Websites

Active Most Wanted and Criminal Investigations

http://www.gunnyragg.com/crimes.htm

Information on the most wanted criminals from various federal, state, and local agencies.

Bureau of Justice Statistics (BJS) Homepage

http://www.ojp.usdoj.gov/bjs/

This site contains BJS statistics on crime, drugs, law enforcement, corrections, and other aspects of the criminal justice system.

City Crime Rates—Carlsbad

http://www.sddt.com/files/reports/statsheets/
cities/carlsbad.html

Crime rate information for the city of Carlsbad, California.

City of Vacaville Police Department

http://www.community.net/~rsanford/police.html

Here, the police department of Vacaville, California, posts a crime and traffic report, a weekly crime map, and information on prevention programs. The page also has links to other law-related sites.

CNSS Analysis of Clinton Administration Counter-Terrorism Proposal

http://www.cdt.org/policy/terrorism/cnss.cti.anal.html

A critical analysis of a bill introduced in the U.S. Senate on February 10, 1995, by the Center for National Security Studies. The site also has links to the center's homepage and a counter-terrorism page.

Crime Bill

http://broadway.vera.org/pub/crimebill/cb.html

Information about the Violent Crime Control and Law Enforcement Act of 1994, with statements on titles 1–33.

The Crime Files Regulations

http://www.emeraldcity.com/crimefiles/crimefiles.htm

Graphic photos accompany information on current unsolved crimes. It would be wise to check the site first before allowing children to use it.

Crime-Free America

http://announce.com/cfa/cfa.htm
The homepage of a grassroots organization with a mission statement, data, a crime forum, and a crime watch.

Crime Homepage

http://timon.sir.arizona.edu/govdocs/crime/intro.htm
A site filled with links to other pages containing legal information; computer and crime statistics; and law enforcement, prevention, and other resources.

Crime Links

http://www.quest.net/crime/links.html
Maintained by the Metro-Dade police department crime lab of Yeknapatawha County, this site has information on forensic science, fingerprint and shoeprint analysis, and current investigations.

Crime Statistics

http://www.electriciti.com/~rweeks/crime.html
This site, which contains sparse information, pertains particularly to Oceanside, California, but also has statistics on other major cities in the United States.

Crime Stoppers of Central Indiana

http://www.inetdirect.net/crime/
Contains press releases, a sample clip from the video *The Consequences of Crime*, a list of new suspects, five of Indiana's most wanted criminals, and links to other Crime Stoppers pages.

Criminal Justice Issues

http://www.mennonitecc.ca/mcc/programs/crime.html
Consists of an article by Wayne Northey entitled "Harsher Punishment for Crime Is Not the Answer." This site is maintained by the Mennonite Central Committee and also has information on victim-offender reconciliation, domestic violence, sexual abuse, gun control, and capital punishment.

CSU Crime Statistics

http://bones.asic.csuohio.edu/dept/csupd/cstats.html
   A small site with campus crime statistics for Cleveland State University.

Dallas Police Homepage

http://server.iadfw.net/dpd/
   Information on crime statistics, prevention, and neighborhood security.

18 USC Sec. 2423 (01/24/94)

http://www.law.cornell.edu/uscode/18/2423.html
   Contains the text of the main section of the U.S. Code devoted to criminal law.

FBI Homepage

http://www.fbi.gov/homepage.htm
   Information on the Federal Bureau of Investigation, with updates on current investigations.

From NameBase NewsLine, No. 8, January–March 1995:

http://ursula.blythe.org/NameBase/newsline.08
   Consists of an article entitled "As Criminal Capitalism Replaces Communism: Organized Crime Threatens the New World Order," by Daniel Brandt.

Gleaning

http://www.vix.com/pub/men/abuse/studies/misc.html
   A limited site with national crime statistics from USENET, and other links.

Internet Resources for Crime Victims

http://timon.sir.arizona.edu/govdocs/crmvctm/home.htm
   This site lists Internet resources for crime victims, organizations that assist victims of crime, and statistics on crime victims. One can also find the Violent Crime Control and Law Enforcement Act of 1994.

Maryland Community Crime Prevention Institute

http://midget.towson.edu:8001/MDCP.HTML

Information on outsmarting crime, sexual assault, and neighborhood watch programs, as well as links to a missing children's network and other crime pages.

Men, Women, Crime, and Prison

http://www.vix.com/pub/men/criminal/stats.html

An article about the prison system and its treatment of women, with links to a men's issues page and a men in the justice system page.

NRA Firearms Fact Card—1995

http://www.nra.org/pub/ila/95_firearms_fact_card

This page is maintained by the National Rifle Association and contains statistical information on firearms.

Operation Safe Streets

http://www.lp.org/lp/lp-oss.html

The Libertarian Party sponsors this page. It outlines the party's approach to crime control.

Opportunity Knocks

http://www.mojones.com/MOTHER_JONES/MJ95/castleman.html

A large page with many links, a resource guide for crime, and information on organized crime, generally presented from a liberal perspective.

Outsmarting Crime

http://midget.towson.edu:8001/outsmart.html

Facts about crime, advice on preventing property crimes and protecting yourself from them, advice on protecting children, and information on fraud and personal security. The Maryland Community Crime Prevention Institute maintains this site.

Peel Police Research

http://www.peelpolice.gov/research.html

The primary focus is police research, with a small amount of information on crime prevention through environmental design, physical design, human resources, and personal safety.

Perilous Times—Crime page

http://www.teleport.com/~jstar/crime.html
This page serves mainly as a links page, providing connections to information on criminal justice, fraud, and other aspects of crime.

Portfolio—Crime Statistics

http://www-portfolio.stanford.edu/104251
Part of Stanford University's crime statistics from the *New Stanford Almanac.* Only a small amount of information is posted.

President's Crime Prevention Council

http://www.whitehouse.gov/White_House/EOP/OVP/html/prevent.html
Information on the Crime Prevention Council created by the Violent Crime Control and Law Enforcement Act of 1994.

Preventing Campus Crime and Sexual Assault

http://msuinfo.ur.msstate.edu/crime/prevent.htm
A summary of campus policy at Mississippi State University.

Representing Victims of Crime: A Perspective on the Disaster of American Public Policy and Proposals for Change

http://tsw.ingress.com/tsw/talf/txt/crime.html
Consists of an article entitled "Representing Victims of Crime: A Perspective on the Disaster of American Public Policy and Proposals for Change," by Richard Alexander.

Results of the National Demonstration Project

http://www.mum.edu/TM_Research/DC_Crime_Project/Abstract.html
This site contains abstracts and charts related to the National Demonstration Project to Reduce Violent Crime and Improve Governmental Effectiveness in Washington, D.C.

Roseville PD Homepage

http://www.sna.com/rosepd/
The homepage of the Roseville, California, police department. It contains links to a wide variety of government resources on crime and criminal justice.

Sacramento Police Department

http://www.quiknet.com/~spdcau/
   Lists rewards, neighborhood alerts, crime statistics, prevention tips, program descriptions, and links to the pages of other police departments.

SAFE AND SOUND

http://www.america.net/~kscdps/
   Maintained by the Department of Public Safety at Kennesaw State College (KSC) near Atlanta, Georgia, this site has information on crime prevention, sexual assault, and KSC crime statistics.

School Violence

http://curry.edschool.virginia.edu/~rkb3b/Hal/School Violence.html
   Contains facts and information on violence in public schools.

Take Back New York's Crime Statistics Page

http://www.users.interport.net/~wave3/stats.html
   Crime factoids, links to the New York Police Department and New York's most wanted criminals make up this site.

Training Manual

http://bones.asic.csuohio.edu/dept/csupd/CWTRM4.html
   The Cleveland State University Campus Watch maintains this site. It contains the text of the organization's training manual, with crime prevention tips.

Uniform Crime Reports—Pre 95: Tables

http://www.fbi.gov/pre95tbs.htm
   Contains *Uniform Crime Reports* for the first half of 1995. The data will likely change as more updated information becomes available.

University of Colorado Police Department

http://stripe.colorado.edu/~police/Home.htm
   Consists of summaries of current police reports, the history of the University of Colorado Police Department, an annual report on crime statistics, and a list of items that have been lost and found on the University of Colorado campus.

UNO—Criminal Justice and Crime Prevention

http://www.ifs.univie.ac.at/~pr2gq1/uno
The UN crime prevention page lists current activities and projects and provides a link to the United Nations Criminal Justice Information Network (UNCJIN).

U.S. House Democratic Leadership—Hot Topics: Crime

http://www.house.gov/democrats/ht_crime.html
This site is part of a larger page of information set up by the U.S. House Democratic leadership. Information is minimal but includes statements from House Democrats on crime, as well as updates on the Oklahoma City bombing.

Violent Crime Control and Law Enforcement Act of 1994

http://gopher.usdoj.gov/crime/crime.html
The text of the Violent Crime Control and Law Enforcement Act of 1994.

Although many of the following computer sources do not specifically deal with crime, information on crime can be found in them. Each database's address is included at the end of its entry, and it will likely lead to the discovery of other information.

Bureau of Justice Statistics (BJS) Documents: This database contains the full text of some BJS publications. To reach it: gopher uacsc2.albany.edu/united nations justice network/Bureau of Justice Statistics.

Congressional Information: Select congressional documents (the North American Free Trade Agreement, the U.S. budget, the Americans with Disabilities Act, and so on) make up part of this database. It also enables one to access directories and committee rosters. To access the database: gopher gopher.lib.umich.edu/social sciences resources/government and politics/u.s. government resources: legislative branch.

Criminal Justice Country Profiles: This database consists mainly of full-text UN reports and statistics on crime in 123 countries around the world. One can access it by: gopher uacsc2.albany.edu/united nations justice network/u.n. criminal justice country profiles.

Historical Documents: Historical documents relevant to the United States are located here. One can access it by: gopher wiretap.spies.com/government docs.

Library of Congress Information System: The Library of Congress Information System (LOCIS) provides access to files on U.S. and foreign law, the Library of Congress catalog, and a national directory of organizations. One can also find detailed descriptions of federal legislation introduced in Congress beginning in 1973. LOCIS provides vast amounts of information and allows its users to perform detailed searches. To get into LOCIS: telnet locis.loc.gov.

Library of Congress Marvel: This gopher provides access to a wide variety of government information, including information on Congress and other branches of government, crime statistics, White House and State Department documents, and more. Its source is gopher marvel.loc.gov.

Speeches and Addresses: This database contains the full text of significant historical speeches in the United States. To reach it: gopher wiretap.spies.com/government docs/us speeches and addresses.

Supreme Court Decisions: One can obtain the full text of Supreme Court decisions since 1989, as well as biographies of Supreme Court justices, through this database. It can be reached by: gopher info.umd.edu/educational resources/academic resources by topic/subject guides/information by subject area/ government, political science, and law/supreme court rulings.

United States Government Gopher Servers: Through this stop on the Internet, one can get into a variety of other government gopher systems. Its source is: gopher stis.nsf.gov/other u.s. government gopher servers.

World Constitutions: The full text of constitutions (both current and historical) of several countries from around the world can be accessed through this database. Its source is: gopher wiretap.spies. com/government docs (U.S. & World)/world constitutions.

Electronic Bulletin Boards

The following bulletin boards provide full or limited public access to information on crime and criminal law. Long-distance charges will apply unless the telephone number prefix is (800) or you live within the local calling area.

Appeals Court Electronic Service (ACES)
(804) 771-2028
Maximum baud: 2400
Location: Richmond, VA

Comments: Address questions to: Systems Office/United States Courthouse/10th and Main Streets, Room 250/Richmond, VA 23219/(804) 771-8009.

Automated Library Information Exchange
(202) 707-4888
Maximum baud: 2400
Location: Washington, DC

Comments: Sponsored by the Federal Library and Information Center Network.

Avalon BBS
(612) 222-6440
Maximum baud: 2400
Location: St. Paul, MN

AZCLU BBS
(602) 271-1180
Maximum baud: 2400
Location: Phoenix, AZ

Comments: Sponsored by the Arizona Civil Liberties Union.

CATCH Resources
(414) 761-2582
Maximum baud: 2400
Location: Milwaukee, WI

CCP-BBS
(215) 568-0356
Maximum baud: 2400
Location: Philadelphia, PA

Comments: Contact Cliff Baumbach (215) 686-4415. This bulletin board is sponsored by the Philadelphia Court of Common Pleas and the Pennsylvania State Justice Institute.

CESAR Board
(301) 403-8343

Maximum baud: 2400
Location: College Park, MD

Comments: Sponsored by the Center for Substance Abuse Research, this board contains current information on substance abuse.

CODE-3 BBS
(714) 534-9196
Maximum baud: 2400
Location: Anaheim, CA

Comments: Some portions of this board are open to the public. Parts of it are restricted to police officers, fire personnel, and ham operators.

Colby Area BBS
(913) 462-2555
Maximum baud: 2400
Location: Colby, KS

Comments: Although part of this board is restricted to police officers, public users can access a question-and-answer area.

Colorado State Judicial BBS
(303) 831-1704
Maximum baud: 2400
Location: Denver, CO

The County Jail
(908) 787-7459
Maximum baud: 14,400
Location: Middletown, NJ

Crime Bytes
(305) 251-2698
Maximum baud: 9600
Location: Miami, FL

Comments: Citizens Crime Watch sponsors this bulletin board, and Metro-Dade police officers operate it.

Criminal Justice Training BBS
(517) 483-9615
Maximum baud: 2400
Location: Lansing, MI

Department of Justice
(202) 514-6193
Maximum baud: 2400
Location: Washington, DC

Comments: Access is prioritized; employees of federal civil rights offices have highest privileges.

El Cerrito Police Public Safety BBS
(510) 235-3273
Maximum baud: 14,400
Location: El Cerrito, CA

Comments: Crime and fire prevention and the Neighborhood Emergency Assistance Program form the focus of this electronic board.

Federal Bulletin Board
(202) 512-1387
Maximum baud: 9600
Location: Washington, DC

Comments: There are two levels of access to the Federal Bulletin Board. To obtain assistance with this board, call (202) 512-1524.

Federal Bureau of Prisons
(202) 514-6102
Maximum baud: 2400
Location: Washington, DC

Comments: Voice number: (202) 307-3104.

FedWorld BBS
(703) 321-8020
Location: Arlington, VA

Comments: This bulletin board serves as a center for more than 100 federal bulletin board systems (BBS). For more information, call (703) 487-4650.

FireNet Leader
(719) 591-7415
Maximum Baud: 14,400
Location: Colorado Springs, CO

Comments: This board is mainly for police and fire personnel; public users have limited access.

Fraternal Order of Police (FOP)
(303) 428-6551
Location: Denver, CO

GSA—Information Resources Service
(202) 501-2014
Maximum baud: 2400
Location: Washington, DC

Comments: The General Services Administration sponsors this board. Call (202) 501-1404 for the voice line.

The Guardian
(510) 644-6806
Maximum baud: 2400
Location: Berkeley, CA

High Tech Crime Network
(201) 729-8276
Maximum baud: 14,400
Location: Sparta, NJ

Comments: This bulletin board contains conferences on high-tech crimes.

Hilton's BBS
(408) 246-0387
Maximum baud: 2400
Location: Santa Clara, CA

Comments: The focus of this bulletin board is child custody.

IdahoLaw
(Idaho Supreme Court Bulletin Board)
(208) 334-2703
Maximum baud: 2400
Location: Boise, ID

Comments: The voice line can be reached at (208) 334-2210.

INFO SOURCE
(908) 821-2530
Maximum baud: 2400
Location: Kendall Park, NJ

The Inns of Court
(402) 593-1192

Maximum baud: 14,400
Location: Dallas, TX

Comments: This board is sponsored by the Texas Bar Association.

JRSA BBS
(202) 434-4867
Maximum baud: 2400
Location: Washington, DC

L.A.W. BBS
(206) 727-8312
Maximum baud: 9600
Location: Seattle, WA

Comments: The Washington State Bar Association supports this board.

LawCat
(302) 478-7728
Maximum baud: 2400
Location: DE

Comments: The Widener University Law School Library sponsors this board.

LawMug (Lawyers Microcomputer Users Group)
(312) 661-1740
Maximum baud: 9600
Location: Chicago, IL

Comments: Users can reach the voice line at (312) 280-8180.

The Lawyers' Lawboard
(503) 484-4344
Maximum baud: 2400
Location: Eugene, OR

Legal Beagle
(603) 883-4466
Maximum baud: 9600
Location: Nashua, NH

Legal Data
(310) 427-5647

Maximum baud: 2400
Location: Los Angeles, CA

Legal Eagle
(402) 592-0442
Maximum baud: 2400
Location: Omaha, NE

Legalease
(509) 326-3238
Maximum baud: 9600
Location: Spokane, WA

LegNet—Jefferson County Legal Network
(502) 561-0742
Maximum baud: 2400
Location: Louisville, KY

Comments: Users can reach the voice line at (502) 584-1135. This bulletin board is sponsored by several local attorneys' groups.

Mouthpiece BBS
(517) 339-0479
Maximum baud: 2400
Location: Lansing, MI

Comments: The Thomas Cooley Law School sponsors this board.

National Center for State Courts Technology BBS
(804) 253-2526
Maximum baud: 2400
Location: Williamsburg, VA

Comments: This board is sponsored by the National Center for State Courts.

NCJRS BBS
(301) 738-8895
Maximum baud: 2400
Location: Rockville, MD

Comments: This board provides users with news, publications, and activities of the National Criminal Justice Reference Service (NCJRS). One can reach the voice line at (800) 851-3420 or (301) 251-2220.

New York Court of Appeals BBS
(518) 426-2220
Maximum baud: 2400
Location: Albany, NY

Comments: Subscribers receive access to the full text of recent court decisions. Public users can get into other files.

North Carolina Supreme Court (SCONC)
(919) 733-0486
Maximum baud: 2400
Location: Raleigh, NC

Comments: The clerk of the North Carolina Supreme Court provides this service. Most information is accessible to the public.

Outpost 69
(912) 729-2384
Maximum baud: 14,400
Location: Kingsland, GA

PACER
(617) 223-4294
Maximum baud: 2400
Location: Boston, MA

Comments: Contact voice registration at (617) 223-9817.

P.C.S.O.
(813) 534-6297
Maximum baud: 2400
Location: Bartow, FL

PD-BBS
(703) 358-3949
Maximum baud: 2400
Location: Arlington, VA

Comments: Users can access public safety information on this board, which is sponsored by the Arlington County, Virginia, Police Department and Emergency Communications Center.

Public Access to Court Electronic Records (PACER)
(804) 771-8084

Maximum baud: 2400
Location: Richmond, VA

Comments: Contact Systems Office/United States Courthouse/ 10th and Main Streets, Room 250/Richmond, VA 23219/(804) 771-8084.

RBBS of Newton
(515) 791-9288
Maximum baud: 2400
Location: Newton, IA

Safe 'n Secure BBS
(602) 870-6004
Maximum baud: 2400
Location: Phoenix, AZ

Comments: This board holds information on law enforcement and safety.

SEARCH-BBS
(916) 392-4640
Maximum baud: 9600
Location: Sacramento, CA

Comments: SEARCH-BBS contains shareware, e-mail, and periodicals.

Serenity in Sonoma
(707) 576-0397
Maximum baud: 9600
Location: Sonoma, CA

Solano Sub-Station BBS
(408) 971-2301
Maximum baud: 2400
Location: Solano County, CA

SOLIS BBS
(408) 971-2301
Maximum baud: 2400
Location: San Jose, CA

Comments: The Santa Clara County sheriff's office runs this board, which contains information on law enforcement.

State Bar of Arizona Electronic BBS
(602) 253-0552
Maximum baud: 2400
Location: Phoenix, AZ

Comments: Contact the voice line at (602) 252-4804.

TexLex
(806) 355-1202
Maximum baud: 9600
Location: Amarillo, TX

University of Minnesota Libraries
(612) 624-4318
Maximum baud: 2400
Location: Minneapolis, MN

The Well of Souls
(503) 741-1829
Maximum baud: 9600
Location: Springfield, OR

Comments: Users can contact either of the voice lines at (503) 741-8224 or (503) 741-6034.

W.F.P.D. BBS
(817) 761-7735
Maximum baud: 14,400
Location: Wichita Falls, TX

Comments: The Wichita Falls, Texas, Police Department operates this board. It contains information on criminal justice.

Computer Databases

National Criminal Justice Reference Service (NCJRS) Document Data Base. Rockville, MD: NCJRS, Semiannual. LCCN: sn94-28493.

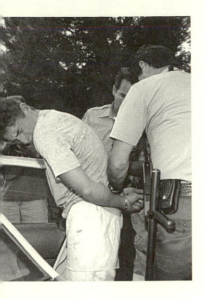

Glossary

abduct To take a person away against his or her will.

abuse (v) To physically or psychologically harm an individual. (n) The act of physically or psychologically harming an individual. Also, (v) to misuse a substance such as narcotics or alcohol; (n) the act of misusing a substance such as drugs or alcohol.

accessory after the fact The aiding of a criminal and/or his or her activity after he or she has committed a crime, for example, by helping to conceal evidence.

accessory before the fact The aiding of a criminal and/or his or her activity before he or she commits a crime.

accomplice A person who helps another commit a crime but is not the primary actor.

acquit To find a defendant not guilty of the charges presented against him or her.

addict A person who cannot control his or her use of a substance such as alcohol or narcotics; a person who would suffer withdrawal symptoms if he or she quit using a substance or substances.

adjudicate To judge or settle a dispute in court.

age of consent The legal age at which a child is considered old enough to make his or her own decision about whether to have sexual intercourse.

alcoholism Addiction to alcohol, sometimes associated with criminal behavior that would not otherwise occur.

287

alias A false or assumed name criminals often use to throw police off of their trails.

alibi A fact that proves that a potential suspect could not have been at the scene of a crime when it occurred.

alien A foreign-born legal or illegal resident of the United States who has not received citizenship.

appeal (v) To contest the outcome of a trial in a higher court; (n) the act of contesting the outcome of a trial in a higher court. Appeals are sometimes submitted through written briefs rather than oral arguments.

appeals court A state or federal court that hears appeals of the rulings of lower courts, usually presided over by a panel of judges.

appellate court *See* **appeals court.**

appellate jurisdiction The authority of a court to hear appeals from lower courts.

arrest To take an individual who is suspected of committing a crime or crimes into custody.

arrest warrant A piece of paper issued by an officer of the court that instructs police to take a suspect into custody.

arsenal A place where weapons are stored legally or illegally.

arson The act of intentionally setting fire to property for revenge, fun, or defrauding an insurance company.

assassin A person who premeditates and carries out the murder of a public figure.

assault To threaten to physically harm another person; assault is often coupled with battery.

attempted murder The act of trying to kill someone but failing to do so.

attorney A person who is familiar with laws and the legal system and serves as legal counsel to plaintiffs, defendants, and people who want legal advice in making decisions.

bail An amount of money set by the court that a defendant must pay to obtain his or her release before trial; bail is set to guarantee that a defendant shows up in court, and it is not refunded unless he or she does so.

bail bond A written guarantee that a defendant will pay his or her bail if he or she fails to appear in court.

bail bondsman A person who issues a written guarantee to pay a defendant's bail if he or she fails to appear in court for a trial; a bail bondsman usually requires collateral before he or she will issue the guarantee.

ballistics The science and study of firearms and their ammunition, used in determining the general type of or exact gun that fired a bullet in shooting cases.

battery The act of striking, hitting, or beating someone with or without using weapons; battery often accompanies assault.

bench warrant A warrant issued by a judge to hold a person in contempt of court or to arrest someone who has skipped bail.

blackmail The act of extorting money from a person through threats to publicize something embarrassing or to turn someone in for a crime he or she committed.

bomb An explosive device that is set to explode at a certain time or under certain conditions.

bomb squad A team of bomb experts within a law enforcement agency that is trained to locate and dismantle bombs.

booking The stage in a criminal investigation at which a suspect is brought to the police station to have a charge entered into the book.

bootlegging Manufacturing, selling, and/or transporting goods illegally, especially alcoholic beverages.

bounty hunter A person who specializes in tracking down people wanted by law enforcement agencies to collect a reward.

Brady Bill A handgun control bill passed in 1993 that established a national waiting period for purchasing handguns and a national instant criminal background check system.

bribery The act of using money to influence an official to alter the outcome of a case, vote, or inquiry.

brief In an appeals case, a written explanation of either the plaintiff's or the defendant's story for consideration by a panel of judges.

brothel A home or haven for prostitutes.

Bureau of Alcohol, Tobacco, and Firearms A federal law enforcement agency that falls under the supervision of the Department of the Treasury; it is commonly called ATF for short.

burglary The act of breaking into a residence or business with the intent to steal.

capital crime A crime that is punishable by death.

capital punishment The death penalty.

cartel An association of organizations in the same business that attempts to control markets and pricing; many specialize in illegal activity such as drug trafficking.

cat burglar A burglar who is able to enter and leave buildings without attracting attention.

chain gang A group of prisoners who are chained together, especially for the purpose of doing work outside of the prison.

charge To legally accuse a person of committing a crime.

check fraud The act of intentionally writing checks that will not clear the bank.

child abuse The act of psychologically or physically harming a child.

civil court A court that hears a dispute between two private parties.

community policing A method of police patrol that involves keeping officers on the streets they are assigned to and having them interact with members of the community on a regular basis.

community service A sentence imposed by a court that requires a convicted defendant to perform such activities as volunteering at a local library, speaking to groups about drug abuse, or working at a park for a set number of hours.

computer crime A crime committed using a computer, such as breaking into other computer systems, altering another person's data, or stealing valuable information stored on computers.

concealed weapon A firearm or other weapon that is carried out of others' view, now legal in many states with a license and a training course.

conspiracy An agreement between two or more people to commit a crime.

contempt of court Disobedience of court procedure or disregard for proper court procedure that a judge determines to be unacceptable.

contraband Illegal goods.

convict (v) To find someone guilty of the charges presented against him or her in a court of law; (n) a person who has been convicted of a crime.

cop A slang term for a police officer.

corporal punishment Physical punishment, such as spanking a child for disobedience.

corrections A generic term used for all aspects of the penal system— prisons, rehabilitation, probation, parole, and other methods used to treat convicted criminals.

counterfeiter One who knowingly manufactures fake items designed to look like their real counterparts; used especially to describe those who print false currency.

court-appointed lawyer A defense attorney appointed as legal counsel for a defendant who cannot afford to hire a private lawyer.

credit card fraud The illegal use of credit cards to purchase goods and services. Illegal credit cards are most often stolen; they can also be legally obtained with no intention to pay the bills after using them.

crime The act of breaking a law.

criminal court A court that hears cases between the state and a defendant who has had criminal charges brought against him or her; the state is the plaintiff and represents "the people."

criminalistics The use of science to analyze evidence in criminal cases.

criminologist One who studies crime and criminals.

death penalty A sentence of death as punishment for a crime, only permitted in murder cases. Some states do not permit the death penalty in any case.

death row An area of a prison designated for inmates who have been sentenced to death.

defense attorney A lawyer who represents a defendant, in either criminal or civil court, and provides him or her with legal counsel.

delinquency Action that is either illegal or unacceptable by normal standards of behavior.

district court A trial court that has original jurisdiction over cases in a certain area.

DNA evidence Scientific evidence that may connect DNA from a suspect's blood or other body tissue to similar specimens found at the scene of a crime.

domestic terrorism Terrorist acts, such as bombings, that occur in the United States.

don The leader of a Mafia organization.

drive-by shooting A murder or attempted murder technique often used by gangs in which members of one gang drive up near the intended victim, shoot him or her, and speed off.

driving under the influence (DUI) Operating a motor vehicle under the influence of drugs or alcohol.

drug abuse The misuse of a substance that alters the mind or body.

Drug Enforcement Administration A federal agency within the Department of Justice that specializes in investigating drug traffickers and dealers.

drug-related crime Crime that occurs as a result of drug use; a crime that occurs in connection with drug trafficking or dealing; a violation of drug possession, use, dealing, or trafficking laws.

Durham Rule A legal rule that requires expert testimony to establish a defendant's mental capacity when he or she uses the insanity defense.

Eighteenth Amendment The constitutional amendment that took effect in 1920 and prohibited the manufacture, sale, and transport of alcoholic beverages.

Eighth Amendment The constitutional amendment that prohibits excessive bail, excessive fines, and cruel and unusual punishment.

electric chair A device used in executing criminals who have been sentenced to death. They are strapped into a chair, and a quick, high-voltage shock is delivered to kill them.

electronic surveillance The use of hidden audio and/or video recording equipment to keep track of the activities of someone suspected of committing a crime.

embezzlement The act of illegally taking or diverting money from an institution or individual for one's own use.

en banc With all justices present to hear a case; court cases heard en banc often involve important or controversial issues.

espionage The use of spies to obtain information about secret government or corporate activities, usually with the intent of passing the information on to rival governments or companies.

Exclusionary Rule A legal rule applied to all states by *Mapp v. Ohio* in the 1960s that prohibits the use of illegally gathered evidence in court; later United States Supreme Court decisions weakened the rule.

extortion The use of force, threats, or other forms of intimidation to obtain money from another individual.

Federal Bureau of Investigation A law enforcement agency contained in the Department of Justice that has broad powers to investigate a wide variety of federal offenses.

federal crime An action that violates federal law.

feds A slang term for federal law enforcement agents.

felony A serious criminal offense, such as rape or murder, that is punishable by more than a year in prison; each state classifies felonies differently.

fence A person or group of people that receives stolen goods.

Fifth Amendment The constitutional amendment that protects a defendant from being tried more than once on the same charge, protects a defendant from having to serve as a witness against himself, and ensures the defendant "due process of law."

fingerprinting The act of obtaining an arrestee's fingerprints to place on file with the local police department and the Federal Bureau of Investigation.

firearms A generic term used for weapons that fire bullets.

First Amendment The constitutional amendment that guarantees freedom of the press, religion, and assembly.

forensics The use of various sciences for analyzing evidence connected with crimes.

forgery The act of intentionally altering or falsifying a document, work of art, or other item; or, a falsely altered document, work of art, or other item.

Fourteenth Amendment The constitutional amendment that guarantees all U.S. citizens civil rights; it stipulates that no state "shall deprive any person of life, liberty, or property, without due process of law, nor deny to any person within its jurisdiction the equal protection of the laws."

Fourth Amendment The constitutional amendment that protects citizens from unreasonable searches and seizures and requires officials to have "probable cause" to conduct a search of someone's person or property.

fraud The intentional misrepresentation of items, circumstances, or people to obtain something from another person or business.

gambling The legal or illegal wagering of money on the outcome of a game or contest.

gang A group of people who come together under a guiding principle or principles. This principle is often a form of criminal activity, and gangs of youths are common.

gang rape The rape of a person by more than one other person.

gangster A member of a criminal organization; often used in connection with Mafia organizations.

gas chamber A chamber into which poisonous gas is released for the purpose of executing someone who has received the death penalty.

godfather The head of an organized crime family or syndicate.

grand jury A body of citizens that considers or investigates accusations against criminal defendants and decides whether to formally indict them.

guard A person who guards prisoners either inside or outside of the compound.

handcuffs A pair of locking metal bracelets, linked by a chain, that are placed around the wrists of arrestees.

handgun A small firearm.

handwriting expert A person who has studied handwriting and can determine if the handwriting on notes or documents is that of a certain person; their testimony is often useful when allegations of forgery surface.

hit-and-run An accident, usually involving automobiles, in which a person involved flees from the scene; the person who flees is usually at fault and flees to avoid having to pay the penalties.

homicide The act of killing a human being, whether it is intentional or unintentional, justifiable or criminal.

hooker A slang name for a prostitute.

indictment A formal criminal charge, delivered by a grand jury, on which a defendant will be tried.

inmate One who has been convicted of a crime and is being housed in a prison or other correctional institution.

inner city The downtown, central, and/or poor areas of cities. They have high crime rates and play host to gang activity.

insanity defense A legal defense a criminal defendant may use to try to persuade the jury that he or she did not understand what he or she was doing at the time the crime was committed; it can be used by people with mental illnesses or emotional problems that rendered them temporarily insane, although rules differ from state to state.

investigator A federal, state, local, or private agent who looks into the circumstances, causes, and evidence surrounding a crime on behalf of the government or a private person.

jail A building designed to hold people who have recently been arrested or who are serving short sentences; jails are sometimes connected to police headquarters and are run by cities and counties.

judge An official of the court who is a legal expert, presides over trials, instructs juries, decides on what evidence may or may not be admitted in a trial, and/or may pass sentence on a convicted defendant.

jump bail To forfeit one's bail money by failing to comply with bail conditions; this most often means failure to show up for a trial.

junk A slang word for drugs and narcotics.

jurisdiction The authority a court or law enforcement agency possesses over legal matters or geographic areas.

jury A body of carefully selected citizens who listen to evidence presented at a trial and return a verdict on the case.

justice A judge; judges on higher courts, such as the United States Supreme Court, are often called justices.

justifiable homicide The legally allowable killing of another human being; justifiable homicides are committed by police officers pursuing armed and dangerous criminals or by private citizens protecting themselves from someone who intends to harm them.

juvenile A young person; in legal terms, usually someone under age 18, although the age varies from state to state.

juvenile court A court that tries cases involving juvenile offenders. Juvenile court systems are not as tightly organized as adult courts, and juvenile cases are tried by a judge rather than a jury.

juvenile delinquency The violating of the law by a juvenile.

kidnap To take a person against his or her will.

larceny The intentional theft of property from its owner.

lethal injection A method of executing someone who has received the death penalty that involves injecting him or her with deadly poison.

lineup A group of people who stand in a room so a witness to a crime can attempt to pick out the criminal he or she saw.

loan sharking The illegal practice of lending money with very high rates of interest and short payback times.

M'Naghten Rule A legal rule that requires jurors to determine whether a defendant using the insanity defense was mentally incapacitated at the time he or she committed a crime.

Mace The name of an incapacitating spray carried for protection and used to fend off attackers.

madam A woman who runs a prostitution house.

Mafia Italian criminal organizations; also used generically for organized crime syndicates.

magistrate A local court official who performs judicial functions such as issuing warrants or settling minor disputes.

magistrate court A court that hears civil cases and/or misdemeanor criminal cases.

mail bomb A bomb that is designed to explode when someone opens the mail package that contains it.

manslaughter The killing of another human being illegally but without malicious intent. First-degree manslaughter occurs when death results from a violent quarrel; second-degree manslaughter involves the accidental killing of a person through negligence.

McNabb-Mallory Rule A legal rule derived from two United States Supreme Court cases, *Mallory v. United States* (1957) and *McNabb v. United States* (1943), that says an arrestee must be taken to a magistrate shortly after his or her arrest, or else incriminating statements he or she makes will not be admissible in court.

Miranda rights The legal rights of a suspect an officer must state to someone he or she arrests; the rights defined by the *Miranda v. Arizona* Supreme Court decision in 1966.

misdemeanor A lesser crime, such as simple drug possession or petty theft, that is not as serious as a felony; offenses punishable by community service, fines, probation, and/or less than a year in jail. Definitions vary from state to state.

money laundering The channeling of profits from illegal activity into legitimate businesses to hide criminal enterprise.

mugging The act of attacking and robbing someone.

mugshot A photograph of an arrested person.

murder The malicious killing of a human being. First-degree murder occurs when someone premeditates a killing and carries it out; second-degree murder occurs when a criminal ends up killing someone in the course of committing another crime such as rape or robbery.

narcotics Drugs that compromise the senses, relieve pain, or relax; also used as a generic term for illegal drugs.

National Rifle Association A powerful political organization opposed to the regulation of firearms.

nightstick A club or baton used by police officers.

Ninth Amendment The constitutional amendment that says that the failure to list some rights in the Bill of Rights does not mean others do not exist.

no-knock provisions Laws that permit a law enforcement agent to carry out a warrant without knocking on the suspect's door.

organized crime The coordinated participation of two or more individuals in a criminal activity; definitions vary from state to state.

original jurisdiction The authority a court has to hear a case for the first time.

pardon An official elimination of a sentence for a crime, usually granted by the president or the governor; pardons may or may not clear a defendant of his or her guilt.

parole The legal release of a prisoner before a sentence has ended, provided he or she complies with certain conditions.

parole officer An official to whom a parolee must report from time to time who makes sure he or she is complying with the conditions of parole.

parolee A convict who is released from prison on parole.

pepper spray A disabling spray derived from hot peppers that people carry to protect themselves from attackers.

pimp A man who finds customers for prostitutes and takes part of the profits.

plea bargain An agreement between a prosecutor and a defendant in which the latter pleads guilty in exchange for lesser charges and/or a reduced sentence; plea bargaining frees prosecutors from the work associated with a trial and gives a defendant a lighter sentence than he or she might have received.

police agency An organization that enforces laws within its legal or geographic jurisdiction.

prison An institution to which convicted criminals are sent to serve their sentences.

probable cause Reasonable grounds for suspecting someone of a crime; the constitutional standard used to obtain a search warrant.

probation The release of a convicted criminal under a suspended sentence, certain conditions, and the supervision of a probation officer.

probation officer An official assigned to keep track of criminals on probation and to report violations.

Prohibition The period in U.S. history between 1920 and 1933 when the manufacture, sale, distribution, and consumption of alcoholic beverages were prohibited by law; also the same period that gave rise to ruthless Mafia bootlegging organizations in major cities such as Chicago.

prosecutor A representative of the state, or "the people," who brings charges and presents legal evidence against a criminal defendant in a court of law.

prostitution The act of engaging in sexual activity for profit.

racketeering The act of carrying on fraudulent or criminal activity using bribery, extortion, intimidation, threats, or violence.

ransom An amount of money demanded by a kidnapper for the safe return of a kidnap victim.

rape The act of forcing a man or woman to have sexual intercourse against his or her will.

reasonable doubt Sufficient uncertainty as to whether a defendant is guilty of the charges presented against him or her to acquit.

reasonable suspicion A lighter standard for performing searches than "probable cause"; an officer need only have reasonable suspicion to search a suspect or his or her property if the situation requires immediate action.

record A file containing a person's criminal history.

reformatory An institution in which delinquent juveniles are sentenced to spend time; reformatories emphasize rehabilitation more heavily than do adult prisons.

rehabilitation The act of trying to reform a criminal so he or she can again participate normally in society.

repeat offender A criminal who repeatedly commits crimes.

robbery The theft of money or property from a person or business using violence or threat of violence.

search warrant A document that authorizes law enforcement agents to search for evidence on the property of an individual suspected of a crime.

Second Amendment The constitutional amendment that gives U.S. citizens the right to bear arms.

sentence The punishment imposed by a court on someone who has been convicted of a crime.

Seventh Amendment The constitutional amendment that outlines a person's right to a jury trial in civil cases involving a contest over more than $20.

simple assault The threat of minor violence against another person that does not involve the use of a weapon.

Sixth Amendment The constitutional amendment that outlines a defendant's right to have a fair trial that is speedy, public, and heard by an impartial jury; to know the charges presented against him or her; to be confronted with witnesses against him or her; to have the right to present witnesses in his or her favor; and to have the right of legal counsel.

special agent A law enforcement agent trained to perform a special task, such as investigating terrorist attacks or negotiating hostage situations.

statutory rape The act of sexual intercourse with a child who has not reached the age of consent.

superior court A state court in which serious criminals are tried by jury; a superior court may also serve as an appeals court above magistrate or other lower courts.

tax evasion The intentional failure to pay any or all of legally required taxes; income tax evasion is a common offense for individuals in charge of profitable illegal businesses.

Tenth Amendment The constitutional amendment that reserves all power not specifically granted to the federal government for the states.

third degree A generic term for harsh interrogation techniques used by police departments to extract confessions from suspects.

three-strikes laws Laws that mandate a sentence of life in prison for third-time violent felons; specific provisions vary from state to state.

trafficking The act of carrying on trade in illegal goods.

treason The attempt to overthrow one's own government.

Twenty-First Amendment The constitutional amendment that went into effect in 1933 and repealed the Eighteenth Amendment, ending Prohibition.

undercover agent A member of a law enforcement agency who poses as someone he or she is not to obtain information on criminal activity his or her department is investigating.

United States Supreme Court The highest court in the United States. It has nine justices appointed by the president, hears appeals from lower federal courts, and has original jurisdiction over cases involving foreign officials or the state as one of the parties.

Untouchables A ten-man force that formed in Chicago during the Prohibition era to combat Al Capone's liquor bootlegging organization. The men were named the Untouchables because they could not be deterred with bribes or threats.

vandalism The intentional damage or destruction of public or private property.

verdict The judgment of the jury on a defendant's guilt or innocence after it has considered all of the evidence presented in a trial.

voice print A short computer file containing a sample of an arrestee's voice.

warden A person who oversees a prison.

Warren Court A term used to describe the noteworthy era (1953–1969) of the United States Supreme Court under Chief Justice Earl Warren, under whose leadership defendants' rights were expanded and constitutional rights were extended to states.

white-collar crime Crimes such as fraud, forgery, and embezzlement that do not physically harm a victim and are often committed by well-paid people; the business or corporation in which a white-collar criminal works is often the victim of his or her crime.

wiretap An electrical invasion into a telephone line that allows investigators to monitor the telephone conversations of a suspect.

witness (n) Someone who sees a crime take place; (v) to see a crime take place.

witness protection program A program that gives witnesses to crimes a new identity, job, and location when they testify in court against someone who is likely to harm them.

writ of certiorari A written order from the Supreme Court that summons a case from a lower court for consideration.

Index